THE
SOCIAL MEANING
OF MONEY

THE
SOCIAL
MEANING
OF
MONEY

VIVIANA A. ZELIZER

PRINCETON UNIVERSITY PRESS
PRINCETON, NEW JERSEY

Copyright © 1997 by Princeton University Press
Published by Princeton University Press, 41 William Street,
Princeton, New Jersey 08540
In the United Kingdom: Princeton University Press, Chichester, West Sussex

Originally published by Basic Books, a division of HarperCollins Publishers,
Inc., 1994

Library of Congress Cataloging-in-Publication Data

Zelizer, Viviana A. Rotman.
The social meaning of money : pin money, paychecks, poor relief, and other
currencies / Viviana A. Zelizer.
p. cm.
Originally published: New York : Basic Books, 1994.
Contents: Includes bibliographical references and index
ISBN 0-691-04821-5 (pbk. : alk. paper)
1. Money. I. Title.
HG221.Z45   1997
332.4—dc21   97–19216

Some material from this book has previously appeared in: "The Social Meaning
of Money: Special Monies," *American Journal of Sociology* 95 (September
1989): 342–77; "Money," in the *Encyclopedia of Sociology*, ed. Edgard F.
Borgatta and Marie L. Borgatta (New York: Macmillan, 1992), pp. 1304–10; and
"Making Multiple Monies," in *Explorations in Economic Sociology*, ed. Richard
Swedberg (New York: Russell Sage Foundation, 1993), pp. 193–212.

Princeton University Press books are printed on acid-free paper and meet the
guidelines for permanence and durability of the Committee on Production
Guidelines for Book Longevity of the Council on Library Resources

Printed in the United States of America

10 9 8 7 6 5 4 3 2 1

For Julian, my dear son

CONTENTS

ACKNOWLEDGMENTS

COMPRESSING GRATITUDE into a judicious inventory of help received, favors bestowed, and obligations accumulated makes a complex array of personal ties one-dimensional. It misses the rich distinctions among varieties of gratitudes, the multiple and very particular sorts of advice, encouragement, and understanding received from different individuals and organizations in the long process of writing a book.

Let me try to describe my many gratitudes. As he has for the past two decades, Bernard Barber listened to my ideas, read each draft, and advised me in this project from its very start. With infinite generosity, Charles Tilly provided indispensable commentaries at critical points. Michael B. Katz's work on American welfare history offered an important guide for my research on changing relief policies, as did his thoughtful comments. I thank other friends and colleagues who gave varied and valuable suggestions: Jeffrey C. Alexander, Sigmund Diamond, Paul DiMaggio, Susan Gal, Albert O. Hirschman, Jenna Weissman Joselit, David J. Rothman, Ewa Morawska, Loïc Wacquant, and Eviatar Zerubavel.

In the past few years I discussed sections of this book in many university seminars, working groups, and conferences. For helpful comments, I am grateful to members of the Russell Sage Seminar in Economic Sociology, Princeton University's Department of Sociology Workshop in Economic Sociology, the Princeton Society of Fellows of the Woodrow Wilson Foundation,

Pierre Bourdieu's seminar at the École Des Hautes Études en Sciences Sociales, and the National Humanities Center's conference on The Gift and Its Transformations, as well as to attentive audiences at the University of Chicago, Columbia University, the Graduate Center of the City University of New York, Harvard University, the New School For Social Research, New York University, the University of Pennsylvania, Yale University, and the Maxwell School of Citizenship and Public Affairs at Syracuse University.

The initial stages of my research were supported by a National Endowment for the Humanities summer grant. A year spent as a visiting scholar at the Russell Sage Foundation in 1987–88 contributed more than generous support and an ideal work setting; there I found a wonderful set of colleagues and friends to discuss my "money" problems. In particular, Robert K. Merton and Eric Wanner asked probing, important questions. Pauline Rothstein and her staff offered extensive and efficient assistance with library sources.

Princeton University, my academic home since 1988, fully encouraged the completion of this project, including providing time off to work on the book. I especially thank Marvin Bressler, then chair of Sociology, for helping my effort in countless ways, organizational and intellectual. With efficiency and care, Cindy Gibson, Blanche Anderson, and Donna DeFrancisco provided invaluable practical support.

At Basic Books, I am happy to acknowledge the collaboration of Kermit Hummel and Martin Kessler as well as the editorial skills of Sheila Friedling.

Three exceptional research assistants worked with me at different stages of this project: Rosann Rovento Bar in its early phases, Victoria Chapman (a virtuoso of the elusive reference) during the long middle years, and Tracy Scott for the finishing touches. Kei Sochi and Katie Pears also provided library assistance.

My family gratitudes come in multiples as well: my brothers Edgardo and Leandro Rotman offered intelligent arguments and found many useful references. From the time this book began, my son Julian helped me, first with his computer expertise as a teenager and, more recently, with valuable critiques and suggestions as a graduate student. I thank Jerry Zelizer for his unstinting support and patience in the busy years spent writing this book. My parents, Rosita and Julio Rotman, were essential companions in this project. Without my mother's encouragement, this book would not exist.

THE
SOCIAL MEANING
OF MONEY

1

The Marking of Money

MONEY MULTIPLIES. Despite the commonsense idea that "a dollar is a dollar is a dollar," everywhere we look people are constantly creating different kinds of money. This book explains the remarkably various ways in which people identify, classify, organize, use, segregate, manufacture, design, store, and even decorate monies as they cope with their multiple social relations. It is a powerful ideology of our time that money is a single, interchangeable, absolutely impersonal instrument—the very essence of our rationalizing modern civilization. Money's "colorlessness," as Georg Simmel saw it at the turn of the twentieth century, repainted the modern world into an "evenly flat and gray tone." All meaningful nuances were stamped out by the new quantitative logic that asked only "how much," but not "what and how." Or as Gertrude Stein put it more succinctly a few decades later, "Whether you like it or whether you do not money is money and that is all there is about it."[1]

Money, according to this conception, also destroys, necessarily replacing personal bonds with calculative instrumental ties, corrupting cultural meanings with materialist concerns. Indeed, from Karl Marx to Jürgen Habermas, from Georg Simmel to Robert Bellah, observers of commercialization in Western countries have thought they saw devastating consequences of money's irresistible spread: the inexorable homogenization and flattening of social ties. Conservatives have deplored the moral decay brought by prosperity while radicals have condemned capitalism's dehumanization, but both have seen the swelling cash nexus as the source of evil.

This book examines changes in the public and private uses of money in the United States between 1870 and 1930. Measured by the range of commodities and services available for cash, the commercialization of American life has unquestionably advanced during the twentieth century. The question, however, is whether or not the expansion of monetary exchange works the way it is supposed to, whether or not it has the consequences ordinarily attributed to it. As monetary transactions multiply, do they render social life cold, distant, and calculating? The standard answer has been an emphatic *yes*. This book contests such strongly held assumptions. It shows how at each step in money's advance, people have reshaped their commercial transactions, introduced new distinctions, invented their own special forms of currency, earmarked money in ways that baffle market theorists, incorporated money into personalized webs of friendship, family relations, interactions with authorities, and forays through shops and businesses.

Consider, for instance, how we distinguish a lottery winning from an ordinary paycheck, or from an inheritance. A thousand dollars won in the stock market do not "add up" in the same way as $1,000 stolen from a bank, or $1,000 borrowed from a friend. A wage earner's first paycheck is not the exact equivalent of the fiftieth or even the second. The money we obtain as compensation for an accident is quite different from our royalties for a book. And royalties gained from a murderer's memoirs fall into a separate moral category from royalties earned by a scientific text.

Unlike an "honest dollar," "dirty" money is stained by its ethically dubious origins. Thus the ubiquitous metaphor: to launder money. One striking example of dirty money comes from the practices of prostitutes. A study of the Oslo prostitution market in the 1980s found a "divided economy" among many of the women: welfare money, health benefits, or other legal income were carefully budgeted, spent for the "straight life," to pay rent and bills. Prostitution money, on the other hand, was quickly squandered on "going out," on drugs, alcohol, and clothes. Paradoxically, the study notes, the women "sweat over, add up, and budget the legal money though the ends will never meet, while simultaneously thousands of crowns can be spent on 'going out.'" Dirty money, it seems, "burns a hole in your pocket and has to be used quickly."[2]

Marty, a new Philadelphia gang recruit during the 1950s, provides a different version of moral earmarking. When asked by his family-services social worker why he would donate to his church the twenty-five cents his mother gave him but not the money he got from the gang's robberies, Marty was clear, "Oh no, that is bad money; that is not honest money." While stolen monies were sullied, his mother's hard-earned money was "honest" and "he could offer it to God."[3] Sometimes, however, "dirty money" is laundered morally by donating a portion to some worthy cause. Consider, however, how that donation differs from an office subscription, a church collection, synagogue dues, or university bequests. Still other monies circulate as different sorts of gifts—a check for a nephew's wedding, a Christmas bonus to an employee, Hanukkah *gelt* for a child, a waiter's tip. Within our households, a wife's income is often distinguished from her husband's, and surely from her child's. Children's monies, too, have multiple meanings: an allowance does not count the same way as the money earned by baby sitting.

Think, finally, of the remarkable range of invented monies we exchange: food stamps for the poor, supermarket coupons for the ordinary consumer, prison scrip for inmates, therapeutic tokens for the mentally ill, military currency for soldiers, chips for gamblers, lunch tickets for institutional canteens, gift certificates for celebrations. Both within the range set by governmental currencies and among the other forms of money created for special purposes, distinction and multiplication appear on every hand.

Yet we know remarkably little about the social life of money. Social scientists treat money paradoxically: although money is considered a basic element of modern society, as a sociological category it remains unanalyzed. Money is ignored, Randall Collins has suggested, "as if it were not sociological enough." The *International Encyclopedia of the Social Sciences* devotes over thirty pages to money, but not one to its social characteristics. There are essays on the economic effect of money, on quantity theory, on velocity of circulation, and on monetary reform, but nothing on money as *réalité sociale*, in Simiand's apt term. Oddly, while sociologists have long recognized social time and social space, social money has eluded them. Sorokin's *Sociocultural Causality, Space, Time*, for instance, devotes separate chapters to the qualitative heterogeneity of time and space, but only a few speculative lines to the possible multiple symbolism of money.[4]

As a result, money as an intellectual construct remains confined primarily to the economists' domain—a world in which unfettered individuals behave as rational participants in market transactions, making distinctions only of price and quantity, a dispassionate sphere where all monies are alike. To be sure, Thorstein Veblen alerted us to the social meaning of what money buys; and, more recently, a new literature on the culture of consumption boldly reverses our understanding of modern commodities.[5] The new revisionist approach uncovers the symbolic meanings of commercial goods, but, curiously, leaves the cultural independence and power of money unquestioned.

Ironically, popular conceptions of money seem to be wiser than academic sociology. In their everyday existence, people understand that money is not really *fungible*, that despite the anonymity of dollar bills, not all dollars are equal or interchangeable. We routinely assign different meanings and separate uses to particular monies. Sometimes the earmarking is quite concrete; for instance, Rainwater, Coleman, and Handel's study of American working-class housewives describes the women's careful "tin-can accounting": monies for separate expenses were kept apart, in tin cans or labeled envelopes—one for the mortgage, another for utilities, for entertainment money, and the like. The wives in Bakke's landmark study of unemployed workers in the 1930s used china pitchers to segregate different types of income earmarked for particular expenses: the rent of an extra room, for example, might serve to pay off the mortgage, whereas a child's earnings were designated to purchase school clothes. And Jean Lave tells us that in Orange County, California, today, residents segregate their monies for special uses by keeping a variety of domestic "cash stashes"—"generally one in the billfold of each adult, children's allowances and piggy banks, a 'petty cash' fund in a teapot-equivalent, a dish of change for parking meters or laundry"—or "banked stashes of money," including Christmas club savings and accounts designated for special expenditures such as property or other taxes, vacations, or home and car insurance payments.[6]

As these concrete variations suggest, we face a serious question: how does money really work? How do people make these sorts of distinctions among monies, when, and for what? But first, why have theorists held so stubbornly to such mistaken views of money?

MARKET MONEY:
A UTILITARIAN APPROACH

Monetization—the increase in the proportion of all goods and services bought and sold by means of money—has been accelerating for several centuries. Many eighteenth-century thinkers saw the monetization of the economy as compatible with or even complementary to the maintenance of a morally coherent social life.[7] But the power of money to transform modern society captured the imagination of nineteenth- and early twentieth-century social theorists. Deeply worried about an ever-expanding market relentlessly invading and desiccating all social spaces, classical social thinkers assumed that money, which Max Weber called the "most abstract and 'impersonal' element that exists in human life," was spearheading the process of rationalization. It was the perverse magical wand that disenchanted modern life. Money turned the world, observed Simmel, into an "arithmetic problem."[8] On purely technical grounds, monetary accounting certainly promoted impersonal rational economic markets. But traditional social thinkers argued that the effects of money transcended the market: more significantly, money became the catalyst for the pervasive instrumentalism of modern social life. In his *Philosophy of Money*, Georg Simmel summed up this nineteenth-century view in his observation that "the complete heartlessness of money is reflected in our social culture, which is itself determined by money."[9]

The task of social theory was thus to explain this uncontested revolutionary power of money. Presumably, it stemmed from money's total indifference to values. Money was perceived as the prototype of an instrumental, calculating approach, in Simmel's words, "the purest reification of means." It was also the symbol of what Simmel identified as a major tendency of modern life—the reduction of quality to quantity, "which achieves its highest and uniquely perfect representation in money." Only money, argued Simmel, "is free from any quality and exclusively determined by quantity." With money, all qualitative distinctions between goods were equally convertible into an arithmetically calculable "system of numbers."[10]

That "uncompromising objectivity" allowed money to function as a "technically perfect" medium of modern economic exchange. Free from subjective restrictions, indifferent to "particular interests, origins, or relations," money's liquidity and divisibility were infinite. The very essence of money, claimed Simmel, was its "unconditional interchangeability, the internal uniformity that makes each piece exchangeable for another." Money thus served as the fitting neutral intermediary of a rational, impersonal market, "expressing the economic relations between objects . . . in abstract quantitative terms, without itself entering into those relations."[11] Simmel unequivocally dismissed noneconomic restrictions in the use of money as residual atavisms: "The inhibiting notion that certain amounts of money may be 'stained with blood' or be under a curse are sentimentalities that lose their significance completely with the growing indifference of money." As money became nothing but "mere money," its freedom was apparently unassailable and its uses unlimited.[12]

This objectification of modern life had a dual effect. On the one hand, Simmel argued that a money economy broke the personal bondage of traditional arrangements by allowing every individual the freedom of selecting the terms and partners of economic exchange. But the quantifying alchemy of money had a more ominous chemistry. In an early essay, Marx had warned that the transformational powers of money subverted reality, "confounding and compounding . . . all natural and human qualities . . . [money] serves to exchange every property for every other, even contradictory, property and object: it is the fraternization of impossibilities." As the ultimate objectifier—a "god among commodities"—money not only obliterated all subjective connections between objects and individuals, but also reduced personal relations to the "cash nexus."[13] Indeed, Marx argued in the *Grundrisse* and *Capital*, money fetishism was the most "glaring" form of commodity fetishism. The "perverted" process by which social relations between people were transmuted into material relations among things peaked with money. For other commodities might retain their more "natural" value or "use value" and therefore some distinctive quality. But as pure exchange value, money necessarily assumed an "unmeaning" form, which in turn neutralized all possible qualitative distinctions between commodities. In their money form, noted Marx, "all commodities look alike." And more incongruously still, money turned even intangible objects devoid of utility—such as conscience or honor—into ordinary commodities. Thus the priceless itself surrenders to price. "Not even the bones of saints . . . are *extra commercium hominum* able to withstand the alchemy."[14]

For Marx, money was thus an irresistible and "radical leveler," invading all areas of social life. By homogenizing all qualitative distinctions into an abstract quantity, money allowed the "equation of the incompatible." Half a century later, Simmel confirmed Marx's diagnosis, dubbing money a "frightful leveler," which perverted the uniqueness of personal and social values: "With its colorlessness and indifference . . . [money] hollows out the core of things . . . their specific value, and their incomparability." Indeed, in his analysis of prostitution Simmel recognized "in the nature of money itself something of the essence of prostitution." Of all social relationships, prostitution, noted Simmel, was "the most striking instance of mutual degradation to a mere means," thereby connecting prostitution to the money economy—"the economy of 'means' in the strictest sense." Max Weber, too, pointed to the fundamental antagonism between a rational money economy and personal ties, as he observed that "the more the world of the modern capitalist economy follows its own immanent laws, the less accessible it is to . . . a religious ethic of brotherliness."[15]

In an essay published in 1913, economist and sociologist Charles H. Cooley submitted a dissenting argument in defense of the dollar. While acknowledging the growth of the cash nexus in modern society, Cooley refused to see money as a necessary antagonist of nonpecuniary values. Instead, sounding much like the eighteenth-century advocates of what Albert O. Hirschman calls the "doux commerce" thesis of the market as a moralizing agent, Cooley argued that the "principle that everything has a price should be enlarged rather than restricted. . . . pecuniary values are members of the same general system as the moral and aesthetic values, and it is their function to put the latter upon the market." Taking honor as "one of those values which many would place outside the pecuniary sphere," Cooley noted that, rather, honor "may call for the saving of money to pay a debt, while sensuality would spend it for a hearty dinner." In such a case, "we buy our honor with money." Progress, Cooley concluded, lay not in depreciating monetary valuation but in assuring the moral regulation of money: "The dollar is to be reformed rather than suppressed."[16]

In his dissent, Cooley aligned himself with the view of those professional economists who saw money as the major rationalizing—but not necessarily corrupting—agent in the modern economy. The great economist Alfred Marshall, for instance, declared in 1885 that "in the world in which we live, money, as representing general purchasing power, is so much the best measure of motives that no other can compete with it." According to Marshall's pragmatic ethics, the fact that "when we want to induce a man to do anything for us, we generally offer him money" does not mean that generosity or sense of duty has disappeared, but simply that money serves as the most efficient measure of the "ordinary motives that govern men in the acts of everyday life."[17]

The influential American economist Wesley C. Mitchell picked up on Marshall's argument, stressing the use of money as one of society's "great rationalizing habits," shaping not only people's objective economic behavior, but their "subjective life." When it came to the intimate world of households, however, Mitchell's argument wavered. Whereas in business "nothing but the pecuniary values of things . . . need be considered, and pecuniary values can always be balanced, compared, and adjusted in an orderly and systematic fashion," domestic accounting was of a different, more "backward" sort: "gains are not reducible to dollars, as are the profits of a business enterprise." How, therefore, could a housewife effectively compare her "costs and gains"? Family values necessarily distorted the rationality and efficiency of the market by introducing unmeasurable matters of subjective value.[18]

Joseph Schumpeter also noted that capitalism "exalts" money, turning it into a "tool of rational cost-profit calculations," a calculus that extended beyond the economic sector into a "type of logic or attitude or method [that] then starts upon its conqueror's career subjugating—rationalizing—man's tools and philosophies, his medical practice, his picture of the cosmos, his outlook on life, everything in fact including his concepts of beauty and justice and his spiritual ambitions." While, on the one hand, Schumpeter suggested that the capitalist process led to "utilitarianism and the wholesale destruction of Meanings," on the other hand, in an only recently published discussion of money he, like Mitchell, acknowledged a sphere, separate from the rational sphere of economic behavior, where money was not culturally barren, as in the use of currency that served also as a meaningful ritual object. This "cultural significance" of money was relevant only in exceptional cases, however, "insofar as it influences the actual behavior of people with respect to money."[19]

The utilitarian model has had a remarkable grip over theorizing about money. Contemporary sociology still clings to the view of money as an absolutely fungible, qualitatively neutral, infinitely divisible, entirely homogeneous medium of market exchange. James Coleman, for example, builds an extremely sophisticated analysis of social exchange, yet continues to treat money as the ultimate impersonal common denominator. Even when analysts recognize the symbolic dimension of modern money, they stop short of fully transcending the utilitarian framework. Talcott Parsons, for instance, explicitly and forcefully called for a "sociology of money" that would treat money as one of the generalized symbolic media of social interchange, along with political power, influence, and value-commitments. In contrast to Marx's definition of money as the "material representative of wealth," in Parsons's media theory, money was a symbolic language—not a commodity, but a signifier, devoid of use-value. Yet Parsons restricts the symbolism of money to the economic sphere. Money, Parsons contends, is the "symbolic 'embodiment' of economic value, of what economists in a technical sense call 'utility.'"[20] Consequently, Parsons's media theory left uncharted the symbolic meaning of money outside the market: money's cultural and social significance beyond utility.

Anthony Giddens complains that Parsons incorrectly equates power, language, and money, since for Giddens money has a distinctly different relationship to social life. He sees money as a "symbolic token," a key example of those "disembedding mechanisms associated with modernity"—detaching social relations from particular times and places. Jürgen Habermas goes so far as to argue that money is the medium by which the economic system "colonizes" the world of routine social life, irrepressibly and systematically undermining "domains of action dependent upon social integration." Sociologists thus still accept with a remarkable lack of skepticism the notion that once money invades the realm of personal relations it inevitably bends those relations in the direction of instrumental rationality.[21]

For a century, therefore, the prevailing interpretation of money shaped an absolute model of market money, based on the following five assumptions:

1. The functions and characteristics of money are defined strictly in economic terms. As an entirely homogeneous, infinitely divisible, liquid object, lacking in quality, money is a matchless tool for market exchange. Even when the symbolic meaning of money is recognized, it either remains restricted to the economic sphere or is treated as a largely inconsequential feature.

2. All monies are the same in modern society. What Simmel called money's "qualitatively communistic character"[22] denies any

distinction between types of money. Only differences in quantity are possible. Thus, there is only one kind of money-market money.

3. A sharp dichotomy is established between money and nonpecuniary values. Money in modern society is defined as essentially profane and utilitarian in contrast to noninstrumental values. Money is qualitatively neutral; personal, social, and sacred values are qualitatively distinct, unexchangeable, and indivisible.

4. Monetary concerns are seen as constantly enlarging, quantifying, and often corrupting all areas of life. As an abstract medium of exchange, money has not only the freedom but also the power to draw an increasing number of goods and services into the web of the market. Money is thus the vehicle for an inevitable commodification of society.

5. There is no question about the power of money to transform nonpecuniary values, whereas the reciprocal transformation of money by values or social relations is seldom conceptualized or else explicitly rejected.

It is not utterly foolish to suppose that the monetization of social life spreads uniformity, precision, and calculation. After all, a money economy made a significant difference to social organization. For example, it facilitated the multiplication of economic partners and promoted a rational division of labor. In the years between 1860 and the early 1930s, the United States saw— among other financial innovations—the creation of postal money orders (1864), travelers' checks (1891), fixed prices (1860s), fixed-priced stores, such as Woolworth's nickel or dime stores (1870), mail-order catalogues (1870s), credit cards (1914), the first electronic funds-transfer system (1918), as well as the intensified use of time-payment plans, such as installment buying and the credit system.[23]

CREATING MARKET MONEY

Starting in the nineteenth century, the American state worked vigorously to create Simmel's "colorless" currency, a standardized national money. How did it do so? It taxed thousands of state-issued paper currencies out of existence, suppressed the private issue of tokens, paper notes, or coins by stores, businesses, churches, and other organizations; and stamped out the personalization of money by individuals. Consider, for instance, the five thousand or more distinct varieties of state bank notes—not including additional thousands of counterfeit issues—circulating during the nineteenth century. Merchants and bankers had to rely on bank-note directories to keep track of the unwieldy varieties of monies since the value (as well as the size and style) of bank notes differed from bank to bank and in different states. It was apparently common for bank customers to specify "in what sort of money deposits were to be withdrawn and with what sort promissory notes were to be repaid."[24]

The government set out to eliminate distinctions among currencies. In 1863 the National Banking Act allowed newly chartered national banks to create a uniform national currency. A few years later the federal government taxed multiple state bank notes out of existence. Earlier, prompted by the financial crisis of the Civil War, Congress had in 1862 authorized the Treasury to print millions of "greenbacks," the country's first paper currency without gold backing, which circulated nationally as legal tender.[25] But even after the National Banking Act, the stock of American money remained highly diversified. The new national bank notes circulated alongside other Civil War currency inventions; not only greenbacks, but interest-bearing legal-tender notes, government demand notes, postage and fractional currency, as well as silver and gold certificates ("yellowbacks"), not to mention the more traditional gold coins and subsidiary silver. These multiple official monies were in many cases earmarked for specified purposes. Greenbacks, for instance, were receivable in most payments, but not for duties on imports nor for interest on bonds and notes. Gold, on the other hand, although designated largely for foreign transactions was also reserved for certain domestic payments, such as custom duties. Limited regional variation persisted; for example, payment in gold continued to prevail on the West Coast. Yet on the whole, after the Civil War, the American state moved toward a more uniform legal tender.[26]

Standardization of money, however, was not a smooth, consensual process. In fact, defining American currency became one of the most explosive political and social issues of the late nineteenth century. Significantly, despite a dramatic post–Civil War increase in people's use of deposits rather than cash, the debates centered on currencies. Were greenbacks "real" money, or did only "hard" metallic money serve as authentic currency? Should gold, as monometalists argued, be the only "true" standard? Or, could silver, as "free silver" proponents maintained, serve as equally sound money? Were national bank notes legitimate? Or, as greenbackers insisted, was only government-issued money acceptable?[27] These were not merely word games or strictly technical distinctions; the "money question" became a fiercely contested public debate, polarizing social groups and shaping the political process of late nineteenth-century American society. *Money* magazine, established in 1897 "specially designed to simplify the present currency question in the United States," noted that voters were being "suddenly called upon to digest arguments and technical essays which would puzzle any man who had not previously investigated the subject." Indeed, as one historian points out, only in the United States did "the argument about the form and function of money [become] public."[28]

By the turn of the century the controversy waned, after free-silver proponents lost the 1896 election and the 1900 Gold Standard Act established the gold dollar as the national monetary standard. In short, within some four decades, the American state had achieved a significant degree of monetary standardization, although not until 1933 did Congress formally declare all U.S. coins and currencies as equal legal tender.[29]

Creating currencies, however, was not entirely state business. At times, stores, businesses, and other organizations—including brothels—privately issued tokens, paper notes, or coins. In fact, Americans often responded to the periodic scarcity of small change by the resourceful production of substitute currency. There are even instances of "church money," such as the fourpence notes issued in 1792 by a church in Schenectady, New York, or the tokens distributed by the First Presbyterian Church of Albany during that same period.[30] Most notably, merchants' copper cents, the "hard-time tokens" of the 1830s, successfully served as both commercial advertising and small change. Other tokens bearing patriotic emblems or political slogans animated economic exchange with timely debates, often satirizing President Jackson's policies. Again in the Civil War, when subsidiary silver became more valuable as metal than coin, privately issued "shinplasters"—paper money in small denominations—along with thousands of tradesmen's and political tokens were used as substitute currency in everyday transactions. Transportation companies, hotels, saloons, restaurants, and retail stores, one historian reports, "that could not carry on business without change proceeded to manufacture their own currency." For example, Boston's Young's Hotel issued a system of checks for 15, 25, and 50 cents signed by the proprietor. Gold coins were also privately issued; between 1830 and 1860 thousands of coins were produced by individuals in California, Georgia, and other states. Indeed, from 1849 to 1855, private gold coins were the main circulating currency in California.[31]

The government stepped in to make this private production of monies illegal. Until the 1860s, private coinage had been tolerated or ignored; the Constitution, for instance, contained no relevant prohibition, while early nineteenth-century counterfeiting laws referred only to fraudulent duplications or imitations of U.S. coins, not to their private issue. But in 1862 state forbearance ended; the postage currency law of that year criminalized shinplasters, declaring that no "private corporation, banking association, firm, or individual" could issue or circulate any "note, check, memorandum, token, or other obligation, for a less sum than one dollar, intended to circulate as money." To meet the critical demand for fractional currency—small change—Congress converted postage stamps into money.[32] Legal restrictions against private monies increased in 1864 and then most forcefully in 1909 with a broad prohibition not only against the private issue of currency "in the resemblance of coins of the United States," but also against currency of "original design." Violators were threatened with a fine of no more than three thousand dollars, imprisonment for no more than five years, or both.[33] Privately issued scrip wages also came under attack. In the late 1800s and early 1900s a number of constitutional and legislative "store orders" or "truck acts" upheld the right of workers to be paid in "lawful money" rather than the scrip, coupons, punchouts, tokens, or trade checks dispensed by "persons, firms, corporations, and companies" often redeemable only at the local company store.

Endorsing and enforcing a single, homogeneous national currency was declared an urgent task; the government, stated one Indiana court case, "should unyieldingly maintain the right to protect the money which it makes the standard of value throughout the country." Even new immigrants were promptly instructed that in America, "the right to *coin money* belongs to Congress alone." When people "manufacture metal or paper money," warned the U.S. Department of Labor's *Federal Textbook on Citizenship Training*, "they must pay a heavy fine and are sent to prison for a number of years."[34] The state moved as well against the personalization of money by individuals; it broadened definitions of counterfeiting and mutilation, pursuing, for instance, the popular late nineteenth-century trompe l'oeil paintings of dollar bills. The government even forbade the common late nineteenth-century practice of inscribing coins with sentimental messages, calling that practice "mutilation." After 1909, a law forbidding the mutilation of coins turned the popular "love token" gifts into an illegal currency. As the Supreme Court of Indiana declared in November 1889, the government "has a right to provide a currency for the whole nation, and to drive out all other circulating mediums by taxation or otherwise."[35]

It was a losing battle. Although the American state did achieve a significant degree of standardization and monopolization in the physical form of legal tender, people continually disrupted monetary uniformity, actively creating all sorts of monetary distinctions. Even Congress resisted when the government's efforts to homogenize currency went too far. Consider for instance the intense debate provoked in 1908 by the proposal to restore the inscription "In God We Trust," which had been removed by presidential order, on United States gold coins. Although a few Congressmen applauded President Roosevelt's sensible decision to remove the motto, insisting that "our coin . . . is a medium of secular, and not sacred, transactions," their more successful opponents argued eloquently in favor of the ritual marker, insisting that while "the removal of [the motto] did not depreciate [money's] monetary value . . . it depreciated its sentimental value." The United States, warned the representative of Georgia, should not coin an "infidel money."[36]

Thus, as Simmel's *Philosophy of Money* went to press in 1900, the real world of money in the United States belied his claims concerning its homogeneity and qualitative neutrality. Indeed, as the consumer society was being established, new forms of earmarking money emerged in a number of different settings. As we shall explore in detail, monies multiplied both within households and in public settings. Even prisons debated the right kind of money for inmates, while some orphan asylums and foster-care supervisors proposed a separate currency for dependent children. Legislatures debated whether tips were an acceptable kind of money or a punishable misdemeanor, while businesses defended in court the legitimacy of coupons, trading stamps, and premiums to promote their products.[37] Therefore, the forms of monetary earmarking multiplied just as official money became *more* uniform and generalized. At least, public discussions of these issues became much more active in this period. That is precisely the irony: while the state and the law worked to obtain a single national currency, people actively created all sorts of monetary distinctions. Outside the world of printing and minting, however, less energy was spent on adopting different objects as currencies than on creating distinctions among the uses and meanings of existing currencies, that is, on *earmarking.*

Clearly, a link is missing in the traditional approach to money. Impressed by the fungible, impersonal characteristics of money, classic theorists emphasized its instrumental rationality and apparently unlimited capacity to transform products, relationships, and sometimes even emotions into an abstract and objective numerical equivalent. But money is neither culturally neutral nor socially anonymous. It may well "corrupt" values and convert social ties into numbers, but values and social relations reciprocally transmute money by investing it with meaning and social patterns.

THE SOCIAL DIFFERENTIATION
OF MONEY

Despite its transferability, people make every effort to embed money in particular times, places, and social relations. Thus I propose an alternative, differentiated model of money as shaped and reshaped by particular networks of social relations and varying systems of meanings:

1. While money does serve as a key rational tool of the modern economic market, it also exists outside the sphere of the market and is profoundly influenced by cultural and social structures.

2. There is no single, uniform, generalized money, but multiple monies: people earmark different currencies for many or perhaps all types of social interactions, much as they create distinctive

languages for different social contexts. And people will in fact respond with anger, shock, or ridicule to the "misuse" of monies for the wrong circumstances or social relations, such as offering a thousand-dollar bill to pay for a newspaper or tipping a restaurant's owner. Money used for rational instrumental exchanges is not "free" from social constraints but is another type of socially created currency, subject to particular networks of social relations and its own set of values and norms.

3. The classic economic inventory of money's functions and attributes, based on the assumption of a single general-purpose type of money, is unsuitably narrow. By focusing exclusively on money as a market phenomenon, it fails to capture the very complex range of characteristics of money as a social medium. A different, more inclusive coding is necessary, for certain monies can be indivisible (or divisible but not in mathematically predictable portions), nonfungible, nonportable, deeply subjective, and therefore qualitatively heterogeneous.

4. The assumed dichotomy between utilitarian money and nonpecuniary values is false, for money under certain circumstances may be as singular and unexchangeable as the most personal or unique object.

5. Given these assumptions, the alleged freedom and unchecked power of money become improbable. Cultural and social structures set inevitable limits to the monetization process by introducing profound controls and restrictions on the flow and liquidity of monies.

Even estimating the quantity of money requires a social accounting involving more than purely rational market calculations. For instance, Simmel posited that money in "extraordinarily great quantities" can circumvent its "empty quantitative nature": it becomes "imbued . . . with fantastic possibilities that transcend the definiteness of numbers." The apparent objectivity of numbers, however, is escaped not only by large fortunes. Ordinary or even small sums of money can attain similar distinction. For example, in civil-law countries that permit monetary compensation for the grief of losing a child in an accident, legal scholars advocate the *franc symbolique:* a token sum of money is perceived as the only dignified equivalent for such a purely emotional loss. Or consider the symbolic calculation of certain charitable gifts; donors to the *New York Times* annual Neediest Cases Fund, for instance, often select the amount of their gift by a personalized sentimental economics: like the couple who took the number of years they had been married (fifty-one) and multiplied it by the cost of their marriage license ($2), or the parents whose $134 donation was reached by adding $1 for each of their daughter's thirty-three years, $1 for good luck, and $100 to keep pace with inflation. During the 1890s Americans made the nickel a socially distinctive currency; a five-cent coin, as one historian puts it, not only "bought anything and everything" but even shaped language ("a nickel's worth," a "nickel nurser," "not worth a plugged nickel," to "nickel and dime" someone, nickelodeon).[38]

The concept of multiple currencies leads us into delicate terminological terrain. Some analysts will prefer to call an object money only when a government issues it and assigns it value. Even there, we have to recognize that, as we've seen, in the United States alone all sorts of governments have issued different bills, coins, and any number of other tender. So have businesses and other types of private or public organizations.[39] Outside the realm of governments, organizations, or business, moreover, people repeatedly do the following three things: they convert selected objects into the equivalent of currencies, as in the case of cigarettes, postage stamps, subway tokens, poker chips, or baseball cards; they create physically distinct markers, such as gift certificates or food stamps; and they adapt government-issued currencies so vigorously that it seems reasonable also to call these variations monies.[40] That is how I will use the term. These objects have no common physical characteristics; they qualify as distinct monies because of the uses and meanings people assign to them, because of the distinctions they represent in everyday social life. Social monies certainly include officially issued coins and bills, but they also include all objects that have recognized, regularized exchange value in one social setting or another. I argue that the earmarking of informal monies is a phenomenon as powerful as the official creation of legal tender.

EARMARKING

How does this process of social earmarking work? After all, the physical homogeneity of modern currency is indisputable. How, then, do people distinguish between monies that can so easily remain indistinct? Anthropologists provide some intriguing insights into the differentiation of monies, but only with regard to primitive money. For instance, ethnographic studies show that in certain primitive communities, money attains special qualities and distinct values independent of quantity. How much money is less important than *which* money. Multiple currencies, or "special-purpose" money, using Karl Polanyi's term, have sometimes coexisted in one and the same village, each currency having a specified, restricted use (for purchasing only certain goods or services), special modes of allocation and forms of exchange, and, sometimes, designated users. For instance, in Rossel Island, a small traditional community in the southwestern Pacific, separate lower-value coins were reserved exclusively for women. In Yap, one of the Caroline Islands in the west Pacific, mussel shells strung on strings served as women's money, while men monopolized the more desirable large stones. Even live human beings have sometimes served as money; Orlando Patterson points out that through much of the ancient world rich people could pay certain debts—brideprice, purchase of houses, compensation for wrongs, and more—by means of slaves, according to well-established scales of value.[41]

As the instance of slaves suggests, special monies are often morally or ritually ranked: certain kinds of money may be good for obtaining food but not for purchasing a wife; other monies are appropriate only for funeral gifts or marriage gifts or as blood money; still other monies serve exclusively for paying damages for adultery or insults, for burial with the dead, or for magical rites. In this context, the "wrong" quality or lesser quality money, even in large quantities, is useless or degraded. This qualitative categorization of monies was also noted by Thomas and Znaniecki in their analysis of the traditional Polish peasant culture: "A sum received from selling a cow is qualitatively different from a sum received as a dowry, and both are different from a sum earned outside." Different monies were used differently and even kept separately. Indeed, Thomas and Znaniecki remarked that a peasant who set a sum aside for a designated purpose, and then needed some money for a different expense, would prefer to borrow it "even under very difficult conditions, rather than touch that sum."[42] These special monies, which the anthropologist Mary Douglas has perceptively identified as a sort of primitive coupon system, control exchange by rationing and restricting the allocation and use of currency. In the process, money sometimes performs economic functions by serving as a medium of exchange, but it also functions as a social and sacred "marker," used to acquire or amend status, or to celebrate ritual events. The point is that primitive money can be transformed from "fungible to nonfungible, from profane to sacred."[43]

But what about modern money? Influenced by economic models, most anthropologists have established a sharp dichotomy between primitive, restricted, "special purpose" money and modern "all-purpose" money, which, as a single currency, unburdened by ritual or social controls, can function effectively as a universal medium of exchange. Curiously, when it comes to modern money, even anthropologists seem to surrender their formidable analytical tools. For instance, over twenty-five years ago, Mary Douglas, in an important essay, suggested that modern money may not be as unrestricted and "free" after all. Her evidence, however, is puzzlingly limited. Modern money, argues Douglas, is controlled and rationed in two situations: in international exchange and at the purely individual personal level where "many of us try to primitivize our money . . . by placing restrictions at source, by earmarking monetary instruments of certain kinds for certain purposes, by only allowing ourselves or our wives certain limited freedoms in the disposal of money."[44]

The word "primitivize" labels these practices as unusual, and perhaps as regressive. Surely these restraints are more than "quirks" or a "clumsy attempt to control the all too liquid state of money," as Douglas suggests. Yet Douglas, who significantly advanced a cultural theory of consumption, does not go far enough with the cultural analysis of money. Likewise, the anthropologist Thomas Crump refers to the existence of what he calls "bounded sub-systems" in modern societies: separate spheres of exchange with special currencies. But his focus is chiefly on economic distinctions between types of monies, such as the simultaneous yet separate use of a national and a foreign currency (usually the dollar) by a country, the selective use of specie versus "scriptural" money for certain goods and services, or the separate economy of credit cards versus cash payments.[45]

Only recently have anthropologists begun to cast off the fallacy of a culturally neutral modern currency. An important collection of essays edited by the anthropologists Jonathan Parry and Maurice Bloch demonstrates the heterogeneity of money, showing how the multiple symbolic meanings of modern money are shaped by the cultural matrix. Parker Shipton's study of "special-purpose" cash among the Kenya Luo also offers a vivid account of how this East African farming community marks certain kinds of legal tender—obtained by a windfall or from the sales of certain commodities such as land, gold, tobacco, or a homestead rooster—as "bitter money" and limits their uses. If money earned from a land sale is spent on livestock, for instance, Luo believe the animals will die; or if tobacco money is involved in a bridewealth payment, the bride will die in fire and smoke.[46] But since such cases are restricted to societies outside the centers of capitalism, they cannot fully challenge established assumptions.

"Cognitive anthropologist" Jean Lave comes closer to the analysis in this book; her investigation of everyday arithmetic practices—which followed thirty-five Orange County, California, men and women in various settings, such as grocery shopping, and examined their household money-management practices—confirmed the futility of distinguishing between primitive special monies and generalized legal tender. Lave's respondents did not treat family income as a "general pool of family funds (like a general mathematics), used for all possible purposes" but instead compartmentalized their funds into distinct "stashes" that "reflected and also supported the social relations and categories of activities into which people organized their lives." Money, concludes Lave, "is employed so as to preserve moral categories and family relations as well as to express them."[47]

The obvious next step is to connect these fascinating findings to the web of social relations in which people are involved. A fully sociological model of money must show how, how much, and why, even in the heartland of capitalism, different networks of social relations and systems of meaning mark modern money, introducing controls, restrictions, and distinctions that are as influential as the rationing of primitive money. Multiple monies in the modern world may not be as visibly identifiable as the shells, coins, brass rods, or stones of primitive communities, but their invisible boundaries work just as well. How else, for instance, do we distinguish a bribe from a tribute or a donation, a wage from an honorarium, or an allowance from a salary? How do we identify ransom, bonuses, tips, damages, or premiums? True, there are quantitative differences between these various payments. But surely the special vocabulary conveys much more than different amounts. Detached from its qualitative distinctions, the world of money becomes indecipherable.

One might argue that the earmarking of money is an individual phenomenon. Indeed, in psychology, new studies now reject the notion that money is psychologically general, maintaining instead that money involves "multiple symbolizations." An exciting literature on "mental accounting" challenges economists' assumption of fungibility by showing the ways individuals distinguish between kinds of money. For instance, they treat a windfall income much differently from a bonus or an inheritance, even when the sums involved are identical. Political scientist Robert E. Lane has also documented a wide variety of ways in which Americans think of money as variable, a meaningful symbol of attitudinal feelings such as personal inadequacy, loss of control, shameful failure, security, or need for social approval.[48] Modern money, however, is marked by more than individual random preferences. As Marcel Mauss observed in 1914, money is "essentially a social fact."[49] The earmarking of money is thus a social process: money is attached to a variety of social relations rather than to individuals.

HOW AND WHEN DO PEOPLE CREATE CURRENCIES?

How, then, are differences among monies created? Although every situation or social relation shapes money to a certain extent, when do people make particularly vehement, visible, and sustained efforts to control monies? And how, specifically, do they mark differences among monies? As this book will demonstrate, people adopt especially elaborate controls over money and establish differential earmarks when and where they are engaged in delicate or difficult social interactions. Here are some prominent examples:

Social Interaction	Earmarked Monies
Creating or dissolving social ties	Courtship expenses, child-support payments, alimony
Making strong attempts to control others	Bribes, token currencies in penal or mental institutions, restricted bequests at death
Establishing or maintaining inequality	Welfare payments for the poor, monies for children, women's "pin money"
Maintaining delicate status distinctions	Tips to mailmen or nurses
Dealing with risk and uncertainty	Contributions of money to secure divine or magical intervention
Managing intimacy	Loans or money gifts to friends or kin; payments to sexual partners; legal monetary compensation for moral or emotional damages
Establishing or managing individual or group identity	Contributions to causes or organizations based on race, ethnicity, gender, or sexual orientation; donations to religious organizations; donor-named bequests to universities
Marking rites of passage	Fees, gifts, donations at weddings, funerals, baptisms, Bar Mitzvahs
Establishing or maintaining honor	"Blood money"
Managing inadmissible conflicts of interest	Payments for birthing or parenting —surrogate mother's fees, black-market payments, adoption fees, board payments to foster parents; payments for organs or blood
Maintaining clandestine social relations	Blackmail, drug-dealing payments, payoffs to spies, payments to concubine

In each of these cases, people create distinct kinds of
monies. Consider for instance a wife's "pin money." As we shall
see in the discussion of domestic currencies, traditional households designate a housewife's funds as a very different kind of
money than a child's allowance or a husband's personal money.
It is used differently, allocated in special ways, and its amount
set by calculations distinctive to gender as well as class.

The examples of differentiated social interactions and earmarked monies listed here belong outside the sphere of the market, but each one finds an equivalent among standard market
transactions. Among other places, earmarking shows very clearly
in wages. A "woman's wage" for instance has historically been a
very different sort of payment from a "man's wage." As Alice
Kessler-Harris persuasively documents, a woman's wage in the
early twentieth century was not set by her efficiency or productivity alone but also by custom or tradition, specifically by beliefs
of what income women needed. Particularly as the ideal of a
"family wage"—income earned by the man sufficiently large to
support his wife and children—spread, women's wages were
defined as supplementary income or an earned version of the
domestic "pin money." Women's earnings, Kessler-Harris suggests, were "not in the same sense as males' a 'wage.'"[50] Indeed,
determining women's wages often involved subtle moral quandaries; for instance, high wages might dangerously encourage a
woman's independence from her family, but overly low wages
might push young women into prostitution. Wages, or market
monies more generally, are thus not exempt from the process of
earmarking. There is no "free" wage economy determined simply
by demand and supply but instead a highly differentiated system
of wages or salaries shaped not only by gender but by such ·
other factors as age, race, and ethnicity.

Even when the sums earned may be comparable, different
systems of payments are not equivalent forms of income; wages,
for instance, differ from commissions, as does a Christmas bonus
from a merit or incentive raise. The forms and amount of payment, moreover, often have significant symbolic value as in the
case of an insurance agent who receives a publicized bonus for

the most sales, or contrariwise, the executive who sees the writing on the wall at year's end when he gets no bonus at all. Types of pay vary as well in the degree of control they exert over a worker's autonomy: payment by result is more restrictive, for instance, than payment by time. And timing itself matters: wage payment by the day or the week is a different sort of income from a monthly or biannual salary.[51] As with nonmarket currencies, each of these cases reflects distinct ways of marking money: for example, paying in certain ways, restricting uses, or determining the proper amount of payments for specified recipients.[52]

The process of earmarking monies—both market and nonmarket—is not only complex and constant but often highly contested. Disputes arise when parties to an interaction have contradictory understandings of the relationship, when their values clash or they are pursuing conflicting interests, or even when they have adopted different techniques for earmarking, especially when the preferred techniques of one party mean something different and undesirable to the other party.[53] For example, burial monies—money earmarked to pay for the dignified funeral of a loved one—illustrate how conflicts arise when money is earmarked to cope with difficult social situations. These monies—discussed in greater detail in chapter 6—have been persistently earmarked by the poor as a sacred expense, often put ahead of other necessities. Death money was, and still is, clearly distinct from rent money, food money, or clothing money. To the poor, a pauper's burial looms as the ultimate personal and social degradation. Which explains why since the late nineteenth century, industrial insurance agents have sometimes been paid ahead of the landlord. To middle-class observers, however, burial monies have typically seemed an irrational form of consumerism. But their attempts to shift poor people's cents or dollars from insurance to a more "rational" expenditure or into savings banks have notoriously failed.

Does this mean that the affluent do not earmark death monies? Spared the spectre of a county burial, upper- and middle-class people may not set aside burial monies, but they still differentiate death monies from other income or routine expenses. Surely, bargaining or comparison shopping for final expenses, such as funerals, however sensible, is deemed sacrilegious, and even negotiating the officiating clergyman's fee has typically involved delicate social work. Death monies are often earmarked to honor the deceased by making special donations to her or his preferred charitable cause. Monies gained by a loved one's death are also treated differently. In child wrongful-death lawsuits, as one example, middle-class plaintiffs tend to ritualize the monetary award by often donating it to charity, safety organizations, or scholarships for poor children. Even life insurance proceeds are set apart from other income, such as Social Security payments. Widows are more likely to use Social Security income for routine living expenses while earmarking life insurance proceeds not only for final expenses but as a "nest egg" to be preserved or else spent on larger nonroutine purchases, such as home repair or a child's education.[54]

How are multiple monies distinguished? How, concretely, do people set death money apart from rent money, or investment money from gift money? As this book will demonstrate, there are a number of different techniques, such as restricting the uses of money, regulating modes of allocation, inventing rituals for its presentation, modifying its physical appearance, designating separate locations for particular monies, attaching special meanings to particular amounts, appointing proper users to handle specified monies, and earmarking appropriate sources of money for specified uses. Indeed, the standard practice of budgeting constitutes a special case of earmarking: the subdivision of funds available to an organization, government, individual, or household into distinct categories, each with its own rules of expenditure.[55]

The phenomenon of earmarking is not restricted to people's uses of state-issued money but applies also to other objects, from tokens and commercial paper to art objects, and even including kitchen recipes or jokes—anything, in fact, that is socially exchangeable. At issue here, however, is to show that precisely

where interpreters of modernity see the utmost depersonalization
of life, in the circulation of state currency, people always introduce distinctions, doubts, and directives that defy all instrumental calculation.

THE BOOK'S AGENDA

To test the argument, this book explores fundamental transformations in the earmarking of money in the United States
between the 1870s and 1930s. It will focus on the creation of
three changing and contested kinds of monies: domestic, gift,
and charitable money. How did family members define and use
their various forms of household income? What if the money
came as a gift? What happened when authorities intervened in
the domestic earmarking process? The period between the 1870s
and 1930s provides a strategic time frame. The earmarking of
monies is a constant process, which preceded that time period
and continued changing afterward. But zooming into those years
makes historical sense. The post–Civil War expansion of the
economy and rise in real per capita income as well as an increasingly consumer-oriented culture and economy gave Americans
the means and incentives for differentiating their monies. In 1914
dollars, for instance, the average employed worker was earning
$375 in 1870 and $834 in 1930, which means that real wages
more than doubled over sixty years.[56]

Meanwhile, the world of goods and services available for
purchase multiplied. An array of useful, aesthetic, entertaining
commodities transformed their purchasers' lives. These commodities competed for the imagination and pocketbooks of
Americans, from automobiles, house furnishings, electrical appli-
ances, radios, and pianos to ready-made clothes, jewelry, stockings, cigarettes, beauty shops, perfume, cosmetics, and mouth-
wash, as well as summer vacations, saloons, amusement parks,
vaudeville, movies, and sports. Mass production and distribution

made at least some of the options available to lower-income customers. General consumer expenditures expanded fivefold between 1900 and 1929, with some discretionary items such as musical instruments and toilet articles increasing ten to twelve times.[57]

Making more money and spending it, however, not only required skillful bookkeeping, but also raised a new set of confusing and often controversial noneconomic quandaries. From the start, consumer experts were caught between the principle of freedom of consumption and the problem of incompetent consumers. What did it mean to spend money well? Who was a competent spender? How "free" should consumers' choices be? The problem of consumption, declared Hazel Kyrk, a noted consumer economist in 1923, was "fundamentally a problem of choice, of selection between values." To spend money is easy, wrote economist Wesley C. Mitchell in his 1912 essay "The Backward Art of Spending Money," but "to spend it well is hard." How should a housewife, responsible for her family's welfare, make objective comparisons "between the various gratifications which she may secure for ten dollars—attention to a child's teeth, a birthday present for her husband, two days at a sanatorium for herself"?[58] Yet the choices mattered greatly. Family welfare, Kyrk maintained, depended at least in part on the wise distribution of family income. Proper spending was differentiated spending; effective spending required earmarks.[59]

Consumerism redefined even thrift. The "new gospel of savings," noted Benjamin R. Andrews, professor of household economics at Teacher's College, Columbia University, and a well-known author, was that the family should "'save to spend,'" earmarking savings for specific worthwhile purchases, such as buying a home, a child's education, a piano, a car, holiday gift expenses, or even "to bring relatives from Europe to America."[60] Making "wise" choices was thus at the core of America's new consumer society.

Struggling for the right answers, Americans wrote about and studied money matters in an unprecedented way. Starting in the

1870s, for instance, household-budget studies richly documented how the working class, lower middle class, and immigrants spent their money. And in anonymous, "confessional" articles ("How We Live on $1,000 a Year or Less") published in popular magazines, middle-class Americans disclosed their own domestic budgets, transforming the spending of money into a public issue. Consumer experts guided popular earmarking practices, while advertisers made their own claims to people's monies. By the 1920s the home-economics movement was booming; textbooks on home management, treatises on family economics, courses in domestic finances, and even the advice columns of women's magazines specialized in the training of competent consumption, seeking a rationalized system for earmarking monies.

Modern money management would also serve to Americanize immigrants properly. Citizenship-training handbooks overflowed with lessons on shopping, banking, transmission of monies, and skillful budgeting. Typical language drill exercises developed newcomers' accounting skills, as students were asked to practice with phrases such as "Next week I shall pay the rent. I shall buy two tons of coal. How much shall the milk bill be?" or write sentences using key words like "will cost," "paid," "expensive," or "bill." Immigrants were also closely tutored on the fundamentals of earmarking. "Do you know," asked one text, "what part of your income goes for clothing, for amusements, for food, or are you guessing? Are you sure you are not spending too much for one thing at the expense of something else?"[61] Thus, paradoxically, the very same government that worried about the standardization and homogenization of its national currency carefully instructed its new citizens on the urgency of differentiating monies.

Budget studies themselves were not simply economic inventories, but, as historian Daniel Horowitz puts it, "morality plays" dramatizing the moral significance of consumption choices, drawing boundaries between legitimate and illegitimate expenses. The growing complexities of earmarking monies were reflected in the "explosion" of budget categories and items in the first decades of the twentieth century. Next to the usual budgetary items now appeared new headings such as "children's allowances, flowers, parcel post, meals outside the home, postage, interest on debt, stationery, taxes, telegrams, and lawn care." It was not merely the complications of affluence. Horowitz shows how a major survey of working-class household budgets conducted in 1918–19 found a notable diversification in "sundry" expenditures; while an 1875 report had found that such funds were spent mostly for newspapers and organizational life, by 1918 monies were divided among "life insurance, church, 'patriotic purposes' gifts, streetcar fare, movies, newspapers, postage, physician, medicine, tobacco, 'laundry sent out,' cleaning supplies, 'toilet articles and preparations,' and barber."[62]

The social differentiation of monies thus became a critical agenda for Americans. The increased use of money in households, gift exchanges, and charities raised particularly delicate and contested puzzles. What sort of money should circulate within the home, as a gift for intimates, or as a donation to a needy stranger? The increasing involvement of households in differentiating expenditures challenged traditional notions of intimacy, domesticity, and social control. The result was not only uncertainty, dispute, and experimentation within households, but also time-consuming public debate and negotiation about proper forms of earmarking. Defining their identities and personal competence increasingly through spending, Americans were engaging in new and difficult forms of social effort. As households became the critical units for expenditure and display, the appropriate earmarking of money became a sign of social competence.

Chapter 2 examines the controversial domestic currency. How did people adapt money to the intimate relations of kinship? How should money be allocated in the family? How, for instance, did families determine how their regular income or extra earnings were used—how much for savings, how much for charity, how much spent for leisure? And, most important, which family members were entitled or competent to control, manage, and spend family funds? To what extent were the husband's wage or his wife's or children's earnings a collective property? How much could they keep for themselves? Defining, allocating, and using domestic monies was not always a consensual process as husbands, wives, and children struggled to divide family funds in often conflicting ways. This chapter focuses on the most problematic, delicate, and debated household currency—the housewife's income—tracing its transformation as women became the family's consumer expert.

Chapter 3 turns to gifts of money. The social relations of kin and friendship also patterned money into a sentimental gift. What distinguished a gift from an ordinary payment for services? And how did people differentiate among various money gifts: ritual tokens, sentimental gifts, remittances? Was a tip a gift or a payment? What about Christmas bonuses? How did men and women differentiate among gifts of courtship; what sorts of transfers distinguished courting from marriage or prostitution?

Chapters 4, 5, and 6 explore the official creation of charitable cash. They extend the analysis of the first three chapters by showing the interaction of state authorities, domestic economies, and gift transfers. This discussion raises the general problem of what happens when the state deliberately sets out to break the homogeneity of money by creating visible distinctions between kinds of money, as it does in establishing ration coupons, scrip, or savings bonds. My account focuses on the persistent conflict between cash and in-kind relief in American social welfare policy. Why did state agencies and private charities resist granting unrestricted money support to poor households and individuals? What sort of money was cash relief? How was it redefined by poor recipients? About what features of charitable assistance did agencies and their clients disagree most vehemently?

Surely the social world of monies extends beyond the doorsteps of households and charities. Why then choose these three areas? Why not examine, for instance, the social construction of market money, confronting economists on their own turf? That is certainly worth doing. But I have selected crucial areas where, according to the traditional dichotomy between the market and personal relations, either money should not have entered at all or should have resulted in rationalization, flattening personal and social relations and commodifying sentiment in family, friendship, charity, death. This book will attempt to show instead that it is very hard to suppress the active, creative power of supposedly vulnerable social relations.

In order to untangle the various uses and meanings of money, the book draws on materials as varied as court cases, etiquette books, instructions for charity workers, annual reports of charitable organizations, immigrants' manuals and memoirs, household budget studies, contemporary novels, plays, vaudevilles, general periodicals, newspapers, and womens' magazines—including feature articles, fiction, letters to the editor, advice columns—consumer economics and home economics textbooks, popular household manuals, and advertisements. Exploring people's changing understandings and uses of money as they manage their multiple, variable, and contested social relations makes us listen carefully to the pronouncements of social arbiters such as etiquette and magazine writers, social workers, or legal authorities. It also takes us, as far as the evidence permits, into people's everyday practices. The challenge is to integrate the changing symbolism of money with people's varied, complex, and often surprising uses of their monies.

2

The Domestic Production of Monies

NELL: You've never been fair with Mother about money. You've had everything—your poker games, your cigars, your holiday fishing trips! . . . And that's why I am asking you to pay her a definite salary instead of making her come to you like a beggar for every penny she gets.

HUGHIE: Most wives have to ask their husbands for money, and I've noticed they don't stutter much.

NELL: There isn't a wife in the world who wouldn't sooner have less money to spend if only she knew it was her own and she could do what she liked with it without answering those everlasting questions: "What do you want it for?" and "What did you do with the last I gave you?"

In the play *Chicken Feed* ("Wages for Wives"), which opened in 1923 in Chicago, twenty-two-year-old Nell Bailey discovers, on the morning of her wedding, that her father had secretly invested his insurance money in risky trolley-company bonds but still angrily blames Nell's mother for spending part of the premium money on her daughter's wedding. Nell insists that she will not get married until her father agrees to give her mother half of his earnings as her rightfully earned wage, explaining to her increasingly concerned fiancé: "Danny, how would you like it if you had a boss and he said—'Look here, Danny, I won't pay you a regular salary. I'll just give you presents when I feel like it. It makes me feel so nice and generous and I like to hear you thank me. And in case you need something, just tell me and I'll see if I think you ought to have it.' What man would ever stand that?" When her father balks, Nell suspends her wedding and organizes a strike—with her mother and a married friend—to secure wives' right to a fair share of family income. The play's "happy ending" has the couples reunited and Nell's chastened father promising his wife, "you're going to get your share of the money—save it or blow it in, as you like."[1]

The battle over the purse strings was more than jocular theatrical entertainment. Starting in the late nineteenth century, it was played out with passion, persistence, and some puzzlement in the privacy of American households. And increasingly in public as well. The domestic "fiscal problem" emerged as a topical news story in magazines and newspapers, in poignant letters to the editor and advice columns, as the topic of conferences in women's clubs, and even from the pulpit. By 1928, one observer concluded that "more quarrels between husband and wife have been started by the mention of money than by chorus girls, blond waitresses, dancing men with sleek hair, [or] traveling men."[2] Indeed, the battle over the domestic finances often ended in court. Between 1880 and 1920, money quarrels increasingly became a grounds for divorce among affluent as well as poor couples.[3] And domestic money raised legal issues even in unbroken marriages. Did a wife have a right to an allowance? If she saved money from her housekeeping expenses, was that money hers? Was a wife a thief if she "stole" money from her husband's trousers? Could a wife pledge her husband's credit at any store? There was also the matter of women's earnings. When was a woman's dollar legally her own? Slowly, but steadily, court decisions began to overturn the common-law dictum that a wife's earnings belonged to her husband.

Why did domestic money become such a controversial currency at the turn of the century? Certainly money conflicts between family members had existed earlier. For instance, in her study of New York working-class women, the historian Christine Stansell tells of one—albeit extreme—1811 case in which a husband beat his common-law wife to death after she took four shillings from his pockets. Yet these disputes remained private, rarely entering the public discourse as a major issue of collective concern. A consensus of sorts existed about the proper regulation of family income, and it varied by class. Among middle- and upper-class households, money matters seem to have been established largely as the husband's business. In her 1841 landmark *Treatise on Domestic Economy*, the household affairs expert Catherine Beecher noted how, particularly among businessmen, a family's expenses were "so much more under the control of the man than of the woman." Likewise, historian Mary P. Ryan's study of family life in early nineteenth-century Oneida County, New York, found men in charge of money matters. After all, the nineteenth-century "cult of domesticity" established home life as an alternative to the dominance of the market: its guardian, the "true" Victorian woman, was a specialist in affect, not in finances. A woman might handle the housekeeping expenses, but "serious money" was a man's currency. Working-class households, on the other hand, managed their limited and often uncertain incomes by appointing wives to be the family's cashier. Husbands and children handed their paychecks over to the wives, who were expected to administer the collective income skillfully, including the cash income women generated on their own. Most of these monies, to be sure, were limited to housekeeping expenses.[4]

But, at the turn of the century, the consensus began to crumble. As the consumer economy multiplied the number and attractiveness of goods while, at the same time, the discretionary income of American households rose, the proper allocation and disposition of family income became an urgent and contested matter. Spending well became as critical as earning enough. In textbooks, classrooms, and magazine articles, home-economics specialists spread the principles of educated consumerism, insisting that "it does not matter so much just how many dollars are in the pay-envelope, as it does what those dollars actually secure and bring into the life of the worker."[5]

Within their homes, families worked hard at earmarking their money. They bought the account ledgers and budget books recommended by experts to carefully register their expenses, or else invented all sorts of strategies to differentiate the household's multiple monies. Take, for instance, Mrs. M's system as she told it to *Woman's Home Companion* in the early 1920s: "I collected eight little cans, all the same size, and pasted on them the following words, in big letters: groceries, carfare, gas, laundry, rent, tithe, savings, miscellaneous. . . . We speak of those cans now, as the grocery can, carfare can, etc." Other families used jars, china pitchers, envelopes, or boxes to distinguish their monies physically, while some stashed them away in stockings or under mattresses and floorboards. Earmarking practices were often quite ingenious, as, for example, that of the father who destined every quarter bearing the date of his child's birth for his education, or of the bargain shopper who built her nest egg by saving the difference between the regular price and the bargain price of her purchases. In a parallel way, immigrants religiously marked a portion of their hard-earned wages for transmission to relatives back in their home villages.[6]

Or else families relied on a variety of outside institutions to safeguard and differentiate their monies, from regular or postal savings banks and school banks to insurance companies, mutual aid societies, budget clubs, building and loan associations, war bonds, and even installment payments. In many cases, this was not just accumulation of homogeneous capital but differentiated savings, most dramatically in the case of the "summer vacation money" or "Christmas money" deposited in the popular Christmas clubs or vacation clubs, which served as collective "piggy banks."[7]

Observers contended that organized budgeting would neatly rationalize household finances: "The more impersonal family book-keeping can become, like that of a store or factory, the more the family will get out of the income, and the less will be the wear and tear on the nerves."[8] But the domestic earmarking of monies was hardly a smooth accounting process. There was too much at stake in how the money was divided, for what purposes, and by whom. As families increasingly depended on the cash wages brought in by the husband, it became more urgent and complex to negotiate husbands', wives', and children's claims to that money. To what extent did the husband's wage become a collective possession? Once his money entered the household, who had the right to control it? Should husbands hand over all their salary to their wives, or how much could they keep for themselves? How much money should a wife receive, and for which expenses? Was that money a gift from her husband, or was a wife entitled to a particular share of the income? What about children: Should they be given their own money to spend or was it their duty to earn it through household chores? How should children spend their money?

This new "tightened competition for the family income," as the sociologist Robert Lynd described it, prompted a general rethinking of economic transfers within households, a search for appropriate domestic currencies for wives, husbands, and children. It was necessary, urged a manual in household accounting, to "consider the amounts [of money] being used by and for the different members of the family, so that there may be always a wise and just division of the family income and no one member will unconsciously have more than a necessary share."[9]

But it was the housewife's money that became the most paradoxical, contested, and uncertain currency. As the tasks of shopping for household needs expanded, women took over most of them. They were charged with transforming their husband's wage into domestic money and repeatedly reminded that a wage was "only money when it comes to your hands, useless to keep, or to wear, or to warm you, or . . . improve the family life. *You* are the one who must change it into food and clothing, a family improvement. . . . " What's more, women were told, "In all the duties of a good woman's life there is none more sacred than this, the duty of Wise Buying." The spinning wheel, observed *Harper's Bazar*, had been replaced by an account book.[10] The twentieth-century version of the nineteenth-century moral guardian was thus expected to serve as the household's purchasing agent and budget expert. To be sure, the financial wisdom of wives had been a concern in the eighteenth century as well. But the expansion of the consumer economy made proper spending skills a dominant and visible measure of domestic expertise. The "good housekeeper" was responsible "for the care of her husband's money, and she must expend it wisely." After all, as one exemplary housewife explained, "a man does not understand the regulation of the household and its expenses."[11]

But there was a fundamental problem with "Mrs. Consumer's" increased financial role; it came without a salary and most often without even a fixed and dependable income. Indeed, turn-of-the-century wives, even those married to wealthy men, often found themselves without a dollar of their own. As Lucy M. Salmon, professor of history at Vassar College, explained in 1909: "Men are still for the most part those whose wages are paid in hard cash, who have a bank account and carry a cashbook, and who therefore consider that they have the right to decide in regard to the way the money they earn shall be spent."[12]

Worse still, women had lost most claims to the economic resources of the family. While the labor contributions of colonial wives were recognized, the nineteenth-century domestication of housewives placed married women outside the productive economy. No matter how hard they worked or how much their families depended on their labors, women's housework was defined—

and valued—as a task of emotional, but hardly material, import. Thus when it came to the household's economic welfare, it was the husband's wage-work—not the wife's housework—that mattered. His money became hers only as his gift, not as her earned share of the income. Tellingly, her money even had a special vocabulary that set it apart from ordinary cash—allowance, pin money, "egg money," "butter money," spending money, pocket money, or "dole."[13] Women were thus caught in a strange predicament of being cashless money managers, expected to spend properly but denied control over money. The success of the home-economics movement, which urged women to run their homes like a business, further intensified the contradiction in women's economic lives.

Women's stratagems to extract some cash from their non-forthcoming husbands were the subject of jokes and a staple of late-nineteenth-century vaudeville routines. But the domestic fiscal problem turned serious, forcing a difficult and controversial reevaluation of women's household money as well as of their earned income. To see what was at issue, we need to distinguish among three possible ways of organizing the transfers of domestic money: as a payment (direct exchange); an entitlement (the right to a share); and a gift (one person's voluntary bestowal on another). Money as a payment implied a certain distance, contingency, bargaining, and accountability among the parties. Money as an entitlement implied strong claims to domestic power and autonomy. But money as a gift implied subordination and arbitrariness. For a long time, women and advocates of women's rights wrestled over which was supposed to be women's proper share of the family income. This chapter examines this struggle, tracing the transformation in married women's money between the 1870s and the 1930s, and showing how gender as well as class deeply marked the meaning, uses, and allocation of domestic currencies.

A DOLLAR OF HER OWN:
DEFINING WOMEN'S HOUSEHOLD MONEY

In terms of evidence, to study money in the family is to enter largely uncharted territory. Although money is the major source of disagreements between husband and wife and often a sore point between parents and children, curiously, we know less about money matters than about family violence or even marital sex. Not only are families reluctant to disclose their private financial lives to strangers, but husbands, wives, and children often lie, deceive, or simply conceal information from each other as well. Perhaps more fundamental still, the model of what Amartya Sen calls the "glued-together family" has meant that questions about how money is divided among family members are seldom even asked. Once money enters the family, it is assumed to be somehow equitably distributed between family members, serving to maximize their collective welfare. How much money each person gets, how he or she obtains it, from whom and for what—these issues are rarely considered. And yet, as Michael Young suggested more than thirty years ago, the distribution of money among family members is often as lopsided and arbitrary as the distribution of national income among families. Therefore, Young argues, we should stop assuming that "some members of a family cannot be rich while others are poor."[14] The period between 1870 and 1930 provides some unusual glimpses into this traditionally secret world of family money; at the turn of the century, as household finances became a contentious issue, the renegotiation of the domestic economy emerged from the usually closed doors of individual households to enter the public discourse.

How was a wife's money earmarked and set apart from other domestic monies? American women, even those whose husbands could afford it, never had a legal claim to any portion of domestic money. As long as spouses lived together, the author of a 1935 *Law Review* article explained, "the wife's right to support is not a right to any definite thing or to any definite amount. . . . Whether the wife will get much or little is not a matter of her legal right but is a matter for the husband to decide."[15] The concept of a family wage—a salary that would support a male wage-earner and his dependent family—further increased married women's dependence on their husband's wages. As a result, the allocation of domestic money relied on unofficial rules and informal negotiation. At the turn of the century, married women—the majority of whom depended on their husbands' paychecks or incomes—obtained their cash through a variety of transfers.

Upper- and middle-class wives received an irregular dole or, more rarely, a regular allowance from their husbands for housekeeping expenses, including household goods and clothing. Sometimes women relied almost entirely on "invisible" dollars, crediting their expenses and rarely handling cash at all. Working-class wives, on the other hand, were given their husbands' paychecks and were expected to administer and distribute the family money. These official monies, however, were supervised and, even in the case of working-class women, ultimately owned and controlled by the husband. Sometimes, husbands openly took over all monetary transactions. In a letter to the advice column of the *Woman's Home Companion* in 1905, a thirty-year-old woman complained that John, her husband, although "liberal in a way . . . keeps the pocketbook himself, buys the provisions, prefers to purchase the dry-goods, the shoes, the gloves . . . and does not see that I need any money when he gets whatever I want."[16] Even if a woman managed to save from her housekeeping expenses, the law ultimately considered that money to be her husband's property. For instance, in 1914, when Charles Montgomery sued his wife Emma for the $618.12 she had saved from the household expenses during their twenty-five years of marriage, Justice Blackman of the Brooklyn Supreme Court ruled for the husband, arguing "that no matter how careful and prudent has been the wife, if the money . . . belonged to the husband it is still his property, unless the evidence shows that it was a gift to his wife."[17]

A wife's legitimate channels to additional cash were thus limited to a variety of persuasion techniques: asking, cajoling, or downright begging. And it was critical to master the rules of asking. Women were reminded that "to ask a tired, hungry man for anything is sheer waste of breath." The woman who "knows how," however, "wears her most becoming gown and puts his favorite dish before a man when she wants something."[18] Sometimes only sexual blackmail worked. A mother of two children whose husband earned $250 a month but gave her only $75 for household expenses confided the secret of her "quick victory" to *Good Housekeeping*: "Last summer I knew I could never stand another year of absolute misery over money matters. . . . On Monday night, after the best dinner I could serve, I told my husband . . . that unless he gave me $175 a month I would never let him so much as kiss me again. . . . In the afternoon I had moved all my clothes . . . from our room to another across the hall." After a week of solitude he relented.[19]

If such techniques of persuasion failed, there was also a repertoire of underground financial strategies, ranging from home pocket-picking to padding bills. In 1890, an article in the *Forum* denounced the "amount of deceit, fraud, and double dealing which grow out of the administration of the family finances." Just to obtain "a few dollars they can call their own," women routinely engaged in systematic domestic fraud; for example, some "get their milliners to send in a bill for forty dollars, instead of thirty, the real price, in order to take the extra ten to themselves . . . [others] overtax their tired eyes and exhausted bodies by taking in sewing without their husband's knowledge; and . . . farmers' wives . . . smuggled apples and eggs into town. . . . " In Elsa Herzfeld's study of families living in tenements on the West Side of New York City in the early 1900s, wives disclosed some of their tricks; one woman told the investigator that while she knew her husband would "whip her" if he found out, she worked on "the sly," building a secret "store" under her mattress. Another wife "served" to earn some extra money, which she used to buy herself dresses for the "rackets." Sometimes, just to be able to send their parents some money, it appears that some immigrant women looked for ways of keeping their letters and money orders outside the home, hidden from their husbands.[20]

Some methods were riskier: in 1905 Joseph Schultz was taken to the police court of Buffalo by Mrs. Schultz. It seems that Mr. Schultz, determined to stop his wife's nocturnal thefts of the change left in his trousers, set a small rattrap in the trouser pocket. At about 2:00 A.M. the trap was sprung, and next morning the husband was taken to court. *Bench and Bar*, a New York legal journal, reported with some satisfaction that the judge turned down the wife's complaint and upheld the right of husbands to maintain rattraps for the protection of their small change. In another case, Theresa Marabella, forty years old, was sentenced to four months in a county jail for stealing $10 from the trousers of Frank Marabella, a laborer from Bellport, New York, and her husband. She had spent the money on a trip to New York City.[21]

But "stolen" dollars were not only taken by the wives of poor men. Indeed, one observer was persuaded that "the money skeletons in the closets of some nominally rich women may be as gruesome as are those in the closets of the nominally poor." While poor women rifled their husbands' trousers looking for some change, the affluent cashless wife used a variety of deceptive techniques. Mrs. Gray, a grandmother married for twenty years but without any money "she could call her own," was described as having "adopted a systematic policy of deceit and fraud toward her husband. . . . When she wants to give a little money to help buy a stove for a poor family, or to assist some sick or starving creature to pay his rent, she tells her husband that the flour is out, or that the sugar is low, and so gets the needful amount." Thus this "strict church member" who never told a falsehood, paradoxically "cheats and deceives" the man "she has solemnly sworn to love and obey."[22]

There were other ways to "circumvent the holder of the purse." Women bargained with dressmakers, milliners, and shopkeepers to add extra items in their bills so that, when the bill was paid, "the rich man's wife may get a rake-off and possess a few dollars." A Parisian-born New York dressmaker complained that American ladies got "costumes made and delivered that they wear one night and then return . . . they get $50 or $100 cash and have it charged as a dress or hats in the bill, so as to deceive their husbands." In search of cash, some women even turned to their servants, selling them their old furniture. A Japanese visitor to the United States in the second decade of the twentieth century was shocked to hear from "men and women of all classes, from newspapers, novels, lecturers, and once even from the pulpit . . . allusions to amusing stories of women secreting money in odd places, coaxing it from their husbands, . . . or saving it secretly for some private purpose."[23]

The relative poverty of married women, however, grew increasingly untenable. How could a wife assume her added financial responsibilities as the household's "wage spender" if she had to ask, cajole, beg, or steal for her money and when so often she did not even know how much money was available to spend? The demand intensified for a more definite and regular housekeeping income for the wife and increasingly for her "private purse," a free sum of unaccounted money to spend for the home, entertainment, gifts, or on the many new consumer goods targeted at a female audience, such as clothes, cosmetics, or perfumes. As a forceful turn-of-the-century editorial in *Ladies' Home Journal* warned, the housewife was simply "not given the tools wherewith to work to the best advantage." While it was "all very well to go into spasms of indignation when one speaks of marriage as 'a business partnership,'" declared Edward Bok, the *Journal*'s editor, marriage "must have a money basis," and domestic income should be treated as the "mutual affair" of husband and wife.[24]

DOLE VERSUS ALLOWANCE:
THE ALLOWANCE AS A SOLUTION

The traditional method of doling out money to women came
under attack by the late nineteenth century in a battle that continued into the first three decades of the twentieth. In 1915 *Harper's
Weekly* observed that "the number of women who find it unthink-
able to ask another human being, 'Please may I have a new pair
of shoes?'" was "rapidly increasing." Anonymous letters to the edi-
tors of women's magazines conveyed the money troubles of
housewives. "What Should Margaret Do?" asked one woman
whose husband in 1909 gave her only $50 a month (from his
$300 salary) to run the house, pay all bills, and clothe herself and
a baby girl. When she asked for more, "John . . . gets very angry
and accuses her of being dissatisfied . . . [and tells her] she is
always wanting something." Etiquette manuals pointed to "the
vexed question of home and personal expenses" as a "chief
source of unhappiness in married life." Part of the problem was
the husband's failure to disclose his financial resources; "thus the
wife, entirely ignorant as to what amount she may safely spend,
errs too often on the side of extravagance, finding too late, when
a storm of reproach descends upon her innocent head, where
and how she has sinned."[25]

While it was true, admitted Edward Bok, the *Ladies' Home
Journal* editor, that "wives, as a rule, get what they want," there
was no reason why they should be obliged to ask for their
money "whereas they are just as entitled to their feminine furbe-
lows as men are to their cigars." Even the most generous husband, noted Bok, seemed to ignore that "nothing on God's earth
humiliates a wife more than to be compelled to ask her husband
for money." Some wives sentimentalized the gift transfer, as, for
example, the woman who told *Ladies' Home Journal* that during
her twenty-five years of marriage she always had enjoyed "asking him for money. We both of us felt that it is as much mine as
it is his, but it gives him pleasure to hand it to me, and it gives
me pleasure to ask it and to see that he is pleased to give it to

me." In most cases, however, the dole was defined as demeaning, appropriate as payment for subordinates but not for partners in marriage. "How would some of our men like it," speculated Bok's editorial, "if every time they wanted some little thing they had to ask their wives for it?"[26] In fact, asking for money made wives feel like their children: "Ada, my little daughter," complained one woman, "has more actual cash than I, for she does not mind giving Daddy a kiss and a hug and asking him for a dollar or two when she wants money to spend. He can deny nothing to her blue eyes and golden curls. But I loathe asking him for money."[27]

Condemning a system that forced women to play the "mendicant before a husband," the well-known and widely syndicated columnist Dorothy Dix remarked on the irony of men who "will trust [a] wife with his honor, his health, his name, his children, but he will not trust her with money." The availability of credit was no solution, since it was simply another form of gift money supervised by the husband. Indeed, observers noted the "anomalous" situation in which men willingly paid "large bills . . . [of] wives and daughters," yet were unwilling "to trust them with the smallest amount of ready money." The rich wife, remarked the widely-read author and theologian Hugh Black, could order "anything from countless stores where they had a charge account." But, often, "she could not give ten cents to a beggar."[28]

The doctrine of necessaries provided wives with some legal recourse by making a husband directly responsible to a merchant for the purchases made by his wife. Yet even this entitlement to pledge a husband's credit was restricted. Necessaries were so ambiguously defined that merchants were reluctant to risk extending credit to a wife for goods that might fall outside that category. Moreover, husbands were entitled to determine where necessaries should be purchased and could terminate a wife's authority to pledge his credit by demonstrating that he had provided the necessaries or a sufficient allowance to obtain them. The law, in fact, was explicitly concerned with protecting husbands from the "mad" expenditures of "extravagant" wives.[29]

Rheta Childe Dorr, a journalist, foreign correspondent, writer, and activist in suffrage circles, recalled how, growing up in the 1880s, "the numerically inferior male members of the family . . . enjoyed a status superior to that of the majority, which was feminine . . . and the superiority consisted in the possession, actual or potential, of money. Mother always asked Father for the money she disbursed for the common household. When any of us wanted to go anywhere, especially if an admittance fee was in question, we invariably said: 'We must ask Father.' When things were needed by any child Mother always said: 'I will speak to your father about it.' Father was no tyrant. . . . But that is how it was in the Eighties." An early twentieth-century nursery rhyme nicely encapsulated Dorr's memories: "Clap hands, clap hands till father comes home, for father has money but mother has none."[30] A better system was needed to assure women, as one commentator put it, "the divine right . . . to the pay envelope." Sociological experts joined the critics, noting that by becoming the household's "treasurer . . . doling out the amount which may be at any time at his command or convenience," a husband controlled "not only the economic but the spiritual life of his wife." Even the courts occasionally agreed, refusing to treat domestic stealing as real theft. In a 1908 case of a wife charged with robbing her husband's small change, Judge Furlong of a Brooklyn court supported the "thief," declaring that "a wife has a perfect right to go through her husband's pockets at night and take his money if he fails to provide for her properly."[31]

But what was a proper money income for wives? For some, the best solution for "penniless wives" was a dowry for every daughter. Wives seemed to prefer a regular weekly or monthly allowance. A 1910 *Good Housekeeping* survey of 300 wives found that 120 supported the allowance system. By 1915, according to *Harper's Weekly*, some young brides "of the ultra-modern type" required the promise of an allowance "before vowing to love, honor and obey."[32] Women's magazines increasingly endorsed the allowance in their articles and even in their fiction. In "Her Weight in Gold," for instance, a short story that appeared in the *Saturday Evening Post* in 1926, Mrs. Jondough, the wealthy female protagonist, declared "that all the gowns and diamond pins in the world were not compensation for even a tiny personal allowance of her very own." That same year, the Women's Freedom League of St. Louis went further, sponsoring a bill that would make a dress allowance for wives legally compulsory. Home-economics experts were in agreement. Mary W. Abel, an editor of the *Journal of Home Economics*, assailed the dole system, arguing that "to achieve the best results in the spending of the family money, the mother should have such control of the income as will ensure her efficiency as manager and buyer."[33] A proper housekeeping allowance seemed to improve domestic harmony. In 1923, the New York Legal Aid Society summarized their experience in handling thousands of domestic conflict cases in a ten-point "Domestic Relations Decalogue" addressed to young men. While the first recommendation was to "be generous according to your means," the second priority was "not to interfere with a woman in the management of purely domestic affairs." The average wife, advised the report, "is far better qualified than her husband . . . to handle economically that portion of his income set aside for household expenses." Even Emily Post certified the allowance with her stamp of approval.[34]

Still, converting female currency from dole to allowance was not easily achieved. A 1928 survey of 200 upper-class men and women found that while 73 used the allowance system, 66 still relied on the "old fashioned system of husbands taking charge of all money, paying all bills and doling out funds to the wife as she asks for them"; the remaining couples had a more progressive joint bank account or an undefined arrangement.[35] Husbands, it seems, were less enthusiastic than their wives about the allowance. As Dorothy Dix pointed out, "One question that is fought out in a battle that lasts from the altar to the grave, in most families, is the question of an allowance for the wife. She

yearns for it. The man is determined that she shall not have it."
As late as 1938, *Ladies' Home Journal* conducted a major
national survey on the topic "What Do the Women of America
Think About Money?" and asked "Should a wife have a regular
housekeeping allowance?" They found that 88 percent of female
respondents answered affirmatively, regardless of marital status
or geographical location. And 91 percent of younger women
(under thirty) were for it. Yet, only 48 percent of the wives actually received an allowance.[36]

Husbands resisted the allowance because it officially carved
out a separate, specific portion of their income and made it
"hers," thereby increasing a woman's financial control. In a "typical case" reported by a reader of *Good Housekeeping*, a clergyman was puzzled by his wife's request for money: "I don't see
any reason why she should have any money. I pay all of the bills
so long as she is reasonable and economical in her ordering."
Critics of the unrestricted allowance regularly invoked women's
alleged financial incompetence. Take, for instance, the lamenta-
tions of the controversial "Mere Man," author of *The Domestic
Blunders of Women*, that it was "to people who cannot put two
and two together, who can not keep money, who do not know
how to spend money, who keep no record of what they receive,
and have no knowledge of what anything should, or has, cost, to
whom we entrust the finances of our homes."[37]

The allowance created yet an additional sort of confusion.
What kind of money was it? If the allowance was no longer supposed to be a dole or gift, neither could it become a payment for
services. In fact "paying" a wife was illegal since it made her "a
menial and a servant in the home where she should discharge
marital duties in devoted and loving ministrations." In 1926,
when a "perturbed housewife" wrote to the governor of Minnesota complaining that "my neighbor's hired girl can draw a
salary of $60 a month, with board and room free. . . . But I, as
housewife, get not one cent for my own needs," the attorney
general's office, according to a *New York Times* report,
responded that there was no law "which compels a husband to

pay a salary to his wife."[38] While occasional observers suggested that since "some money must pass . . . between the head of a house and the members of his household," the transfer might as well be treated as a business contract, most supporters of the allowance were careful to distinguish it from a payment. "To the man who says, 'But I cannot pay my wife like a servant,'" recommended a writer in the *Forum*, "the answer must be 'Certainly not.' She is a partner and as such is entitled to a share in the dividends." In fact, some allowance advocates reasoned that an equitable domestic currency protected women from the necessity to earn market wages in order to supply some "little extra money" without having to ask their husbands.[39]

If the allowance was difficult to define, it was also hard to regulate. Since it was not a payment, the actual amount of money involved could not depend on the performance of wifely duties. While usually it was expected to be "proportioned to the earnings of her husband," in practice, as a *New York Times* editorial pointed out, it remained a "delicate question," often creating a "sharp difference of opinion about [its] size."[40] The uses of the allowance remained unclear as well. Was it exclusively for the household? Who "owned" the surplus, if there was one? Did it cover women's personal needs?

ALLOWANCE VERSUS A JOINT ACCOUNT: THE ALLOWANCE AS "BAD" MONEY

In February 1925, Reverend Howard Melish, rector of the Holy Trinity church in Brooklyn, addressing the New York Women's City Club on the importance of a wife's economic independence, related the following anecdote: "Yesterday," Melish told his audience, "I asked an old lady . . . what her idea was of a happy marriage. Without an instant's hesitation she replied 'An allowance.'" But the anecdote backfired. The next day, in an editorial entitled "They Want More Than That," the *New York Times* expressed the new, critical view of allowances: "Admitting . . . the equality of service rendered by wife and husband in . . . the family unit, why should the one rather than the other have an 'allowance' and . . . why should the 'allowance' be determined by the husband and be granted as a favor?" Allowances, concluded the editorial, "are for inferiors from superiors," and therefore an inappropriate currency for the modern woman.[41]

In the 1920s, even as popular support for allowances intensified, there was also a growing criticism of the allowance system from those who saw it as an inequitable and even degrading form of domestic money. Christine Frederick proclaimed it a "relic of some past time when women were supposed to be too inexperienced to handle money." Frederick, a leader of the popular household-efficiency movement, rejected the allowance as an "unbusinesslike" scheme that undermined the modern goal of running the home as rationally as a factory or an office. Benjamin R. Andrews, a noted authority in home economics, explained that a housewife's "compensation as worker is of the same kind as that of all workers—it is the living that she enjoys." That her wages were not "in the form of money income as is the pay envelope of her husband for his outside employment" hardly mattered. The wife received "real wages," meaning her "food, clothing, shelter and cultural satisfactions of all kinds," which were equal to her husband's benefits after his cash income was "transmuted by family expenditure into food, clothing," and the like. "His pay and her pay," Andrews concluded, "are ordinarily identical."[42]

Most "anti-allowance" advocates, however, did not press for domestic salaries but supported a democratic "joint control of the purse." The modern "good husband," according to a playful definition in the *American Magazine*, was a "fifty-fifty" man who "takes his wife into his confidence as a real partner and plays fair with her in every detail . . . (hardly ever) short-changing her." "Bad" husbands were either "fog throwers" who "never let their wives in on a thing. . . . They take their wives 'to have, to hold, and to baffle'"; or they were "dime tossers" who concealed their finances but told their wives they make "barely enough to live on. He gives her a dollar on Monday with the air of a philanthropist, and asks her on Friday where and how she squandered it." The "holdout," on the other hand, pretended to allow his wife to handle their family funds but "always holds out a substantial part of it through various misrepresentations."[43]

The new, improved domestic money was to be shared, designed to minimize gender as well as age inequality. Families were urged to "hold a periodic council around a table, with frank and courteous discussion of its ways and means, and with due consideration of how, and how much, each member can contribute in work, in money, in cooperation, toward . . . this whole business of the home." The father and mother would act as a family board of directors, allocating money according to its diverse needs. The new financial system would also include a specified sum for each family member's personal expenses, to be considered a budgetary entitlement and not a gift. The "personal purse" was not just a man's privilege: As the *Ladies' Home Journal* explained, "whether it be in the few pennies of childhood or the . . . many dollars of maturity, [personal money] seems to be a sacred possession. . . . There is no liberty without some money that belongs to us and not to a budget." Husbands were reminded that it was "dishonesty" to claim, "'I will keep this much or that much for myself and the rest belongs to the home.'" If the "family purse" was to become a true "partnership fund," according to the new financial agenda, then "all belongs to the home and the man's share for personal spending cannot . . . take precedence over the shares of other members of the family."[44]

But how many couples actually adopted the new domestic dollar? The 1928 *Harper's* study "Marriage and Money" found that, of 200 respondents, only 54 had what the magazine described as the more "feminist" financial arrangement: a joint bank account or common purse. In 1929, in *Middletown*, the Lynds reported that most couples depended on "all manner of provisional, more or less bickering" financial arrangements. And some two decades later, *Crestwood Heights*, a study of suburban life, discovered that despite democratic norms dictating cooperative spending of the husband's income, "the wife does not know, even roughly, how much her husband earns." Wives still had to "manipulate their household allowances" in order to obtain "unreported" personal funds. Tellingly, vaudeville comedians of the 1920s continued to get laughs by joking about women's domestic strategies: "Oh, how she always liked to clean my clothes; she often used to take spots out of my clothes. One night she took three spots out of my trousers—a five, ten, and a twenty spot." If women wore trousers, went another standard joke, a wife "would get up in the middle of the night and steal money from herself."[45] Although the actual finances of housewives may not have significantly improved, by 1930 the symbolic meaning of a wife's allowance was changing from a sign of independence and domestic control to a form of financial submissiveness.

A HUSBAND'S ALLOWANCE: DOMESTIC MONEY IN THE WORKING CLASS

Domestic money was not defined only by gender, but also by the social class of the household. The working-class wife, suggested one home-economics textbook, could well be envied by wealthier women. Although the latter seldom have "ready money in hand," the wife of a workingman often "determines the . . . financial policy of the family and has control of the necessary funds." Indeed, in her 1917 study, the social investigator and settlement house activist Mary K. Simkhovitch found that as a family's income increased, "the proportion controlled by the wife diminishes till often she becomes simply a beneficiary of the husband." Paradoxically, class—in most ethnic groups—seemed to be inversely related to gender in the power structure of domestic money. In her 1910 study of Homestead, Pennsylvania,

Margaret F. Byington discovered that the men "are inclined to trust all financial matters to their wives." On payday, workmen turned over their wages to their wives, asking "no questions as to what it goes for."[46] In working-class families, the allowance usually was designated for husbands and children, not wives. The social investigator Louise B. More's analysis of wage earner's budgets found that an allowance for "spending money" was made in 108 out of the 200 families she investigated: 94 men received all or part of the amount given; and in 29 families one or two children had an allowance. In most working-class families, it seems to have been the wife who "doles out spending money according to the needs and the earnings of each." The historian Leslie Tentler's study of working-class women from 1900 to 1930 concludes that this financial arrangement of working-class families granted a great deal of economic power to wives, making the home "their fief." Indeed, to contemporary middle-class observers, it appeared that husbands "who accept a daily dole from their purse-keeping wives are usually subject beings."[47]

But these studies and observations may have idealized, and thus overestimated, the economic clout of working-class wives. To be sure, administering the family income involved women actively in domestic finances, allowing them a degree of managerial control. What remains unclear, however, is their actual discretionary power. In the first place, money management in families with limited money incomes was an arduous task. Although working-class standards of living improved at the turn of the century, family budget studies show the precariousness of their financial lives. Husbands' and children's wages went almost exclusively to food, clothing, shelter, and insurance. And being the cashier put a heavy burden of responsibility on wives: household money troubles could be conveniently blamed (by family members as well as outsiders) on female mismanagement rather than on a tight budget or an irregular labor market.[48]

More important, as soon as there was any surplus income, a

wife's apparent grip over the purse strings quickly loosened. Although the ideal good husband was indeed expected to turn over all his wages intact to his wife, receiving one or two dollars a week for his personal use, many did not. Studies of New York's West Side conducted in 1914 found that while "there is a current belief that the American workingman turns his wages over to his wife on Saturday night and allows her to apportion all expenditures," how much the wife actually received from the husband's wages and what he kept back "depends on the personal adjustment between them and not on a recognized rule." Evidence on precisely how the money was allocated is very limited. But the West Side study suggests that the outcome was usually rigged in favor of the husband. As one Italian wife explained: "Of course they don't give all they make. They're men and you never know their ways." The settlement-house worker Elsa Herzfeld's 1905 investigation of New York's West Side families found that while some husbands gave their wives their entire wages, receiving back their carfare and "beer money," other men gave "as much as 'he feels like' or 'as much as he has left after Saturday night.'" One husband deposited most of his earnings in the bank and put the amount "he thinks necessary for the household in the glass on the mantel." Sometimes, noted Herzfeld, "the husband does not tell the wife the amount of his wages."[49] Similarly, a later study of unskilled Chicago wage earners in 1924 found that, when asked about their husbands' weekly earnings, over two-thirds of the wives gave lesser amounts than the actual earnings found on the payroll. The investigator concluded that the man "may not give his entire earnings to his wife, but may simply give her the amount he thinks she should spend for the family."[50]

Thus, the idealized view of a solidary family economy coordinated and controlled by the wife concealed competing claims for money within the family. The husband's pay envelope was not always intact on arrival. Neither were the children's. Tantalized by the attractions of a consumer culture, children increasingly withheld or manipulated their earnings. David Nasaw found that, in the early part of this century, wage-earning children "who were obedient in every other regard did what they had to to preserve some part of their earnings for themselves. They lied, they cheated, they hid away their nickels and dimes, they doctored their pay envelopes." Indeed, according to one report, mothers did not like it when their sons worked in places where they were tipped "because it is then impossible to know how much money is rightfully his." Unlike the wage, a child's tip was considered "his own." While working girls were more likely than their brothers to hand their wages over intact, not all of them did. Italian working girls on the New York West Side told investigators how easy it was to "knock down" a paycheck when they made overtime: "Whatever you make is written outside in pencil. . . . That's easy to fix—you have only to rub it out, put on whatever it usually is, and pocket the change."[51]

Even the portion of money that the wife did receive and control was limited to housekeeping money. As with wealthier women, the working-class wife had no right, and much less access, to a personal fund. Pocket money for personal expenses was a male prerogative, or a working child's right. The working-class husband's allowance was thus a very different kind of money than the allowance of middle-class wives. Although partly allocated for useful expenses, food or clothing or transportation, it was also a legitimate fund for personal pleasures. Indeed, the historian Kathy Peiss's study of leisure among working-class women in turn-of-the-century New York clearly shows that men could afford to pay for their amusements—drinking in saloons, attending movies and the theater, or buying tobacco—but their wives had no money left for personal recreation. Looking back to the life of his parents in the early twentieth century, sixty-four-year-old Monsignor Lorenzo Lacasse recalled: "When my father brought his pay home, he'd lay his envelope on the corner of the table, to the last penny. My mother handled it. For a few extra cents, he sold chocolate bars in the mills." The extra "little money," however, was "for his expenses, for a glass of beer once in a while."[52] Thus, women's money retained a collective identity, whereas men's and children's money was differentiated and individualized. If a working-class wife needed more money, her options were limited. With little access to credit accounts, she turned to kin or neighbors, but often also to pawnbrokers and moneylenders. Sometimes women relied on their younger children for extra cash. During a government investigation of industrial home-work conducted in 1918, one mother explained that her little boy helped her to wire rosary beads at home because she needed "some money of her own." Another mother needed false teeth and "thought the children might just as well help to buy them."[53]

Novelists captured some of the contest, confusion, and pain involved in the earmarking of working-class domestic monies. Take, for instance, Maisie's indignation—in John Dos Passos's *The 42nd Parallel*—when she went to the savings bank to deposit, in the children's schooling account, her baby's five-dollar "birthday money" sent by her brother Bill only to discover that her husband Mac had secretly withdrawn $53.75. When Mac comes home that evening, she angrily confronts him for "stealing money from your own children" to surely squander it "on drink or on some other woman." She did not know that Mac had needed the money to pay for his Uncle Tim's funeral. When Mac promises to replace the money, she ridicules him for not being "man enough to make a decent living for your wife and children so you have to take it out of your poor little innocent children's bank account." The incident ends with Mac walking out on his family.[54] In Anzia Yezierska's 1925 *Bread Givers*, a semi-autobiographical account of growing up in New York's Lower East Side, the popular—and recently rediscovered—narrator of Jewish immigrant life tells of her parents' disputes over their children's earnings. Her father insisted that a tenth of the children's wages be donated to charity (as prescribed by Orthodox Jewish law); "and he belonged to so many societies and lodges that even without our ever getting anything we wanted for ourselves, the money didn't stretch enough to pay for all the charities Father had to have." When his wife reminded him that the children needed money for clothes, accusing him of giving charity with the "blood money of your children's wages," the father countered that to "stop my charities . . . It's like stopping the breath of God in me."[55]

As home-economics experts began to encourage joint control of the domestic dollar, the working-class financial system lost its legitimacy. Studies of English working-class families suggest that there was a shift to the middle-class system of housekeeping allowance for wives. Limited data make it difficult to determine whether the same was true for the United States. During the 1920s, when the Lynds studied Muncie, Indiana, they reported that it was rare for a husband to turn over his paycheck and allow his wife control over the household economy. But class differences seem to have persisted: by 1938, according to the *Ladies' Home Journal* national survey on money, only 38 percent of women in income groups under $1,500 received an allowance, compared to 62 percent of those in families earning more than $1,500.[56]

PIN MONEY VERSUS REAL MONEY:
DEFINING WOMEN'S EARNINGS

What happened when women's money did not come from their husbands' paychecks? When women worked for nonrelatives, whether at home or for wages, the boundary between that income and serious money was still preserved, only in different ways. In the working class, for instance, a married woman's income, usually earned by caring for boarders, taking in sewing or laundry, or, among farm families, by selling butter, eggs, or poultry, did not have the same visibility as her husband's paycheck.[57] Since her labor was part of a woman's traditional repertoire of domestic tasks, the money she made was merged into the family's housekeeping money and usually spent on home and family, for clothing or food. Legally, in fact, until the early

decades of the twentieth century, those domestic earnings
belonged to the husband. And the courts staunchly opposed
converting a wife's money into her tangible property. In a growing number of personal-injury cases, where the law had to
decide whether the husband or the wife was entitled to recover
for a woman's inability to work, as well as in claims brought up
by creditors, the courts insisted on distinguishing between the
domestic dollar and an earned wage. If a wife worked at home,
even if her labor was performed for strangers, caring for a
boarder or nursing a neighbor, that money was not a real earning and therefore belonged to her husband. Ironically, but significantly, in some states a wife's domestic earnings could become
her property but only as her husband's gift.[58]

Earned domestic money, much like the allowance, thus
retained a separate identity as a gift, not as real money. Money
earned by married women in the labor force was also special
and different. It even had its own name. The term "pin money,"
which in seventeenth-century England had meant a separate,
independent income for a wife's personal use—and was
included as a formal clause in upper-class marriage contracts—
lost its elitist British origins in turn-of-the-century America, and
now meant the supplementary household income earned by
wives. Still it was treated as a more frivolous, less serious earning
than the husband's. As a 1903 article in *Harper's Bazar* aptly
remarked: "No man works for pin money. The very idea makes
one smile."[59]

The boundary between women's earned income and the
husband's salary was also marked by their different uses.
Historian John Modell, for instance, suggests that among late
nineteenth-century, native-born American families, "all dollars
were not equal," and women's income (as well as children's)
was spent differently and less freely than the husband's.
Among farm families, women's egg money and butter money
were distinguished from husbands' wheat money or corn
money. The historian Joan Jensen suggests there existed a dual
economy, with women and children providing for living

expenses while husbands paid for mortgages and new machinery. An Illinois farmer's wife, who enjoyed writing and kept a large correspondence, explained that despite her husband's complaints about the costs of her writing materials, "as a matter of course, I pay for it out of my own scanty income." Her neighbors, however, criticized her unprofitable pastime, while they proudly bragged about "how many . . . eggs and old hens they have sold." For urban middle-class women, discreet forms of earning pin money at home (making preserves, pickles, or poundcake; knitting shawls or sweaters; or raising poultry or Angora cats) were approved, but, again, only for certain types of expenses—charity, for example, or "a daughter's lessons in music or art." A "little stream of silver will flow into her exchequer," observed an article in *Woman's Home Companion*, "and at a pinch buy a new bonnet or provide a treat for a birthday, subscribe to a magazine or take tickets for a concert."[60]

During the 1920s and 1930s, as more married women entered the labor force, their earnings, regardless of the sums involved, were still defined as pin money, categorized as supplementary income, and used for the family's extra expenses or earmarked by more affluent couples as discretionary "fun" money. For instance, in 1928 one woman told an *Outlook* reporter that she reserved her income exclusively to buy clothes. Another explained, "We blow my money on extra trips abroad, antiques, anything extravagant." Others used their salary to pay the maid's wages and saved the rest. A story in the *Saturday Evening Post*, four years later, reported on the persistent "wife-keeps-all-theory" of wives' earnings. Couples in which the wife was employed were asked what her money was used for: "Keeps it all for herself . . . saves it, spends it, just as she likes," was a common response: "the important thing [is] . . . she mustn't help her husband out."[61]

KEEPING MONEY DOMESTIC

Domestic money is thus a very special kind of currency. It would be difficult to understand its changing meanings, allocation, and uses in the United States between the 1870s and 1930s without an awareness of the new cultural "code" and accompanying social changes. In the case of married women, their money was routinely set apart from serious money by a complex mixture of ideas about family life, by a changing power structure within the family, and by social class. Conventional expectations of the family as a special, noncommercial sphere made any overt form of market intrusion in domestic affairs not only distasteful but a direct threat to family solidarity. Thus, regardless of its sources, once money had entered the household, its allocation, calculation, and uses were subject to a set of domestic rules distinct from the rules of the market. Family money was nonfungible; social barriers prevented its conversion into ordinary wages.

But family culture did not affect its members equally. Gender introduced a further type of nonmarket distinction in the domestic flow of funds: a wife's money was not the same kind of money as her husband's. When a wife did not earn wages, gender shaped many things:

1. *The allocation of her money.* In the hierarchically structured family, husbands gave wives part of their income as a gift or, more rarely, as an entitlement. To obtain additional money, wives were restricted to asking and cajoling, or else stealing.

2. *The timing of this allocation.* It either had no prescribed timing (dole method), so that to obtain money a wife had to ask each time; or it followed a weekly or monthly pattern (allowance).

3. *The uses of her money.* Wives' money meant housekeeping money, a necessary allotment restricted to family

expenses and excluding personal spending money. Pocket money was a budgetary expectation for husbands and children, but not for wives.

4. *The quantity of her money.* Wives usually received small sums of money. The amount of an allowance was not determined by the efficiency or even the quantity of a wife's domestic contributions, but by prevalent beliefs about what was a proper amount for a wife to receive. Therefore, a larger paycheck for the husband did not need to translate into a rise in the housekeeping allowance. On the basis of gender economics, it might in fact simply increase a husband's personal money.[62]

Changes in gender roles and family structure influenced the meaning and methods of allocation of married women's money. The traditional dole or "asking" method became, as the consumer role of women expanded, not only inefficient but also inappropriate in increasingly egalitarian marriages. The allowance, praised as a more equitable method of allocation in the early part of the century, was in turn condemned by home-efficiency experts of the 1920s and 1930s as an unsatisfactory payment for modern wives. The joint account emerged as the new cultural ideal. What about the uses of married women's money? In contrast to the variety of allocation methods, the earmarking of a wife's housekeeping income for collective consumption remained remarkably persistent. Despite the increasing individualization of consumption patterns and the encouragement by home-economics experts to allot personal funds for each family member in the domestic budget, personal spending money for wives still was obtained by subterfuge or spent with guilt.

Gender influenced women's money even when their income was earned. A wife's wages or pin money, regardless of its quantity and even when it brought the family a needed income, remained a less fundamental kind of money than her husband's wages. It was either collectivized or trivialized, merged into the housekeeping fund and thus undifferentiated from collective income, or else treated as a supplementary earning designated either for family expenses (a child's education or a vacation) or for frivolous purposes (clothing or jewelry). The trivialization of women's earnings extended beyond the private domestic economy. For the opponents of women's labor, pin money was a socially irresponsible currency, a luxury income that threatened the wages of the real provider. Thus, despite strong evidence that pin money was often in fact a "family coupling pin, the only means of holding the family together and of making ends meet," women's earnings were systematically stigmatized as "money for trinkets and trifles."[63]

The circulation of domestic money was not shaped by gender alone, however. Social class added an additional set of restrictions on the liquidity of money. The middle-class method of allocating household money was reversed in the working class, where wives handed out allowances instead of receiving them. The working-class wife's managerial power was thus greater than her middle-class counterpart, although her discretionary power may not have differed significantly. The complex cultural and social "life" of domestic money thus shows the limits of a purely instrumental, rationalized model of market money that conceals qualitative differences among kinds of money in the modern world.[64] Domestic monies are distinct transfers; not simply a sanitized, impersonal type of economic exchange, they are meaningful, socially constructed currencies, shaped by the domestic sphere in which they circulate and by the gender and social class of domestic "money handlers."

Children also handled domestic money. In fact, between the 1870s and 1930s, children's money became the subject of enormous controversy within families and among educational experts. Children, like their mothers, were caught in the predicament of practicing consumerism without having income of their own. As child labor laws put most children out of work, the dilemma involved children of all social classes. Authorities agreed that money should not be doled to the child: such gifts from parents, relatives, and friends made "a beggar of the child." Nor was a domestic wage appropriate: such payments threatened the boundaries between home and marketplace. The allowance—as the child's rightful portion of the family income—emerged as the proper income for children. But it had a different meaning, method of allocation, and uses than the allowance of middle-class wives or working-class men. Closely supervised by parents, the allowance was defined primarily as educational money, teaching children proper social and moral, as well as consumer, skills.[65]

To be sure, Marx and Engels were partly correct when they accused the bourgeoisie of reducing family relations "to a mere money relation." As we saw, money concerns did increasingly permeate the American household. In fact, in the 1920s some observers ironically predicted that the national enthusiasm for rationalized housekeeping and budgeting would turn "Home, Sweet Home," into "Home, Solvent Home," with "Ma and Pa a couple of cash registers, and the kiddies little adding machines."[66] Yet, such nightmare visions of a commercialized world failed to capture the complexity, and reciprocity, of the monetization phenomenon. Money came into American homes, but it was transformed in the process, becoming part of the structure of social relations and meanings of the family.

As we reach the turn of the twenty-first century, this domestication of legal tender still remains somewhat of a mystery. As households are being revolutionized by high divorce rates, as remarriage creates new kin networks, as single-parent units dramatically multiply while unmarried heterosexual or homosexual couples form new families, as women's paid employment expands and as home-based employment reappears, we barely know how it all shapes domestic monies.[67]

Although work such as the cognitive anthropologist Jean Lave's indicates that domestic earmarking is alive and well today, researchers have been primarily concerned with how the relative earnings of a couple modify the domestic power structure, in particular, the effect of a wife's increased earnings. And they find that indeed a married woman's higher income will generally increase her financial autonomy and domestic influence. But as they probe further, scholars of family life uncover some puzzling patterns. Take, for instance, the findings of *American Couples*, an extensive survey of contemporary households, that sometimes a wife's paycheck—even when she earns more than her husband—makes little difference to her domestic power: she still "places her financial destiny in his hands, granting him ultimate control over their money." A financial adviser reports similar cases, such as the client who "used to fight tooth and nail to win commissions at work, then would return home and obligingly hand her checks over to her husband. He would then determine the amount of her monthly allowance."[68]

When it comes to the division of household labor, a woman's income also works in unexpected ways. Although her money does have some impact on how much her husband will participate in domestic duties, the effect is remarkably small, and sometimes paradoxical. When sociologist Arlie Hochschild—as part of her study of dual-career families—looked at husbands who earned *less* than their wives, she discovered that none of them shared the housework.[69] What Hochschild calls the "logic of the pocketbook" also fails when it comes to the uses of women's wages. Especially in cases where wives provide the secondary income, her earnings are often earmarked for particular expenses, such as children's education, mortgage payments, baby-sitting and housecleaning expenses, or luxuries. The authors of *American Couples* point to the "interesting accounting system" in which the husband's money is defined as family money but "the wife may think that the money she earns is outside the joint account." Significantly, however, despite the prevalent assumption that her money is for personal frills while his money is communal property, in fact the wife's extra income is more likely than her husband's to be spent for family needs than on her personal needs. An important British study of money and marriage provides further evidence of how the differential use of money by women works; it appears that when wives control household finances, a higher proportion of the collective income is apt to be spent on food and daily living expenses than when husbands are in charge. It seems that husbands are still more likely than their wives to retain personal spending money.[70]

As they try to explain contemporary domestic transfers, researchers have begun to examine more closely what happens to income as it becomes part of the household. Most analysts conclude that the meanings, allocation, and uses of domestic money depend primarily on the relative persistence of the "male-provider" ideology. As long as couples adhere to the notion of the husband as the primary earner of income, it does not really matter how much a woman earns; her income will be treated as different, less significant, and ultimately dispensable. For Arlie Hochschild, it is the couple's beliefs about the relative power of men and women that shape the household's "moral accounting system"; wives who earned more than their husbands actually "balanced" their greater power by doing more housework.[71] Other scholars focus on the effects of accounting systems in the household, suggesting that separate accounting systems for husband and wife produce more equitable and rationally allocated household finances, while pooled incomes lead to unequal domestic arrangements. In the end, however, as two experts in contemporary couples have argued, the effect of separate incomes is tied to gender ideology: If couples reject the male-provider role, then a separate accounting system will increase wives' domestic power; yet in traditional households a woman's separate income is marginalized as pin money, bringing her no additional power.[72]

The sociologist Kathleen Gerson's recent research moves a step beyond these findings. Her look at variations in the family participation of American men shows that wives' earnings help shape the domestic economy, although not in the expected ways. The wife's share of earned income does not translate directly into power within the household, but the combination of her income and long-term career prospects may redefine the social relations of some couples as well as the husband's identity, shifting away from that of a traditional breadwinner to the more equal arrangements of what Gerson calls "involved fathers." And while traditional husbands continue to treat their wives' income as—in the words of one of her respondents— extra "gravy," the more egalitarian couples, albeit still a minority, pooled their monies, treating all dollars as equal.[73] From one perspective, this interpretation corresponds closely to my observations on the changing organization of money in American households. Contrary to the simple equation of money with power and rationality, amounts of income do not in themselves determine their uses or control; the allocation of household money always depends on complex, subtle understandings about relations among household members. Furthermore, an ideological explanation looks quite incomplete: in situation after situation, we have seen ideologies themselves changing in interaction with existing practices and social relations: remember how the exigencies of managing increasingly commercialized consumption undermined the view of a wife's domestic funds as her husband's gift. It would be surprising not to find a similar interaction among ideology, practice, and social relations operating today.

In addition, ties to third parties—employers, relatives, authorities, and, of course, children—strongly affect the ways that household members organize their use of money; the remainder of the book will explore these relations in much greater detail. It seems likely that those kinds of ties affect household monetary practices today. For example, a recent study documents children's access to family income, estimating that, on average, a child receives about 40 percent of an adult share of that income. Clearly, in this and in other ways, the presence of children significantly affects the allocation of household income.[74] If a wife's share of the household income is no longer defined as a gift from her husband, the same is true, to some extent, of the children's share. However, this does not mean at all that gift transfers—monetary or otherwise—are disappearing in favor of some market-driven neutrality. Let us look more closely at the place of money gifts in American life.

3

Gifted Money

IN ITS DECEMBER 1909 issue, *The Ladies' Home Journal* added an unusual option to its yearly inventory of new and appropriate Christmas gifts. Why not send Christmas money to friends and family? proposed Lou Eleanor Colby. Confessing how at first she had dismissed money as an inadequate gift "not to be dreamed of," Colby told *Journal* readers she decided to "disguise the money so that it would not seem just like a commercial transaction," searching for ways "in which I could put a bit of my own personality into the gift." Her mother, reported Ms. Colby, was thrilled to receive $10 skillfully transformed into artwork: A ten-dollar bill had been changed into ten one-dollar bills and inserted into a couple of posters. One picture showed five sad dollar bills not knowing where to go while the second poster depicted a happy ending: "five little dollars speeding joyfully" toward her mother's purse. A "dollar ode" completed the gift, its final verse suggesting that sometimes:

> *to rake in the shekels is the right thing to do*
> *So the heart of this mother had no grief to rehearse*
> *As she welcomed the dollars to a home in her purse.*[1]

Turning money into a proper gift, however, was not just Lou Eleanor Colby's ingenious creation. Other articles in women's magazines reported on "New Ways to Give Christmas Money," while readers sent in their own elaborate designs. As one woman discovered, "To be able to give money acceptably is to possess an accomplishment that is not too common." Yet Americans were remarkably resourceful. In the late nineteenth century they had converted thousands of ordinary coins into "love tokens" by engraving sentimental messages that made the coins a popular romantic gift for lovers as well as a present for family celebrations—birthdays, weddings, or anniversaries. To be sure, in some niches of American life people had made gifts of money even earlier in the nineteenth century: gold coins to children or Christmas presents to slaves. But gifts of money to equals were rare.[2]

By the first two decades of the twentieth century money entered the gift economy transformed into "gift money" by a number of new and more formal disguises. For example, in 1910, American Express first began advertising money orders as "the acceptable Christmas gift." Agents received special display posters and instructions showing them how the same money order that American Express had sold since 1882 as a safe and efficient way to pay bills or send money abroad could be also sold as a gift. Western Union joined the American Express gift business with distinctive telegrams for sending money as a gift for special occasions. Greeting-card companies produced a remarkable assortment of inventive and popular money holders to send coins or bills to friends and relatives for birthdays, Christmas, and other holidays. And after 1905, specialty stores and department stores designed an entirely new currency: gift certificates for a specific sum of money to be spent either on a designated type of merchandise—gloves and shoes were popular items—or in a particular store.[3]

The emergence of money gifts was part of a more fundamental transformation of the gift economy. Ironically, the expansion of gift giving in the midst of a generally commercializing economy made money a more problematic gift; both donor and recipient increasingly faced the dilemma of distinguishing gift money from other monetary transfers. This was no easy matter, since the standardization of legal tender increased the superficial resemblance between transfers of money as a gift and transfers in such forms as wages, tips, charity, or repayment of debts. Where the donor or recipient was already uncertain as to the character of the relationship between them, a misunderstanding could be very damaging.

By the 1900s, as America's consumer society vigorously expanded, people bought goods not only for themselves but increasingly as gifts for others. Most notably, after 1880, Christmas gift giving multiplied as relatives, friends, and even acquaintances exchanged holiday gifts. The same was true with wedding gifts. A couple marrying before the Civil War expected nothing but a gift of cash or property from close relatives. But by the end of the nineteenth century, part of the middle-class wedding ritual became the proud display of gifts received not only from close family members but also from distant relatives, friends, acquaintances, and even co-workers. Gift-giving opportunities multiplied: birthday celebrations, for instance, rare in the nineteenth century, became popular events during the 1900s. Or gift-giving events were invented: Mother's Day—created in 1908—turned flowers into the perfect sentimental gift for mother. Gift cards were printed for every possible holiday or personal anniversary, while gift shops and catalogues identified, classified, and promoted gift goods.[4]

New immigrants soon remade their own holidays into gift-giving rituals. After 1887, for instance, gift cards for Jewish holidays became a popular item. Or consider how Jews shaped an American Hanukkah, mirroring the gift exchange extravaganzas of Christmas. Historians suggest that, at the turn of the century, shopping for Christmas presents was, to many Jewish newcomers, a symbolic marker of their Americanization. But gradually Jews began to shop for Hanukkah gifts, celebrating their own December festival in a new, modernized American way. In its earlier form, Hanukkah had been a minor festival marked by the giving of "Hanukkah gelt," or gift coins, to young children. In its American version Hanukkah *gelt* was transformed into Hanukkah money and, by the 1920s, spent much like Christmas gift money but for "Hanukkah Pleasures." Bar Mitzvahs and confirmation ceremonies also came to be major gift giving celebrations for Jews. By the 1920s, suggests historian Jenna Weissman Joselit, "the social component of the bar mitzvah had begun to rival, if not eclipse, its ritual function." Jewish gift giving spawned a special category of "Jewish" gift goods: a Jewish book was a different kind of gift than an ordinary book, a Jewish picture carried different meanings from an ordinary painting.[5]

To be sure, America's enthusiasm for gift giving was highly profitable for business and advertisers; turning holidays into shopping days was a marketer's delight. And, indeed, observers increasingly bemoaned and despaired over the greedy commercialization of American celebrations. Each December there were calls to stop "this miserable and foolish business of *giving because we have received*, encouraged . . . by shopkeepers, fed by our own mean ambition and vanity."[6] But gift giving was not merely the product of crass commercial manipulation; people chose to set aside some of their income to spend as gifts for others at the expense of their own consumption. Household budgets reflected this deliberate earmarking of "gift" monies: along with food, shelter, clothing, life insurance, and other expenses, the increasingly detailed account ledgers of early twentieth-century households included gifts as a separate expense category, sometimes even distinguishing among allocations for Christmas, birthdays, graduation, weddings, and anniversary gifts. After 1910, Americans formally segregated their "Christmas money" by depositing holiday cash in the savings banks' enormously successful "Christmas Club" accounts. Somewhat before Christmas clubs came into being, poor people already had been putting their monies into Penny Provident banks, which, as we will see in chapter 4, were invented by charity organizations societies and used by the poor as a way to set aside small sums for designated expenses.

Home-economics experts—chief proponents of rational budgeting—applauded this spending for others, claiming that "the family budget needs to make some provision for that giving to relatives and friends which is part of the grace of life." These "friendship gifts" were perceived as distinct from contributions to religious or charitable organizations, more an "expression of affection to those within the family and to those outside for whom one has personal esteem." Mothers were urged by home-economics specialists to train their children early in choosing gifts "as an expression of their love and friendship" so that "in later years they shall be generous . . . and wise givers."[7]

The "how-to"s of gift giving were spelled out by the widely read etiquette experts. Recognizing "the uncertainty regarding the appropriate selection of the present, the time and way of sending it, the note or card which should accompany it," manuals added special chapters on gift etiquette for weddings, anniversaries, birthdays, visiting, christenings, sometimes even including a "gifts in general" category. Aside from "regularly appointed occasions for gift-making," one writer advised in 1905, there were now many "irregular ones, occurring constantly in the circle of mutual acquaintances and friends." Gift-giving possibilities seemed limitless: "Whenever a wish is felt to express sincere appreciation of any sort, whenever it is desired to extend a cordial congratulation, whenever a graceful deed can tell a thought more eloquently than mere words—in all such instances gifts are appropriate."[8] Even immigrants' manuals instructed their readers on gift decorum. For instance, Alexander Harkavy's popular text on letter writing for Jewish newcomers included samples of proper notes to accompany different types of birthday, bridal, or New Year's presents.[9]

As the personal web of gift giving expanded, so too did gift goods. While a flower or a book or a traditional hand-made item were still welcome gifts, so increasingly were all sorts of new manufactured luxury or practical items. In the 1910s, even washing machines, vacuum cleaners, or automobiles were declared Christmas gifts. As was money. Christmas money, explained a column in the *Ladies' Home Journal*, "supplies dearly cherished wishes, adds small luxuries, prevents worriment and gives opportunities for helpfulness as no other gift does." Etiquette experts certified money's gift potential, noting that it often was the "most welcome gift"; a wedding check could, for instance, help the couple "purchase what others have omitted to offer, to gratify some special desire, or to lay aside for future need or emergency." Gift certificates, the "self-gift method," as noted in Lillian Eichler's 1924 best-selling etiquette book, were increasingly "finding favour in good society. One presents the bride with a credit slip for $10, $20, or $50 . . . and the bride may go to the shop and select whatever she likes." And, as a graduation gift, checks were "always welcome." Home-economics experts concurred: the giving of money gifts, declared a leading home economist, was a "desirable custom."[10] Money gifts were not just the luxury of an elite. On December 13, 1911, the *New York Times* reported that foreign residents in America that year had sent over $4 million in "Christmas offerings"—money orders to their families abroad.

Yet gift money was a peculiar, puzzling, sometimes troubling currency. How could the same legal tender used to pay salaries, bribe officials, tip porters, help the poor, or provide a wife's housekeeping allowance also serve as a sentimental gift that expressed personal care, affection, or joy? How did gift givers and recipients know when a dollar was a gift dollar? And what did it take to coin sentimental monies? This chapter explores the "invention" of gift money, turning first to the nature of gifts in general, then to the ways in which gift money is differentiated from other sorts of currencies, and, finally, to the production and earmarking of gift money during the first decades of the twentieth century.

INTIMATE CURRENCIES

It is remarkable how little we still know about gift giving in modern industrial societies. Until recently, sociologists, obsessed by the corrosive effects of modernization, disregarded gifts as sentimental residuals of a lost world of intimacy and community—made further invisible by the feminization of the gift economy.[11] Or gifts were relegated to exotic, precapitalist, primitive societies. Not surprisingly, when it comes to gift giving, anthropologists have done the lion's share of the work, producing a rich, extensive, and often controversial literature.

One of the central concerns of anthropologists has been to determine the extent to which modern markets displaced gift transfers, the traditional developmental view that markets did wipe out the more socially embedded gift exchanges being increasingly contested by those who argue that different forms of exchange coexist in modern society. As John Davis puts it, "we have available to us . . . a repertoire of socially acceptable practices which are culturally, morally and even economically distinct."[12] As part of this argument, anthropologists also debate the relative opposition or affinity of gift exchange and commodity exchange. Scholars who dwell on the profound contradictions between the reciprocal, affective, socially bound gift and the impersonal, instrumental, socially "free" commodity are strongly challenged by those who insist that the dichotomy is false. Not only are commodities—as well as market exchange more broadly—cultural and social processes and objects the same as gifts, but, some analysts contend, if one observes gift exchange closely enough it turns out to be as pragmatic, calculating, and obligatory as market transfers. Or else gifts serve primarily as display commodities, visible symbols of a donor's wealth or refinement.[13]

What, then, is the meaning in our modern, commercial world, of personal gifts, with whom we exchange them, and how? Consider, for instance, how we define a "good" birthday gift. Surely it must express the intimacy of a particular social tie, convey affection, denote thoughtfulness. The meaning of gifts varies. Wedding gifts, for example, represent an additional communal symbolism of collective solidarity, while gifts to a doorman frequently reinforce the inequality and distance between donor and recipient. The form and manner of a gift—monetary or otherwise—symbolize the character of the relationship between the parties.

Certainly some gift transfers waver at the borderline of market exchange. But if they cross that boundary they cease being gifts. Therefore, equating gifts with market transfers misses the point: there are multiple types of modern transfers rather than a single market exchange of commodities. Gifts constitute a range of transfers distinct from payments or entitlements and corresponding to a different range of social relations. Gifts are bestowals marked by intimacy as well as by the relative equality of donors and recipients. In keeping with such relationships, gifts do not call for immediate reciprocation except in the form of appreciation, and they assume the long-term duration of a relationship. A gift to inferiors, on the other hand, quickly slips into charity, while a gift to superiors becomes a tribute. That is why the personalization of gifts matters greatly: gifts must be appropriate in character and value to the relation between the parties, revealing the degree of intimacy and equality between giver and recipient. The good gift bears the mark of its donor and is clearly intended for a specific recipient. What makes gift selection an elaborate and difficult task, however, is that gifts not only reflect social ties but can redefine them. Giving an overly personal gift to a mere acquaintance, a much too expensive gift to a fiancée, or an impersonal gift to one's mother confuses, annoys, or offends by implying or forcing a mistaken definition of the social relation.

At the turn of the twentieth century, as their gift exchanges multiplied, Americans contemplated, debated, and publicly defined gift transfers. Who were gifts for? In the initial enthusiasm for gift offerings, people distributed Christmas gifts to a broad range of acquaintances ranging from close relatives to business associates, but after 1910 the more "lavish or intimate" Christmas gifts were designated primarily for family and close friends. Flowers, candies, or books were appropriate presents for friends "who are not so near." Christmas cards were sent to everyone else. Similar distinctions were made with regard to wedding gifts, as etiquette books recommended that expensive presents be sent "only by most intimate friends."[14] Thus, not only were gifts marked as transfers for intimates but gifts also served to distinguish degrees of intimacy.

What did a "good" gift for kin or friends mean? Above all, its value was not to be determined by its price; a gift was thus to be set apart from a payment. The "soul" of a present, explained Mrs. Ward's *Sensible Etiquette* as early as 1878, was not "mere costliness" but the "kind feeling that it manifests." Gift giving, cautioned Mrs. Ward, should never be regarded as "a mere question of investment or exchange." The best Christmas gifts did "not imply money . . . they have nothing to do with debtors or creditors." In fact, "if the motive is mercenary . . . or perfunctory," warned Ethel Frey Cushing's *Culture and Good Manners* in 1926, the gift would fail as "an expression of real friendship." In the world of gifts, "no account should be taken of a possible return."[15] Significantly, early etiquette manuals sharply condemned the growing practice of exchanging wedding gifts. The anecdote of a bride who returned her presents to the silversmith where they had been made and, "asking credit for their value, proceeded to select whatever took her fancy" served as a negative morality tale to show how exchange reduced "sentiment to a most mercenary spirit." Unique gift goods were not to be treated as ordinary interchangeable market commodities. By the 1920s, the new etiquette approved the exchange of wedding presents *except* "if the gift carries with it a definite significance, or if it's marked with the bride's initials," or if the gift was chosen by the family of the bride or groom.[16] Intimacy thus made a gift item unique.

To mark the transfer as a gift, donors needed to distinguish their offerings not only from a payment or an entitlement but also from other—unequal—bestowals. Distinctions were often delicate. Only certain kinds of food, an observer in *The Living Age* noted in 1904, made appropriate gifts: "Chocolates and sweetmeats are . . . permissible, and even cakes and biscuits of the more frivolous kind; but it would be regarded as a gross breach of decorum to offer a friend anything which could appease his hunger or sustain his life."[17]

If some gifts were uncomfortably close to charity, others, such as Christmas gifts from employees to employers, or students to their teachers, were condemned as inappropriate tributes. In 1912 the popular and widely publicized SPUG (Society for the Prevention of Useless Giving)—Theodore Roosevelt became the first male SPUG—was created to stop the quasi-compulsory collection of money among working girls in shops and stores to buy Christmas presents for their superiors. Such presents, declared the society's sponsors, were not gifts but blackmail or graft "as unavoidable to its victims as any payment to a politician by an office holder ever was."[18] SPUG organizers made it clear that such "useless" giving did not include authentic gifts, such as "[the] hand-painted silk sachet bags for Father, nor tomato-shaped red flannel pin cushions for Brother, nor any other gifts that come from the heart." The "charm of a gift," explained SPUG advocates, "lies wholly in the fact that it is given by a friend. It ought to show unselfishness, some personal effort to please by thoughtful selection, appropriateness."[19]

To certify the equality of gift exchange and the intimacy of a gift, givers as well recipients carefully personalized gift goods. Thoughtfulness was upheld as the hallmark of excellence in gift giving; the gift should show "that you have thought of the person for whom it was intended." A birthday gift, instructed one etiquette expert, should "carry the suggestion of a warm hand-clasp, a tender kiss." While a handmade gift might bear the most tangible signs of its donor, even the manufactured useful items that became popular after 1910 could convey "the personal touch," if the gift showed "that the giver really took the trouble to see what his friend needed and then had the patience to find that particular thing."[20] Gift cards also became increasingly particularized. While the earliest cards displayed only pictures, after about 1905 greeting cards left sufficient space for hand-written messages and the sender's name.[21]

Recipients personalized gift exchange in their own ways. Etiquette experts prescribed hand-written thank-you notes, which "refer to the gift in some way, that the giver may feel that it is a personal one and not a duplicate of many others." Engraved cards were "rude. . . . Nothing but a personal note on personal stationary will do." Always, urged another writer, mention the "type of gift received." Miss Leslie's 1859 *Behavior Book* had provided more forceful directives on how to personalize gifts; "when an article is presented to you for a specified purpose," stated Miss Leslie, "it is your duty to use it for *that* purpose, and for no other, according to the wish of the donor."[22]

But personalizing gifts was not enough. As gifts multiplied and monetized, the gift needed to correspond closely to the degree and type of intimacy of a particular relationship, distinguishing among friends, different relatives, or acquaintances. Recognizing that "very few of us have the gift of knowing what to give," etiquette manuals guided their readers along the complex social maze of gift exchange. Take, for instance, *Correct Social Usage*'s typical instructions on wedding gifts in 1905: although house furnishings and linens were appropriately provided by a bride's near relatives, "bachelor friends should not choose such things for their wedding gifts, nor any article of wearing apparel." Casual acquaintances, on the other hand, "frequently send only flowers." Or consider birthday gifts for young girls: while most friends sent books, flowers, or candy, her sisters or "very dear friends" could offer "dainty underclothes." Jewelry was appropriate only from "a close relative."[23] Modern gifts were thus distinct, deeply personalized transfers shaped by particular social ties of kin and friendship, marked by and marking intimacy and equality. The best gift displayed detailed, affectionate knowledge of the recipient and the relationship. The worst gift was the indifferent gift, most notably a gift selected merely on the basis of price—the people, as a *Harper's Bazar* put it, who "come at Christmas time and say: 'I want to buy a present for ten dollars—I don't care what.'"[24]

Surely this view made money an unlikely candidate for gift giving. How could money define a social tie as intimate and equal when the same legal tender bestowed as a gift was used for all sorts of other unequal and impersonal transactions—payments to strangers, children's allowances, charity to the needy, tribute to the powerful? Indeed, as we saw, the state had worked long and hard to make dollars an anonymous currency fit for all social transfers. The range of social relationships involving monetary transfers, moreover, had multiplied, which meant that the number of distinctions people made by the form, manner, and meaning of transfers likewise multipled.

Bringing money into the territory of gifts therefore posed a problem. Other commodities—a book, a tie, a Christmas food basket, gift cards—could, albeit with some effort, be marked as gift goods.[25] But aside from differences in denomination, age, or condition, how could people distinguish between physically identical dollars? For some the task was impossible. Significantly, in his *Philosophy of Money* Georg Simmel singled out the peculiar inadequacy of money as a gift. A sum of money with its "uncompromising objectivity," Simmel contended, can never become an "adequate mediator of personal relationships." "A gift in the form of money," he explained, "distances and estranges the gift from the giver much more definitely." Money was the fitting medium only for the impersonal social relations of the market, where "business is business . . . [and] the person completely indifferent to us." That is why, explained Simmel, "among refined and sensitive people presents that are

meant to pay tribute to a person must make the money value
imperceptible." But not only was the money gift "incompatible
with the standards of the upper circles of society"; as Simmel
observed, "even servants, coachmen or messengers often
appreciate a cigar more than a tip of perhaps three times its
value."[26]

Almost a century after Simmel's remarks money gifts are still
seen as a contradiction, or a corruption. In *The World of Goods*,
Mary Douglas and Baron Isherwood insist on the distinction
between cash and gift as essential for preserving the critical
boundary between commercial ties and personal relations. Colin
Camerer, an economist, explains that "inefficient" gifts—unlike
cash—are better "signals" of information about the nature of an
enduring personal relationship. What's more, notes Camerer, the
"strikingly cold" gift of money may serve to signal the end of a
particular social tie. Money, the sociologist David Cheal confirms
in his original study of gift exchange in Winnipeg, is an "inferior
symbolic gift" because it "removes all traces of the persons upon
whom the personal relationships . . . depend." Yet Cheal found
that two-thirds of the wedding gifts given in Winnipeg consist of
money. Practical gifts such as money do enter the "moral economy" of gift giving, he concludes, but, like other practical gifts,
remain in a slippery periphery, uncomfortably close to the "limits
of the gift economy," not quite an equal member of the gift
world.[27]

Anthropologists, meanwhile, report that in certain rural
non-Western societies, such as the Mendi of the southern high-
lands of New Guinea or the Merina of central Madagascar,
modern money often circulates as a legitimate personal or ritual
gift. Parry and Bloch imply that this is possible because the
economy is still seen as a morally and socially regulated sphere
and modern money is not yet a central currency. Until monetary relations are defined as the antithesis of bonds of kinship
and friendship, they suggest, "there is nothing inappropriate
about making gifts of money to cement such bonds."[28] However, gifts of money create and sustain intimate bonds in

advanced market economies as well. In fact, in the United States the forms and meanings of monetary gift-giving seem to have multiplied as commercial life expanded and official money became *more* uniform and generalized.

How, then, was money turned into a gift in the early part of this century? People were certainly aware it was a sensitive task. As a *Ladies' Home Journal* article acknowledged, although the "future" of Christmas money "far outstrips the charming gift one's neighbor is untying at one's elbow" on Christmas morning, "when all the rest of the world is receiving holly-decked packages and ribbon-bound gifts of beauty and utility, money—plain and unadorned—hardly strikes the Christmas note."[29] The paradoxes of "gifting" money did not escape humorists. Consider the following 1920s vaudeville act:

> HE: It's bad form for a person to leave the price mark on a gift, isn't it?
>
> SHE: Yes, and I knew a woman who was so absent-minded that when she gave a fifty-dollar bill for a Christmas gift, she tried to rub the price mark off of it. . . . She was giving the fifty-dollar bill to her married daughter, and didn't want her to know how much it was worth.
>
> HE: And what did her married daughter do with the fifty-dollar bill, when she got it?
>
> SHE: She took the money, and paid the grocer what she owed him.
>
> HE: And what did her mother do?
>
> SHE: Her mother cried, and said, although she loved to give a Christmas present, there wasn't much fun in paying her son-in-law's grocery bill.[30]

True, the price tag of a money gift could not be removed. And, of course, gift money once bestowed could easily be turned into a payment, spent in ways the donor did not intend or even like. The challenge was thus to turn that apparently autonomous, socially indifferent currency into a sentimental personalized gift. How was this earmarking done? We turn now to the methods for creating gift money, which involves: (1) the *invention* of a currency that did not circulate in other social relationships; and (2) the *delimitation* of currency, which includes several related techniques such as the physical and symbolic differentiation of legal tender, segregation of gift monies, and restricted spending. Note that money gifting occurs at four distinct occasions: (1) on receiving money designated as a gift; (2) when money thus received is set aside for future use; (3) when money *not* acquired as a gift is set aside for future giving; (4) and on giving money as a gift to someone else. Each of these gifting occasions sets its own problems of demarcation, and each generates its own distinctive series of social techniques.

GIFTING MONIES

The "old-fashioned" nineteenth-century rule had been plain: gifts of money could only be exchanged between near relatives or closest friends. Deploring the new expansion of money gifts, an article published in 1898 by the English *Spectator* reaffirmed that a money gift was honorable only "if there is natural love and affection, as of parents or very close friends." Although these discussions often focused on loans of money, the distinction between family members or quasi-kin, on the one hand, and friends or acquaintances, on the other, was also critical for gift giving. With remarkable consistency, etiquette manuals reaffirmed the rule that "money should not be presented" as a wedding gift "except by members of the two families or old and intimate friends."[31] The same was true for christenings. The child's godfather—especially if the child was named after him—gave money but other guests brought presents of silver or jewelry.[32] A gift of money from an ordinary friend or mere acquaintance would have been considered distasteful, at least in middle- and upper-class circles.

The "family rule" made sense in the context of the middle-class domestic economy of the nineteenth century. To a certain extent, any financial household transfer was a money gift. The sentimental family, after all, was upheld as a privileged, noncommercial sphere immune to instrumental market concerns. Once a husband's wage or his salary crossed the domestic threshold it was transformed, distributed to his wife and children as his gift, not his payment.

But as all forms of gift giving multiplied in the early twentieth century, gift money became no longer just a family currency; Christmas money cards, for instance, were now sent to friends and distant relatives. New forms of gift money emerged, such as tips for the worker or a Christmas bonus for the employee. What's more, as we saw, within families gift money became an increasingly contested currency: the traditional method of allocating money by the husband to his wife and children as "a gift and an indulgence" was vehemently assailed as unjust and demeaning. A wife, protested Susan B. Anthony, "is made to feel [the money] is a mere gift and not her just due—her earnings in truth."[33] As new household currencies were established in the form of entitlements rather than gifts—housekeeping allowances for wives, educational allowances for children—gift money was differentiated from other domestic transfers and earmarked for the creation, celebration, and sustaining of intimate ties. The gift of a gold coin to a child, as one example, was now set apart from that child's allowance.

As a sentimental currency, gift money became women's money. Shopping for gifts was a new, demanding, and central task for the modern housewife. And it posed an additional financial dilemma for cashless wives. Although domestic budget experts urged the inclusion of a separate private fund for each family member "unmolested and uninspected" that could be used partly for gifts, women repeatedly complained that their housekeeping allowances left them with little extra money. Married women, observed a writer in *Harper's Bazar* in 1901, lacked "the privilege of bestowal." "The little gift she felt like sending a friend . . . or the small surprise for the children," noted another critic of domestic finances, "had to be passed by with sometime a rising lump in her throat." It reportedly drove some women to shoplifting, stealing from department stores "ribbons or laces to adorn the babies' clothes . . . or often little gifts for [their husbands]." Or as in the case of one middle-aged woman who stole a $50 table cover from a department store explaining when she got caught "tearfully . . . that she had wanted it for a wedding gift for her daughter."[34]

With little personal money, wives were thus routinely put in the peculiar predicament of asking their husbands for additional gift money, which, of course, was partly used to buy the husband's own present. To make matters worse, unearned gift money was esteemed as a somewhat less valuable currency than money earned independently. As a result, in the early 1900s many married women who stayed out of the regular labor force took a seasonal job simply to earn their own Christmas money. Even when it came to the children, home-economics advisers, noting that "the gift that costs us nothing is of small value in the giving," urged mothers to make their children "earn the money, or at least a certain portion of it, with which to buy their gifts for Christmas." Women were not just gift buyers but gift sellers as well; most of the new fashionable gift shops of the 1910s were apparently run by "charming and cultured women."[35]

Was gift money the privilege of the prosperous? After all, etiquette manuals and women's magazines catered primarily to a middle- and upper-class audience, guiding the social economy of the affluent. After paying for food, fuel, lodging, and other necessities, working-class families had little discretionary cash left for gifts. Yet, although the evidence is incomplete, it looks as though working-class immigrants, for whom remittances of money to relatives abroad were an everyday fact and the pressures of surviving in the new country urgent, still routinely earmarked money for gifts. A separate category for gifts appears in working-class budgets sometimes specifically labeled "gifts of friendship," as distinct from loans, church contributions, or charitable donations. One early-twentieth-century study of wage-earners' budgets in New York City found that while native-born and "Americanized" immigrant groups allocated more of their income for recreation and personal spending, foreign-born families spent more on religious contributions and gifts to friends.[36] And increasingly they saved their money either at home or in special savings accounts specifically to spend on holiday gifts. Gifts of money were an important part of immigrants' gift giving—not only the Christmas dollars shipped each December to their families back home but money gifts sent to relatives for name days, Easter, weddings, and other festive occasions. In their letters home, Polish immigrants clearly distinguished their Christmas rubles or other personal gift monies from nongift remittances, money for ship tickets, loans, offerings for the church, or donations for a mass.[37]

We happen to have particularly rich documentation for Jewish immigrants. Jews—mostly working class—carried over a long tradition of incorporating money into their ritual and social life, including gift giving. Indeed, a remarkable survey of traditional Jewish religious texts and literary sources identifies some seven hundred categories of socially or religiously distinct monies drawn from different places and times in Jewish history. These *Yiddishe gelt* (Jewish monies) range widely from *domestic currencies*—the wife's *knipl*, or secret savings, a child's pocket money, *pushke* money set aside for charity in special "pushkes," or charity boxes; to *holiday money*—*maot hittim* or Passover money designated for the holiday needs of the poor, Hanukkah *gelt*, Purim *gelt*, *Rosh Hodesh* (new month) money offered to a teacher in addition to his pay; to a multitude of different *rites-of-passage monies,* which included "bath money" given by a boy's godfather when the child is bathed the night before his circumcision; *pidyon haben* (redemption of the first-born male) on the thirtieth day after birth, when five silver coins are received by a *kohen* (priest) from the child's father as a symbolic redemption from God; multiple wedding monies, such as special payments for those who accompanied the couple to the *chuppah* (wedding canopy); coins thrown at the couple under the canopy—gold and silver from the rich, *kopeks* from the less affluent (the money was then picked up by the poor); money given to the *hazzan* (cantor) for the glass that is broken by the groom during the marriage ceremony; "veil money" given to the bride after her hair had been cut off and a veil or hairpiece put on her head marking her as a married woman; and, finally, "burial monies" paid to the burial society for individuals who stayed with the body and prayed before the burial; "shroud money" for the poor; *yizkor* money, offerings for charity given after the recitation of *yizkor*, a prayer for the remembrance of the dead. There were *moral* monetary distinctions as well: between "kosher" and "nonkosher," or dishonest money—for example, the profits from a prostitute could not be used for religious purposes; or *magical* earmarkings, such as *mikvah* money offered to the poor by women returning from their ritual bath for good fortune, or the "good luck" coins put in the pocket of a new garment or a new purse. "Charity" money was distinguished from money to be saved or from *mazel tov* (congratulations) monies. And within traditional synagogues, Jews engaged in *shnuddering*: inviting monetary pledges (at times by auction) from congregants for the honor of participating in ritual, such as the privilege of being called to the Torah.[38]

We know only a little about how many of these monetary distinctions persisted among American Jewish immigrants and in what forms. Sometimes traditional forms of gift money must have created conflicts for new immigrants, as in the case of the "greenhorn" who wrote to the *Bintel Brief* (letters to the editor) section of the *Jewish Daily Forward* in 1906, asking how to spend part of his first American earnings. Before he left Russia, he explained, he had promised his blind father "that I would send him the first money I earned in America." But now, fearful that his job would not last, he needed advice: "Shall I send my father a few dollars for Passover, or should I keep the little money for myself?" He was told to send his father the money.[39]

Clearly, gift money was not an exotic or anomalous currency in Jewish social life. And, as shown by the multiplicity of remittances, or transfers of money abroad, the complex differentiation of monies was not peculiar to Jews. Other immigrant groups too marked their religious and family celebrations—weddings, christenings, first communion—with gifts of money. Consider wedding gifts. On the Lower East Side of New York at the turn of the century, money or a useful household article was the customary gift for Italian as well as Jewish weddings. As it was for Polish weddings. Sophonisba P. Breckinridge's account of immigrant life in the 1920s documents the popular Polish custom of "buying" a dance with the bride with a present of money. The practice, she reports, was sometimes carried to excess: "the men divided their gifts into small parts and demanded many dances with the bride, often causing her . . . serious fatigue." In other Polish weddings, an older woman or a flower girl passed a plate to collect money, and sometimes paper currency was pinned on the bride's dress, or else money was collected from male guests who tried to smash tough dinner plates by throwing silver dollars at them. Wedding money gifts served partly to subsidize the wedding but also provided a nest egg for the new couple. Breckinridge suggests, however, that second-generation immigrants may have become less comfortable and even somewhat embarrassed with money gifts.[40]

In the working-class domestic economy, women, too, were the principal gift givers, putting money aside for the special transfers of kin and friendship. Women appear to have been the typical depositors in Christmas Club accounts and, along with their children, in the Penny Provident funds organized by charity organizations and often reserved as holiday funds. Working-class men, on the other hand, devised their own gift-giving activities; in late-nineteenth-century saloons, workingmen were expected to treat their mates to rounds of beer as a symbol of solidarity and community.[41]

Gift money was thus a distinct currency earmarked for friends and kin, reinforcing the intimacy of particular social ties. Money as a gift was problematic precisely because the call for display of intimate, affectionate knowledge of the recipient and the relationship contradicted, to some extent, the impersonality of the many other settings and relations in which money transfers took place. Let us see how these principles worked out in three situations involving increasingly delicate social relationships—Christmas bonuses, tipping, and courtship gifts.

BONUSES AND TIPS

Some gifts of money became delicate precisely because they took place at the boundary between relationships that differed greatly in their significance. Let's see first what happened when money gifts were bestowed outside the intimate network. At the turn of the century, the expanding gift economy spawned a different category of gift currencies, such as Christmas bonuses and tips, which captivated, confused, and sometimes angered donors and recipients. Unlike money gifts for kin and friends, these currencies were offered in mostly impersonal and clearly unequal transfers, from employer to employee, from patron to server. And yet they were not the same legal tender used for wages or salaries; the transfer was legally optional, informally bestowed, the amount unspecified, variable, and arbitrary. Did these currencies qualify as gifts? What kind of relationship did they mark between giver and recipient?

Consider the Christmas bonus. On December 23, 1913, headlines in the *New York Times* disclosed that in Chicago alone that year banks and large industrial corporations would distribute over a million dollars in Christmas gifts to their employees. These Christmas offerings were of many kinds. Take, for instance, Montgomery Ward's gift to each of their 7,500 employees in Chicago, New York, and other cities of a "Christmas dinner and basket containing a turkey and other incidentals." Or the $5 gold coins offered by Swift. A Brooklyn Company celebrated its fiftieth anniversary by spending over a million dollars for their Christmas gift of group life insurance for their employees, while another company donated cash to the employees' pension fund and sick benefit association. The New Orleans Railways Company made Christmas a "keep the change" day for its conductors, offering them as well a percentage of the fares collected that day.

Employers thus found ingenious ways to earmark their Christmas gifts as a form of transfer different from an ordinary paycheck. In the nineteenth century they had done so by giving in-kind gifts—turkeys, watches, or candy—or gold coins. They further gifted Christmas offerings—in-kind or money gifts—by distributing them at a special holiday celebration for all employees. In some cases, one observer noted, gifts were distributed with such "formal courtesy and a personal greeting" that for "a brief time" the office was transformed "into a reception-room of a host and his guests."[42] Working girls were advised by women's journals to recognize the "kindly spirit lying behind the gift" and urged to convey to their superiors an "appreciation of whatever the firm has given her." Some workers did so, such as the saleswomen in a department store who, according to one report, "sent scores of letters to the manager's office, telling what had been done with the "Christmas fund," thus proving that "holiday commissions ... meant more to them than wages."[43]

But employers entered riskier territory when they started making money gifts. The *Times* reported that while many firms in 1913 still adhered to the "time-honored custom of presenting turkeys and gold pieces of varying denominations," there was an increase in the number of corporations offering "profit-sharing plans organized on a systematic basis of remuneration for length of service"—or a cash bonus. As early as 1902, J. P. Morgan & Co. had apparently broken the record by giving each of their employees a full year's salary as a Christmas present. Gifts of cash were increasingly standardized, calculated as a percentage of the wage. By 1911, a 10 percent bonus was considered "liberal." Some banks went as far as substituting the Christmas present for a first-of-the-year merit increase in salary.[44]

Most employers, however, continued to want to treat the bonus as a discretionary gift; after all this custom of "remembering the workers" served them well in overseeing and regulating workers' productivity as well as assuring their loyalty. Indeed, it is reported that Woolworth's first Christmas cash bonus to employees in 1899 ($5 for each year of service, with a limit of $25) was meant to match competitors' higher wages and avoid a salesgirls' strike. It was probably also a cheaper way to pay overtime; around 1910 a twenty-five-year-old saleswoman working in a New York department store told a National Consumers' League investigator that in the week before Christmas "she worked standing over fourteen hours every day. . . . So painful to the feet becomes the act of standing for these long periods that some of the girls forego eating at noon in order to give themselves . . . a foot-bath." For this overtime the store gave her $20, "presented to her, not as payment, but as a Christmas gift."

Significantly, while some companies offered a bonus to every employee, others made the Christmas present contingent on length of service or a worker's efficiency record. Or on a worker's proper disposition of the bonus; in Christmas of 1914 a large Minneapolis flour-milling company reportedly gave each of their employees a $25 check to be deposited at a savings bank, the gift check being valueless otherwise.[45]

But the similarity to other forms of payment invited recipients to treat the bonus as an entitlement, pressing for a definition of the additional income as a right. As early as 1903 a report on the role of Christmas in business life deplored the fact that some employees were in the "habit of reckoning with this 'present' as a part of their income," thus losing "the flavor of the holiday season." Too many working girls, similarly lamented the *Woman's Home Companion* in 1905, "accept this voluntary remembrance from the firm as their right."[46]

It became increasingly difficult to distinguish Christmas cash from wages. The personalization of a business gift from employer to employee was hard to sustain when the bestowal was standardized and expected. By the 1950s the Christmas bonus officially lost its status as a gift: when a firm announced a reduction in its annual Christmas bonus as a way to make up for the expense of introducing a costly new retirement plan, the union tried to negotiate the employees' holiday bonus. After the company refused any bargaining, the union appealed to the National Labor Relations Board. The board ruled that the Christmas bonus could no longer be considered an employer's discretionary gift but an expected and negotiable component of a worker's wage. Although a dissenting board member protested that a "genuine Christmas gift has no place at the bargaining table," it was generally agreed that the bonus was no longer a present but a separate category of payment from the regular paycheck.[47]

Tipping involved an even more difficult, confusing, and often contentious social interaction between donor and recipient. A tip, unlike the bonus, was not just a Christmas offering; it was a secular, yearlong bestowal affecting many parties in a variety of social exchanges. For some people, the tip was indeed a gift, the emotional supplement to the wage, a singular transfer of money that personalized commercial exchanges; it "lets me show," explained a commentator in *The Atlantic Monthly* in 1911, "my measure of fraternity, good-will, affection, obligation, that is not susceptible of measure." But for others the tip was a crass corruption of the gift, a mercenary bribe that paid for a stranger's personal service, "the waiter's smile or immunity from the terrible look." The proof, argued William R. Scott in *The Itching Palm*—an exposé of tipping—was that those who tipped "would not think of offering a friend money and would be insulted if any one offered them money."[48]

This was not an isolated disagreement. In the early 1900s, as tipping became increasingly popular, it provoked great moral and social controversy. In fact, there were nationwide efforts, some successful, by state legislatures to abolish tipping by turning it into a punishable misdemeanor. In countless newspaper editorials and magazine articles, in etiquette books, and even in court, tips were closely scrutinized with a mix of curiosity, amusement, and ambivalence—and often open hostility. When, in 1907, the government officially sanctioned tipping by allowing commissioned officers and enlisted men of the United States Navy to include tips as an item in their travel expense vouchers, the decision was denounced as an illegitimate endorsement of graft.[49] Periodically, there were calls to organize anti-tipping leagues.

Why was the tip such a troublesome gift? After all, it involved only small change. Partly, it was simply a nuisance, difficult to calculate and awkward to present. Indeed, the etiquette of tipping became increasingly complex, instructing not only how much to tip, but whom to tip, when to tip, and how to tip. But tipping presented a more fundamental puzzle: it lay at the boundary of other critically different transfers, not quite a payment, not quite a bribe, not quite charity, but not quite a gift either. The confusion extended to the effects of tipping on the relationship between tipper and tip taker.

Some observers had no trouble in treating tips as another version of modern money gifts, sentimentalizing the "charm and poetry of personal relation." Different from a payment, the tip, as one etiquette expert explained, served to "remember" those "giving personal service." In fact, according to Scott, many courts declared anti-tipping laws unconstitutional because they interfered with the common-law right to make gifts.[50]

But how could it be a gift, objected critics of tipping, if the giver barely knew the recipient? Distinguishing between "the tribute of friendship," offered to "faithful, long-tried servitors" at Christmas, from the "pernicious custom" of distributing money gifts to "people who have no claim whatever on [the giver's] generosity," a *New York Times* editorial denounced tipping as "ineffectual bribery."[51] Worse still, tipping generated fake displays of concern: "a deceptive show of friendliness which may in a moment be thrown off," thus lessening "the chance of genuine friendliness." Widespread concern with political graft at the time made tips suspect reminders of other corrupting transfers that were unearned, unjustified, illegitimate. "The gift of a quarter to a waiter as a tip," explained one commentator, "is an unsound transaction because the patron receives nothing in return—nothing of like substantiality." Moreover, unearned money was more likely to be dissipated: "abnormal gains," noted a writer in *The Law Quarterly Review*, "produce abnormal extravagance; and to give any man a remuneration which exceeds the economic worth of his services is to disturb his estimate of the value of money."[52]

Even when not morally corrupting, tips were denounced as socially demeaning. What sort of gift was it, queried some critics, if it humiliated the recipient? "We do not believe," declared the editor of *Harper's Monthly Magazine* in 1913, "that it is possible for a man earning an honest living to take money which he has not earned without the misery which even the mendicant must know from alms." Since the recipient was not indigent, tipping was, in fact, worse than charity, "a gross and offensive caricature of mercy . . . it curses him that gives and him that takes."[53]

Thus, unlike money gifts between kin or friends, tips indicated distance and inequality between donor and recipient. What could you expect, critics contended, from an offensively "un-American," aristocratic European import? Tipping, Scott asserted in *The Itching Palm*, was "what one American is willing to pay to induce another American to acknowledge inferiority." Imagine, Scott continued, "what would happen if a tip should be offered to the average 'gentleman' who patronizes restaurants, and taxicabs and barber shops?"[54]

Significantly, when the relationship between donor and recipient of tips was equalized, the tip became an embarrassment. A writer in *Everybody's* told of the man who, after years of tipping his barber, did not quite know what to do when the barber bought his own shop. So he asked the barber: "Now that you are proprietor, you and I are equals, and I do not tip my equals. Which shall it be in the future, conversation and no tips, or tips and no conversation?" The matter was complicated when the barber lost his shop, creating a new dilemma for the patron: "Should he resume his former tipping and thus humiliate his quondam friend?"[55]

The fact that, unlike an employer's salary, the tip was discretionary, "dependent upon the whim of the patron," further established the inferiority of the recipient. It could be used, as one observer approvingly recognized, as an "instrument of moral and social discipline. The withholding or diminution of it should be a punishment, as the bestowal or enlargement of it a reward." Not only did the tip display the inferiority of the recipient but, some critics insisted, it perpetuated inequality by allowing employers to pay lower wages with the assumption that tips would supplement the worker's income.[56]

That is why turning down a tip was a such a powerful symbolic statement of independence and dignity—offensive to the patron who bestowed the tip as charity, admired by those who saw tipping as degrading. Consider the experience of a young immigrant working as a delivery boy for Wanamaker's, as recounted by his sister in 1918. Once after delivering a ninety-eight-cent parcel, the woman who placed the order gave him a dollar and told him to keep the change: "He said, a little huffily, I imagine, that he did not take 'tips' and held out the two cents. She looked him up and down and shut the door in his face. So he laid the two pennies at her door and went away." Two days later he was fired.[57]

It was, of course, not only the donor but the recipient who marked tips either as gift, charity, payment, or bribe. A young Japanese immigrant working as a cabin boy in a steam yacht recalled—in one of the "life stories" collected by Hamilton Holt for *The Independent* in the early 1900s—how he "thankfully accepted" a tip "from a lady who give me the money in such a kind and sympathetic manner," or the gentleman who gave him a dollar and said, "I wish this were ten times as much; still I want you to keep it for me to help your study." Although this dollar felt "precious," the cabin boy angrily rejected the dollar from a "fastidious" lady who had repeatedly scolded him and treated him badly. He threw "the paper money to her feet," saying, "Madam, this is the bribe and graft. I am amply paid from the owner of the yacht to serve you . . . no tip for me."[58]

Nevertheless, those observers who insisted on the gift elements of the tip denied the social inequality involved in tipping, asking whether "the waiter [is] more demeaned by the coin in his palm than the parson by the obvious envelope furtively slipped in his hand by the best man?" or "the physician . . . by the gratuities of grateful patients after their bills have been paid?"[59]

But gifting tips was, in most cases, an impossible task. The transfer was marked by the inequality and impersonality of the exchange; it resembled a payment too much. In fact, by 1917 the appellate division of the New York State Supreme Court ruled that tips were not a gift but "a payment made in order to obtain reasonable service . . . [they] are a part of the wages of the employee." The appeal was filed by the Rochester Taxicab Company to contest an award made in 1916 under the Workmen's Compensation Act to the parents of one of their deceased cabdrivers. The issue was whether the State Industrial Commission should have included tips along with wages in computing the amount of compensation; the cabdriver's weekly wages had been $12, while his tips averaged $5.10 a week. The Court of Appeals argued that tips were much like other legally compensable advantages provided by an employer, such as board, lodging, or rent. Furthermore, noted the court, the tip was "so usual and the amount so uniform" that the "person rendering the service considers that the tip is his as a matter of right and involves no particular favor." An "extra large" tip might be "appreciated," but the "ordinary tip" was considered "a payment of money actually due."[60] The court unanimously affirmed the award.

A dissenting editorial in the *Virginia Law Register* objected to the decision, claiming that until a recipient of a tip could sue for it, tips could not "any more enter into the legal wage than the actual drink which used to be given in kind." However, tips were increasingly pushed into the realm of payments, with fixed percentages or tip tariffs, and, more dramatically, considered as taxable income.[61]

Thus, when it came to gifts of money between employers and employees or patrons and servers, the personalization of money did not work well. Without intimate knowledge of the recipient and where relations were clearly unequal, the transfer resembled charity. Although donors tried to label the money as a gift, increasingly recipients pressed to define the bonus or the tip as an entitlement or a payment.

MONEY IN COURTSHIP

What happened when gifts were intended to create intimacy, as with the courtship gifts exchanged between men and women? Unlike bonuses and tips, these gifts linked people forging affective, possibly sexual ties. It mattered greatly to carefully differentiate courtship relations from ordinary nonsexual friendships, from marriage, and from prostitution. In the early twentieth century, as courtship was being transformed by the new dating rituals of the young, such distinctions became increasingly harder to make. Moreover, men and women often had conflicting definitions of a relationship and of the nature of proper behavior for each relationship. Courtship gifts were therefore extremely delicate transfers.

Etiquette books endlessly struggled to identify proper gifts between men and women, aware that the wrong gift could easily confuse friendship and a permanent romantic commitment, or even imply the purchase of sex. Expensive or excessively intimate gifts were therefore suspect: fancy jewelry or wearing apparel were fit for a kept woman, or perhaps a man's wife, but not as tokens of respectable courtship. An early 1859 "behavior book" was emphatic: "To present a young lady with articles of jewellery, or of dress, or with a costly ornament for the centre-table (unless she is his affianced wife) ought to be regarded as an offence, rather than a compliment." A "dignified" woman could accept only objects "that derive their chief value from

associations": "autographs of distinguished persons ... a few
relics or mementos of memorables places," or a simple bouquet
or a book. Perishable gifts such as "fruits, flowers, or confec-
tions" were preferable, explained another etiquette expert, for
they left "no obligation resting upon the lady."[62]

The improper gift had to be returned immediately: much
like turning down a tip, rejecting a gift was the best way for the
recipient to correct the donor's inappropriate definition of their
relationship. It was "bad form," noted a *Dictionary of Etiquette*
in 1904, "for a man to send expensive presents to a woman who
may be compelled to return them." Etiquette writers harshly
condemned not only the men who violated or abused the gift
code but also women who accepted the wrong gift or, even
worse, extorted gifts by pretending romantic interest or even
daughterly affection: those "young ladies who profess a sort of
daughterly regard for certain wealthy old gentlemen, are so kind
as to knit purses or work slippers for them ... for they know
that he will reward them by a handsome present of some bijou
of real value."[63]

Some twenty years later, the distinctions among gifts persisted; Eichler's *New Book of Etiquette* asserted that no "well-
bred" girl could accept "valuable gifts" from men acquaintances.
Whereas the range of acceptable gifts had expanded from the
traditional flowers, candy, and books to items such as tennis
rackets and ice skates, the etiquette still excluded anything "that
costs a great deal of money."[64]

Even after the couple became engaged, gifts remained sensitive markers of the relationship. Turn-of-the-century etiquette
was strict: expensive presents "unless it be the engagement ring"
were "not in the best taste." Nor was wearing apparel, especially
not the wedding dress: a very plain trousseau was preferable to
"the elaborate outfittings towards the purchase of which the
groom-expectant has largely contributed," even when the bride
was "as poor as a church mouse." The first edition of Emily
Post's famous *Etiquette*, which appeared in 1922, although

somewhat more liberal about a "bridegroom-elect's" gifts to his future bride, still made it clear that any item, such as wearing apparel, a motor car, a house, or furniture, considered to be "maintenance" was off limits. Post was quite specific: "It is perfectly suitable for her to drive his car, or ride his horse. . . . But, if she would keep her self-respect, the car must not become hers. . . . He may give her all the jewels he can afford, he may give her a fur scarf, but not a fur coat." The scarf was an "ornament," Post explained, but the coat was "wearing apparel" and thus an unfit gift for a bride.[65]

The severity of the gift code reflected the concern with distinguishing courtship relations from marriage or prostitution. The wrong gift, warned Emily Post, cast the bride "in a category with women of another class."[66] Until the couple was married, the ambiguity of the relationship persisted. That is why courtship gifts were supposed to express affection or admiration without suggesting payment or support.

It all changed when the bride became a man's wife; her husband's gifts and his money then turned into domestic transfers, no longer ambiguous although subject to a different set of rules and expectations. Etiquette manuals reminded brides of the distinction between courtship and marriage transfers: "until the fateful words are spoken that make the twain one flesh," wrote one etiquette writer, the bride "has no claim whatever on the purse of her future husband." As she approached marriage, however, the bride was advised to start treating her husband's money with wifely concern and discourage, as Post put it, any "charming, but wasteful, presents." Unless the fiancé was very wealthy, noted Ethel Cushing's *Culture and Good Manners*, "a young girl prefers to have [her fiancé] save his money for the home and its furnishings."[67]

The dilemmas of gift giving between men and women became more acute as money increasingly entered courtship. At the turn of the century, new forms of middle- and working-class courting, such as dating and treating, involved the purchase of goods and services in a transformed public world of consumption and commercialized leisure. As "going somewhere," Beth Bailey tells us in her history of courtship, replaced the old system of "calling" at a girl's home or "keeping company," "money—men's money—became the basis of the dating system, and thus, of courtship." How was this courtship money to be distinguished from the same legal tender used in prostitution or in domestic payments? In fact, as Beth Bailey reports, many young men defined dating as a form of "promiscuous buying" of female companionship.[68]

But even though they may have paid for a girl's dinner or an expensive corsage, young men did not offer their dates a direct payment or even a gift of cash. Indeed, within the zone of courtship, Americans never arrived at a point where a man could make a gift of legal tender unless there was the presumption of marriage or a sexual relation. Note that the popular turn-of-the-century love tokens did not qualify as gift items until the coins were put out of circulation, defaced, and inscribed with sentimental messages. Thus, while brothels created special currencies such as brass tokens for payment of prostitutes, courting couples invented romantic tokens without exchange value to be used as gifts.[69]

To be sure, other transfers of legal tender from men to women outside of courtship or marriage were legitimate, such as a charitable cash offering or a salary. But even a man's tips were suspect as dangerous enticements to prostitution; consider, for instance, the statement in 1912 by the Juvenile Protective Association of Chicago that tipping was a "vicious" system encouraging young girls "who would . . . not dream of accepting money from a man" to accept his tip, thereby establishing "a relationship of subserviency and patronage which may easily be made the beginning of improper attentions."[70]

Twentieth-century courting did not involve direct gifts of money, but it routinely called for a man's joint purchase of goods or services, ranging from the girl's corsage to paying for dinner, theater tickets, and transportation. Etiquette books in the 1920s took on the problem of distinguishing more closely among such indirect transfers of money from men to women: carfare,

for instance, was "so small an item" that a women could allow
the man to pay, but the woman who met an acquaintance in a
restaurant "does not permit him to pay for her meal unless he
has specially invited her to join him." Only if the woman was
"invited to a matinee, or a tea, or to attend a ball game" was the
man expected to assume "all obligations."[71]

Working-class courtship rituals made the distinctions between
gift transfers more difficult than in middle-class dating. "Treating,"
as shown in Kathy Peiss's study of single working-class women in
New York at the turn of the century, became a popular arrangement by which women received financial help, gifts, and access to
entertainment from men in exchange for a variety of sexual favors,
from flirting to sexual intercourse. Young working women who
earned low wages and were obligated to contribute to their families' income had little spending money left for their own clothes or
entertainment. So they relied on men friends to "treat" them to
dancing, drinks, theater, or dinner. As Peiss reports, informal
working-class etiquette allowed a much broader range of
respectable indirect payments for women than in the middle class;
working girls accepted not only recreation and food from a man
but also gifts of clothing or even a vacation trip.[72]

Many such in-kind transfers were paid by a woman's fiancé
or her "steady," but some women reportedly accepted treats from
casual acquaintances as well. Yet the transfer remained within the
realm of courtship gifts. Distinctions between courtship and prostitution, however, grew thinner with "charity girls," women who
offered sexual pleasures to strangers they met in the popular public dance halls in exchange for presents or other "treats." There
were also the "taxi-dancers" who made their living by dancing
with paying customers. Leo Rosten recalled a Saturday night tour
of three New York taxi-dance ballrooms; at Seventh Avenue's
Honeymoon Lane Danceland, Mona led him to the dance floor,
letting "her body, all marshmallow, flow against mine . . . and
murmured . . . a voluptuous 'Mmmm-mmh!'." After dancing for a
moment "approaching ecstasy," a buzzer loudly "honked," and
Mona quickly "disengaged her clutch," instructing him to get

more dance tickets. When Rosten protested that he thought his ticket was for a whole dance, Mona announced that "a dance is every time the buzzer buzzes"—which was every minute. After Rosten promptly returned with ten more tickets, Mona was once again "warm and yielding in my arms—until the buzzer finished its tenth pecuniary decree." Jean later explained that the dancers kept half the price of their tickets, plus "you have to add the *presents* . . . like nice lingerie, a bracelet, a purse, a piece of jewelry, maybe an evening gown." Or sometimes cash. At the Majestic Danceland, Honey told Rosten about a St. Louis real-estate dealer who dated her: once "'he leaned over in the cab he was taking me to some scrumptious Chinese food in, and without one single word he leaned over and kissed me—nothing rough or forcing, just a real sweet little kiss. Then he handed me ten dollars without a peep.'" With taxi-dancers, noted Paul G. Cressey in his more systematic account of Chicago dance-halls in the 1920s, the date—"a conventionally accepted means for young people to get acquainted"—acquired "a suggestion of immorality." Yet, like "charity girls," taxi-dancers were not prostitutes, but committed to an "intermediate" occupation. In the form of dance tickets, taxi–dance-halls even had their own currency that marked the particular sexual economy of patron and dancer. Cressey observed five distinct relationships between dancer and client, each with its own rules of payment, not only the standard dance payment but also "free dances" for more "favored suitors"; "mistress" arrangements; an "alliance" in which, for a few months, a man paid for the dancer's rent or groceries; the "plural alliance," where the girl "enters an understanding by which she agrees to be faithful to a certain three of four men," who through "separate arrangements" meet her "financial requirements" of rent, groceries, or clothes; and the "overnight date," which "quickly takes on the character of clandestine prostitution."[73] In general, only a stipulated cash payment at the time of sexual relations marked a woman's activities as prostitution. As Peiss explains, as long as they did not accept money from men, "charity girls" retained a degree of sexual respectability.

We've seen, then, how people employ a wide range of techniques in order to personalize their gifts and distinguish intimate, affectionate social relations from other social exchanges. With money gifts, the challenge was more urgent, delicate, and time-consuming. As the uses of legal tender multiplied it took skill, determination, and care to personalize money. Let us now explore how it was done.

TRANSFORMING LEGAL TENDER INTO GIFT MONEY

Recall Lou Eleanor Colby dressing up her dollar bills before sending them to her mother as a Christmas gift. Gift-wrapping legal tender was one of the most dramatic ways in which people distinguished gift money. They also did so by selecting or creating distinct gift currencies, segregating monies, or restricting the uses of money gifts.

Consider, first, the physical alteration of currency. In primitive societies, gift monies were easily identifiable. For instance, on Rossel Island in the Pacific, only one specific shell-coin of a particular shape and color could be used to conduct a valid marriage.[74] For Americans, gifting money was harder: they had to create their own distinctions within a standardized currency.

They did so with remarkable originality and skill. Women's magazines describe the many time-consuming and often elaborate strategies for converting legal tender into gift money: gold coins hidden in cookies or concealed by Christmas seals; dollar bills decorating a belt-buckle or encased within a picture frame. A bride received a "carefully wrapped package" from her physician. Inside she found one of his "dreaded pill-boxes" filled with gold coins and labeled "to be taken before or after meals." The better the disguise the more successful the gift. Indeed, women boasted that it took "a long time before the recipient realized that she had received a present of money." Sometimes the gift-wrap was so unique that it became "a shame to take the money." One example was the "check shower" tea party organized by a "bunch of busy girls" who had no time "to embroider or crochet." Yet they found time to produce a gift offering that "didn't seem mercenary at all the way it was done": "there were checker-board sandwiches . . . checkerberry candies . . . the tea cloth was a pink-and-white checked gingham . . . [and] there was . . . a pink-and-white checked holder for a hot teapot handle. . . . When the engaged girl unbuttoned the flap of the tea-pot holder she was quite overcome at finding it filled with the neatly folded personal checks of the girls."[75]

Husbands were urged to display similar imagination when giving gifts of money to their wives, so that the gift would be distinguished from her allowance; "If you . . . give her a check," advised the *Ladies' Home Journal,* "put it in an embroidered purse, or a leather sewing basket, or a jewel box which will be a little gift in itself. Whatever you give, don't let it mean just so much substance." Housewives made similar efforts to distinguish a maid's Christmas gift from other payments: one woman reported how she made the money for her helper "more Christmassy by slipping it inside a tiny purse or a pretty handkerchief," thereby making "a distinction between the gift and the monthly wages."[76]

The greeting-card industry added to the gifting of money by what one historical account of the business calls an "almost endless variety" of money holders, as designers apparently "vied with one another to produce original ideas as carriers for coins, bills, and checks."[77] Some cards—both commercial and domestic—used religious symbols to gift money. Homemade Christmas money was often decorated with ritual reminders—the pine cone of the Christmas tree, for instance, used as a money holder. And greeting-card companies manufactured money holders in the shape of a Christmas tree or presented by a Santa Claus.

Money was also gifted by turning it into a playful item. Humorous English Christmas cards in the 1870s had often used

fake coins as a pun. And both in England and America in the mid-
nineteenth century, cleverly fabricated bank notes were sent as a
Valentine's gift of "love money." But by the twentieth century,
Americans played with real money. Housewives penned witty
messages to better personalize their money gift: "This introduces
you to my friend Bill. He is a good sort, ready to spend and be
spent. Take him with you next time you go shopping." Hallmark
money cards displayed cute images of children, animals, or jolly
versions of Santa Claus with amusing messages. Humor, like ritual,
served to differentiate money as a gift. So did language; in gift
cards, money became a "bit of cheer" or some "little thing."[78]

A second way to differentiate gift money physically was to
use only special kinds of money such as gold coins or brand-
new dollar bills. Each Christmas, the demand for gold coins and
crisp new bills created much additional work for the Mint as well
as for the banks that distributed the money. In November 1910
when the Treasury, for the sake of economy, decided not to
issue new coins for the forthcoming Christmas, the "wall of
protest . . . the indignation of the shoppers and the demands of
the merchants" were such that, according to a *New York Times*
report, Treasury officials considered ordering a few million silver
coins for the holiday business.[79]

Special currencies were also used to pay for services associated with ritual events, as, for example, the clergyman's fee for a
wedding ceremony. Etiquette manuals were careful to specify
not only who was expected to pay the clergyman's fee (the
groom, through the best man) but also how to present the
money. The standard procedure in the early 1900s was to give
the clergyman at least five dollars in gold, clean bills, or a check
enclosed in a sealed envelope.[80] But sometimes not even a physically distinct currency was enough. In December of 1907, when
his congregation offered Rev. Dr. Jones, the pastor of a Presbyterian church in Pittsburgh, a Christmas purse containing $100 in
new golden coins, according to a *New York Times* headline, the
pastor "tossed the gold into his hat and handed it back." The

"nice new money" was missing the motto "In God We Trust," which recently had been removed by the president. For the pastor, such "godless coins" could not qualify as a gift: "I swore," he told his congregants, "I would take no money that did not bear the old motto."[81]

Others earmarked legal tender as a gift by withdrawing it from circulation altogether and inscribing their own personal messages. Significantly, studies of primitive money tell how sometimes gold and silver coins were converted into a kind of jewelry known as "dead money." Turn-of-the-century etiquette manuals document many such symbolic "murders" that turned money into an ornamental gift. An "exquisite" christening present, for instance, was a gold chain and locket made of five-dollar gold pieces given by each of the father's groomsmen and melted down by a goldsmith.[82]

A more radical way of gifting money was to invent new currencies. Here, again, business stepped in with such innovations as the Christmas money order or the gift certificate. To convey the difference with ordinary transfers of money, gift orders—like money cards—were 'also often dressed up in ritual costume. American Express advertised its first Christmas money orders with the picture of a woman sitting next to the manger where Christ was born. The woman, explained the advertisement poster, sat near the spot where the three wise men had presented Christ with gifts. By December of 1917, the company made use of both domestic and wartime themes. That Christmas it printed two streetcar cards to promote money orders as "the most suitable war-time gift": One portrayed a soldier displaying his gift order; and another—most likely targeted for immigrants as remittances—showed an elderly couple holding the money order along with a note from their son explaining, "Not knowing what you would wish most, I am sending you this practical present."[83]

Gift certificates—also called merchandise coupons or gift bonds in this early period—were a clever device to meet people's expanding gift obligations in the early 1900s. On purely practical grounds, as the ads noted, they solved "the problem of 'what to get'"; the donor was not only "saved all the bother," but assured that "your gift will not be duplicated." But, surely, the main appeal of gift certificates was not their efficiency; it was simpler, after all, just to send cash. Certificates skillfully managed to turn cash into a gift. Donors paid the store to transform their money into an often "handsomely engraved and embossed" document, usually personalized by the name of the donor and the recipient. This new gift currency was further set apart from legal tender by restricting its spending to a particular store or even a particular item. Nor was this currency convertible into ordinary cash: their gift certificates, warned New York's Simpson Crawford Co. in a 1906 advertisement in *The World*, were "good for merchandise any place in the store" but were "not transferable for cash."[84]

Although we know little about the actual circulation of gift certificates, it seems that these currencies were appropriate mostly for friendly, but not overly intimate, relations or for the more impersonal and unequal transfers. Macy's ads are instructive: When "in doubt what to choose for a friend, for employees or charitable gifts," their store bonds would "solve the problem"; as a gift to friends, the ad explained, "[the bond] must please, because it secures the recipient whatever he or she may desire." Or consider Simpson Crawford's glove certificates targeted for "the busy man in the office—every clerk he has will appreciate them." Part of a certificate's appeal, after all, was that some of the work of personalizing gifts was delegated to the recipient: their glove certificate, the Mark Cross ad explained, "may be purchased and sent instead of the gloves themselves, permitting the recipient to choose her own gloves."[85]

The physical manipulation of legal tender was a powerful, tangible technique of transforming money into a gift. But money was gifted also at an earlier stage, as people segregated certain monies from other domestic currencies to be spent for gifts; families often kept their gift money in a special, separate box or a tin bank or, after 1910, in a Christmas Club bank account. The banks' Christmas savings-account plan was a stunning success:

by December 1926 it was reported that some $400 million were distributed nationally to about 8 million depositors by some 8,000 banks. For fifty weeks during the year, each club member, using a coupon book, punch cards, or bankbooks, deposited a small amount—the average deposit during the 1920s was $1 but the amounts ranged from 25 cents to $20—that was redeemed in a lump sum just before Christmas.[86]

The appeal of Christmas accounts had little to do with economic incentives. Although a few banks paid the same interest rate on club accounts as on regular savings accounts, most banks offered a much lower rate and, increasingly, no interest at all. And yet people kept bringing their holiday monies to the bank to be put aside for Christmas. A 1940 report in *Banker's Magazine* noted the great "popularity of this systematic method of accumulating a definite sum for a definite purpose . . . regardless of dividends." Bankers protested that they made little or no profit from these small deposits and only kept them as a way to attract new wage-earning customers; yet, banks actively advertised their "smile checks," urging prospective depositors to "light a Christmas candle every week" by making a deposit. As one banker confided to an interviewer, the slogan "'Christmas money' . . . gets 'em by the hundreds and the thousands. Gets 'em in a way that thrift or poverty or security and the rest of those bank-advertising bywords can't begin to touch." Jews furthermore apparently adapted the Christmas Club concept to Hanukkah: by the mid-1920s "Save For Hanukkah" ads by the East River Savings Institution appeared in *Der Tog* and *Morgen Zhurnal*, two Yiddish newspapers. Although printed in Yiddish, the ad pictured a young couple standing next to a Christmas tree.[87]

We know little about Christmas Club depositors. There may have been some affluent customers, but most club members were workers, most typically the workingman's wife who, according to a study of eight Boston banks in 1926, was "obliged to and . . . willing to save in smaller amounts than men." In fact, some of the men interviewed were reportedly "ashamed to be seen at the Christmas Club window." For women, and possibly also for some children, the Christmas Club—much like the Penny Provident banks that preceded it—was a useful institutional device to safeguard monies from the household economy for use by them for gift giving or other domestic expenses.[88]

RESTRICTIONS ON GIFT MONEY

We have seen how money was set aside for gift giving and then transferred as a gift item. But the gifting of money did not stop there; it also mattered how gift money was spent by the recipient. A birthday check was not supposed to be cashed for groceries, or Christmas money used to pay a gambling debt. In order to complete the gifting process, donors and recipients found ways to restrict the spending of gift currencies. Although money gifts were praised as "the most useful" since they allowed the recipients freedom to choose their own gift goods—the ultimate privilege of a consumerist culture—recipients were not as free as supposed. Marking money as a gift imposed obligations on spending it that did not exist with a wage. We saw how, in fact, certificates were highly restricted currencies.[89]

It was, of course, easier for donors to control the gift transfer by choosing an object. Etiquette guides recognized the donor's rights by insisting that a recipient's thank-you note should always make specific mention of the item received, and by placing certain restrictions on the exchange of gift goods. With money the task was complicated; etiquette books, however, increasingly urged their readers to acknowledge precisely what they had or would buy with a relative's money gift. It was expected, for instance, that a wedding gift be spent in furnishing a couple's new home or on a wedding trip. Even a birthday gift of cash could be used by friends or relatives to influence the consumption pattern of the recipient: an aunt's $50 birthday present, for instance, was designated for the repapering of her niece's parlor.[90]

Deeply concerned with the rationalizing of household finances, home-economics experts had their own reasons to recommend the earmarking of gift money. The "danger from gifts," warned Benjamin R. Andrews, professor of household economics at Teachers College, Columbia University, was the "receipt of something not earned" and therefore less likely to "stimulate a sound economic reaction in the receiver." Andrews advised treating gift money "apart from current regular income, not to use it for current needs, but to add it to one's personal capital." Gifts to children, for instance, were best destined for a savings account, held as the child's "education or start-in-life fund." Money gifts, concluded Andrews, "are wisely given when conditioned."[91]

Indeed, when it came to children's gift monies—even small sums—the earmarking was justified as an educational process. Even as the allowance was upheld as the best source of income, most children still received gifts of money from parents, relatives, and visitors at Christmas, birthdays, or other occasions. Concerned with their children's consumer skills, however, parents wavered between the value of free choice and the urgency of wise spending. Consider a typical situation raised by an early-twentieth-century "practical book on home management": a young girl decides to spend the five-dollar gold piece she received as a gift from her grandmother by giving half to her brother and spending the other half herself, feeling that "it was her personal property, to do with as she pleased." But the girl's mother "wanted to dictate to her what she should buy with it." When the grandmother reluctantly intervened, advising her grandaughter that "she had better spend it the way your mother wants to," the girl returned her gift. Although early supporters of children's rights urged that "nobody should insist upon telling [children] how to spend their own money," in fact most parents seemed to have closely supervised their children's spending, including their money gifts.[92]

Often gift money was earmarked as a charitable gift, thereby making cash a morally superior bestowal than an ordinary present. Thus the *Ladies' Home Journal* reader who told how each year she looked for "some deserving case of need: some girl struggling for a musical education or some young man aspiring for college; some woman who should be in a hospital." She then asked her friends to bring her the sum of money they had anticipated spending on her Christmas present in "a sealed blank envelope, unmarked," then added the money she would have spent for their gifts, and turned the entire gift fund into a charitable donation. Often gifting money was the only way to offer financial assistance to a friend or a relative; as Mrs. Colby explained, her "jolly little messengers of Christmas cheer" could be sent "into some homes where money, although sorely needed, might not be sent through ordinary channels."[93] Gifting the exchange defined the relation between donor and recipient as one of equals, thereby making the transfer affectionate rather than embarrasing.

Restricting the uses of gift money was not merely a refinement of the upper classes. SPUG, which by 1913 was renamed as the Society for the Promotion of Useful Giving, boasted that the graft money spent by working girls in gifts to their superiors had been redirected into "good giving." Many of the young women were using their savings "for little gifts to families poorer than theirs." Immigrants' letters home clearly reveal how they, too, cared deeply about how their gifts of money were used: donors routinely instructed parents, siblings, wives, or children how to spend their gift remittances, whether on a suit, a dress, or Christmas celebrations. Surely their instructions were sometimes modified by the recipients but, at least from the evidence, it seems that the recipient felt obliged to provide an accounting of how and why the money was spent differently. "You wrote us, dear son," the parents of one Polish immigrant responded on January 1902, "that we might make [from the 10 roubles he had sent them] a better Christmas tree . . . and make ourselves merry during the holidays." But, instead, the money had been divided, they reported, to pay a debt of eight rubles to the carpenter, one ruble spent for a holy mass, and only the rest they "took for our Christmas festival."[94]

The restrictions on spending gift money did not work magically. At stake were the long-term intimate ties between donor and recipient. As the correspondence of immigrants poignantly discloses, money remittances were a way of "remembering" and upholding family ties.[95] Contesting a gift of cash was in part a rejection of the donor's feelings and of the relationship itself.

People thus cared deeply about differentiating money as a gift; they did so by decorating, inventing, segregating, and restricting currencies. In fact they used a variety of other techniques as well, for example, labeling certain sums as gifted amounts, like the Jewish designation of 18 as a gift of *chai* or life, so that an $18 gift becomes a unique and distinctly more meaningful transfer than $19 or $20.

What mattered was to mark standardized currency in some unmistakable way that would allow the same legal tender used in other impersonal transfers to be bestowed as a sentimental gift, to display a donor's particular knowledge of the other person and their relationship. This was especially difficult for the most intimate, reciprocal, long-term relationships, and people had to make great efforts to certify the affectionate rather than instrumental value of their money gift—except, of course, in certain ritual bestowals, like those of a wedding or christening, where the money gift of a relative or an intimate friend was socially defined as a proper transfer. Moreover, with the invention of gift certificates and money orders, gifts of money multiplied in less intimate or equal but still friendly relations. Here the problem was to display cordiality without either making the gift too intimate or confusing the money with a payment, an entitlement, or charity.

In the more impersonal, unequal, although sometimes cordial relations of employer and employee or patron and server, gifting money created a different sort of quandary; it bordered on charity, thus potentially demeaning rather than rewarding the recipient. As a result, while the problematics of a gift of money between intimates were resolved by personalizing money, the ambiguities of gift giving among more distant and unequal parties were managed by standardizing and routinizing the transfer—as from tip to a service charge, from bonus to salary. Gifting was even more radically standardized in the absolutely impersonal relations between business and consumers, as with the popular turn-of-the-century coupons and premiums offered by a growing number of companies to promote their products.[96]

The remarkable range of money gifts contests standard accounts of the effects of commercialization and rationalization on social life: gift exchanges were supposed to be squashed by the hard-nosed instrumentalism of the modern world—not to flourish and diversify. To be sure, analysts and critics were not all wrong; we have just traced, after all, the profound commercialization of the gift economy. And, of course, business and advertisers created their own profitable stratagems to make money acceptable as a gift. But the conventional assumption that monetization would deplete social life of meaning, dry up social relations, and annul gift exchanges was mistaken. In fact, what people did was to mark an array of different forms of money to discriminate among a surprising range of meaningful social relations.

The work of what John Davis has called the "gifting of the market"—including gifting money—still goes on. According to one study conducted by American Express, over $54 billion are being spent by Americans annually on money gifts, including cash, personal checks, and gift certificates. Money cards are available for almost any occasion, including Valentine's Day. And gift certificates are sold not only by department stores but by a wide variety of specialized businesses including restaurants, beauty salons, and telephone companies. In 1987, American Express successfully launched its Gift Cheque, "in an elegant gold envelope with a distinctive card for the gift-giver to sign," as a new gift currency "more personal than a personal check." At Tiffany's, special "Tiffany Monies" gift coins from $25 to $1,000 are advertised as Christmas gifts redeemable in merchandise. Meanwhile, Christmas Club accounts, which seemed to be withering away a few years ago, are reportedly having a comeback.[97]

People still care deeply about distinguishing their gift money from other transfers. *Emily Post's Etiquette* 1992 edition offers advice ranging from when and how to give money gifts, special formulas for acknowledging money gifts, and even techniques for the tasteful display of wedding-gift checks. Post's manual offers detailed instructions on personalizing money: "When a gift is a sum of money," advises Post, the recipient "should indicate how it will be used. 'Your check for $50.00 is going into our "sofa fund," and we can't tell you how pleased we were to receive it.'" If the couple have no immediate use for the money, they should still mention some particular use, "say that it will be such a help in furnishing your apartment, building up your savings, or whatever."[98] Or take also the persistent concern with camouflaging the "price tag" of money gifts. Early editions of Emily Post had declared it against good taste to display checks as wedding presents or to divulge their amounts; but by the 1950s a special new section on "displaying checks" approved the exhibit of wedding-gift checks—as long as the amounts were strategically concealed. Precise instructions were included: the checks were to be laid out on a flat surface one above the other so that the signatures alone were disclosed. The amount of the check on top was covered with a strip of opaque paper and then a sheet of glass was placed over all of them. The glass, recommended the manual, had to be sufficiently large to cover the edges with presents and to "keep a curious someone from lifting it."[99]

The gifting of money, of course, goes even further; we have hardly touched, for instance, the rich world of monetary gifts, loans, and other transfers *within* families. Nor have we fully explored the age, racial, and gender earmarking of money gifts.

We know that women are still in charge of choosing and shopping for Christmas and other gifts, that the wife is more likely than her husband to make Christmas Club deposits, but we need to examine more closely gender patterns in the giving of cash, or the apparent division of labor between handling small sums of gift money by women and larger amounts by men. Furthermore, we have not looked at parallels to monetary markings in adjacent areas such as the giving of time in voluntary services and displays of friendship.[100] Again, there are fascinating similarities between the dilemmas of gift transfers for households and for the state.

We also need to ask how the gifting of money works in other societies. In Japan, for instance, where gift giving is extensive—ranging from Mother's Day and St. Valentine's Day gifts, to gifts for childbirth, entering school, graduation, birthdays, as well as gifts for building a new home, starting a new business, moving, or traveling—the giving of money is widespread. Japanese money gifts include "congratulations on schooling" (*Nyugaku iwai*—gifts for the family of children who start school) wedding gifts, funeral offerings, and *Toshidama,* money gifts presented by relatives on the New Year, usually to children. The Japanese take enormous care in differentiating these gifted monies: they use only new bills (although not for funerals), present their gifts in elaborately and meaningfully designed envelopes personalized with the name of the recipient, and avoid certain sums as unfit for gifts—four, for example, because in Japanese the numeral sounds too much like the word "death." The gifting of money in Japan is so effective that it apparently serves as legal evidence to identify bribes: if the money is offered without its gift envelope or is wrinkled, dirty, or used, the transfer is more likely to be a bribe than a gift. Indeed, bribes are often disguised as gifts by placing clean bills in a money envelope or by using properly wrapped gift certificates sold by department stores.[101]

As money entered the sphere of personal gift giving in early twentieth-century America, we have seen that it did not corrupt, repress, or debilitate people's social exchanges. Instead, new gift currencies were created to mark their multiple social relations. This earmarking of monies took place in other parts of American society as well, from the differentiation of monies within households that we discussed earlier to the more bureaucratic and formal world of business and public institutions. These institutions include the many charity organizations involved in the bestowal of money to the poor. In their work we can see the interaction of state authorities, domestic economies, and gift transfers. For that reason, we will explore them in considerable detail.

4

Poor People's Money

THE 1910 *Guida degli Stati Uniti per L'Immigrante Italiano* (Guide to the United States for the Italian Immigrant), published by the Connecticut Daughters of the Revolution and translated the following year into English, reassured newcomers that "the United States have always been the land of the immigrants," discovered by one Italian and named for another. It then gave them advice on how to make it in America, how to find work, how to travel, how to become a citizen. Among other things, the guide also offered recent immigrants practical tips on how to handle *il dollaro*. It was not just a matter of adopting a different currency; these new Americans had to learn the modern rational approach to money management. "It is dangerous," warned the guide, "to carry money in your pocket or leave it at home." Special sections offered careful guidelines on how to deal with savings banks and on "safe" ways to send money abroad or within the United States.[1]

Those many immigrants who fell into poverty encountered a much more deliberate and organized restructuring of their financial practices. Convinced, as visitors of a prominent New York relief society put it, that poor Italians were "unintelligent in the use of what they have," charity organizations became determined to teach their clients how to use money properly.[2] Consider the case of Mrs. C, a widow who had come from Italy to the United States shortly after her marriage. When her husband died, their small savings were dissolved in doctors' bills and funeral expenses. In the early 1920s, the Columbus Family Service Society gave Mrs. C and her six young children $10 a week in grocery orders to be spent at a designated grocery store. To prepare her for a money allowance, Mrs. C was then asked to keep a written account of her purchases, watch grocery lists, and identify where staple foods could be bought cheaper. But when a visitor discovered that twenty-five cents recorded for tomatoes, supposedly canned, had been spent for one pound of fresh tomatoes—Mrs. C admitted she had been "extravagant" and could have bought "just as good tomatoes at another store for twenty cents a pound"—the agency felt that she still needed further training and supervision before being given a money allowance. For the first few months, a visitor met with Mrs. C twice a week, usually for a whole afternoon, to discuss, among other matters, "food preparation, buying . . . and discipline." She accompanied Mrs. C to the grocery store, attempting "to point out economies." At the time of the report, Mrs. C had become "very careful in recording expenditures . . . laying a good foundation for later budget plans." Even the grocer recognized that she now was "a very close and efficient buyer." Still Mrs. C was not given a money allowance.[3]

American welfare experts have persistently viewed charitable cash as a redoubtable, multifaceted currency. In the hands of the morally incompetent poor, experts have declared, money could turn into a dangerous form of relief, easily squandered for immoral purposes. Indeed, for most of the nineteenth century and the early 1900s, state agencies as well as private charities directly regulated the household economy of the poor, allocating clothing, fuel, and food to the needy, but seldom cash. Or else, as with Mrs. C, agencies dispensed grocery orders that specified not only *which* goods recipients could purchase but also *where* to buy them.

Concern about the dangers of cash formed with respect to three classic, interrelated distinctions in Western charitable practice. The first was *public versus private* relief—assistance dispensed by state and public officials versus relief distributed by individuals or voluntary benevolent associations; the second distinction concerned *outdoor versus indoor* relief—the support of the poor in their own homes or their institutionalization in almshouses; and the third distinction was *cash versus in-kind*—assistance provided in the form of monetary support versus goods and services. When, in what manner, and how directly to use money for relief thus raised fundamental questions about the organization of charitable practice as a whole. Defining cash as dangerous inclined charitable organizations toward the more restrictive arrangements in each of these three concerns.

In a modern consumer society, however, properly supervised money could serve as an important instructional currency to rehabilitate the morally righteous but technically incompetent poor, teaching them how to spend properly. By 1899, an authoritative handbook for charity workers dismissed the preference for in-kind relief as an outmoded "charitable superstition." About a decade later, Frederic Almy, secretary of the Buffalo Charity Organization Society and an outspoken critic of public outdoor relief, made the startling pronouncement, via a much-cited article in *The Survey*, that money relief awarded by private charity "can be made quite as spiritual in its effects as the alms of good advice." By 1922, an analysis of the methods used for dispensing relief by eighteen leading charity organizations throughout the country recommended the money allowance as the preferred method of giving, "in all cases possible," but especially for long-term assistance. A major history of the charity organization movement, published that same year, also found that "the weight of opinion seems to be in favor of relief in money."[4] And, starting in 1911, the highly controversial but enormously successful mother's pension movement made public cash available for the relief of widows and their dependent children.

Mirroring the new general enthusiasm for turning money into a ritual or sentimental gift, charitable workers declared that cash was preferable even as a Christmas gift for the poor. Rather than giving old clothes or food, charity agencies were now urged to give "funds to buy them." Or a gift certificate: New York's Siegel Cooper Co. promoted their "Christmas dinner certificates" signed by the purchaser and delivered to the beneficiary, who then exchanged it for a dinner basket. As "gifts of charity," explained a Macy's ad, merchandise bonds "enable you to avoid the delicate point of giving money." A pension, however, made the best gift. By substituting the degrading Christmas basket dinner for the more dignified gift of a yearly allowance, the poor could be offered the security of a regular income rather than a token one-day feast.[5]

What had turned dangerous money into legitimate cash relief? Sounding very much like consumer economists, social workers, during the first few decades of the twentieth century, defended the discretionary freedom of the money allowance as a necessary training tool to cope with the modern market by allowing the family "to handle money, to learn its value, and its buying power." If you "deprive a person of the function of spending," explained Emma Winslow, the influential home economist at the New York Charity Organization Society, "you make that person poor indeed." Unlike in-kind relief, asserted Joanna Colcord, the superintendent of the New York Charity Organization Society, cash conserved "family independence and self-respect." In the same way, better than food or other traditional forms of in-kind "Christmas cheer," Christmas money would allow dependent families to "make their own plans," even if it meant to "have as foolish and poorly planned a dinner" as they wished.[6] Of course, it had to be the "right" kind of money. Whereas sentimental alms-giving degraded the recipient, rationally budgeted monies trained competent consumers—or so the practitioners reasoned.

Yet, despite the rhetoric, the alleged freedom of monetary payments was an illusion. Cash relief was still treated as a very different kind of money from a wage. The poor, after all, were not ordinary consumers. As one charity official bluntly put it, "if these families had been able to manage their own affairs successfully they would not be knocking at our doors." How, then, could they be trusted to spend their money freely but not foolishly? Even consumer theorists, while staunchly supporting freedom of consumption, recognized that free "choosers" of goods had to learn how to avoid "blunders and waste"; the "successful purchaser" was not born, but trained in the "art of expenditure."[7]

If competent consumers needed instruction in making "wise" choices, then surely recipients of relief needed the expert guidance of social workers to correct "defects in expenditures." Indeed, recognizing the hazards of "incapable management" A. C. Pigou, in his classic statement on welfare economics first published in 1920, urged "some degree of oversight" when transfers to the poor were made "in the form of command over purchasing power." American welfare practitioners concurred. It was necessary, as the general secretary of the Brooklyn Bureau of Charities explained, "for counsel, instruction, and other help to accompany funds that come to the family through no labor of its own." Only a "carefully supervised cash allowance," noted Colcord, could assure that "the money will really be expended for the purposes designed." Administrators of public mothers' pensions were equally persuaded that close surveillance of pensioned families was needed "in order that the public money granted . . . may serve the purpose for which it is appropriated." The trick, suggested a speaker at the 1901 meetings of the National Conference of Charities and Correction, was to make money "as safe as groceries."[8]

How did social workers create this new kind of "safe" instructional currency for their clients? How did they mark the differences between modern "constructive" pensions or allowances and the old-time corrupting gifts of money, alms, and the dole? And how was cash relief set apart from an earned wage? Unlike the social "domestication" of family money and the personalization of gift money, the earmarking of cash as relief was bureaucratically prescribed and officially imposed. Charity organizations, teamed with home economists, devised all sorts of formal and informal strategies to remake the earmarking systems of the poor by "directing the spending of money of families under their care."[9] In the process, although social workers insisted on the liberating effects of cash relief, the supervision of relief probably intensified. Welfare workers undertook the reform of family budgets with the zeal formerly spent in upgrading family morality. Armed with budget books and account ledgers, social workers visited the homes of the poor, showing them what to buy and where.

What happens when authorities intervene in the process of earmarking? We have seen how, as money increasingly entered into domestic and gift exchanges, people created new currencies to circulate within the family or to give as gifts. These personalized economic worlds were not homogenized through the use of money, since people invented new ways to earmark their intimate currencies. When it came to the poor, however, charitable authorities mistrusted their methods of earmarking; they set out, therefore, to remake the domestic economies of dependent families. In the process, they devised new monies that provided the poor not only with purchasing power but also with lessons in spending.

Thus, paradoxically, just as the American state was struggling to enforce a single, generalized, freely circulating legal tender, public and private charities alike invented multiple alternative monies for the poor by producing either materially distinct currencies, such as grocery orders or food stamps, or by closely restricting the uses of ordinary money. As we will see, at times the boundaries between cash relief and other monies blurred as visitors of the poor felt entitled to earmark even dependents' own money for "proper" expenses.

The next three chapters will examine in depth the earmarking ideologies and strategies of welfare authorities. But first, why did nineteenth-century charity experts worry so much about poor people's monies? This chapter looks at their reasons for viewing money as a dangerous form of relief and then examines authorities' techniques to keep money, as much as possible, out of poor people's hands. Chapter 5 proceeds to the earmarking of the new charitable cash. How did social-welfare officials coin their instructional currency? And how successful were they? Could official earmarks stamp out the diversity of poor people's monies? Chapter 6 will show that recipients of relief nevertheless maintained their own systems of earmarking. What donors dismissed as incompetent, foolish, or immoral economic choices were often shaped by a competing set of monetary distinctions. At times a sort of contest took place between official and private systems of earmarking as people found strategies to subvert bureaucratic restrictions on the uses of their money, often spending in ways that puzzled or outraged middle-class observers.

To be sure, American charitable practices and ideologies varied considerably from place to place and from time to time. More specifically, most private or public agencies, after the eighteenth century, did not adhere to a single method of providing assistance to the poor but, in fact, often mingled in-kind and cash relief. Nevertheless, a close look at the record reveals decisive changes and discernible national patterns in the ideas and practices of dispensing relief. Indeed, as Michael Katz has noted in his analysis of nineteenth-century poor relief, one of the "great themes of American social experience" is precisely the "continuities in institutional patterns across a sprawling, decentralized, and diverse nation." "All over the country," Katz tells us, "those nineteenth-century Americans who controlled social policy made similar choices about poor relief."[10] Historians have focused on policy debates over *whether* or *where* to give relief—tracing closely, for instance, the nineteenth-century enthusiasm for poor-houses and the persistent struggle against supporting the poor in their homes—but we still know little about changing methods for dispensing outdoor relief. In order to understand *when* and *why* Americans shifted among in-kind relief, grocery orders, or cash, this account will make no effort to document all local and state variations, but will stress instead major changes in practices and ideologies.[11]

DANGEROUS CASH

The Benevolent Societies of Boston, organized in 1834 to address the city's growing concerns with its poor, specified in their first annual report that relief "is to be not in money, but in the necessaries required in the case."[12] Nine years later, in its first statement the New York Association for Improving the Condition of the Poor (AICP) likewise restricted relief to "necessary articles." Visitors to the poor were not allowed to give money, except when authorized by the association's advisory committee.[13]

Some accounts suggest that cash relief may have been somewhat less disturbing during the early part of the nineteenth century. Until the 1830s, for instance, New York, Baltimore, and Boston apparently paid their pensioners with money. Consider more closely the case of Philadelphia. Although there was some opposition to cash aid as early as the 1760s, cash relief had been the most important kind of public as well as private assistance in the early 1800s. Curiously, the guardians of the poor were sometimes encouraged to give *only* money (or wood) instead of groceries.[14]

But in 1828, the city's new poor law virtually abolished cash aid. And after a new almshouse opened in 1835, public cash relief became illegal under state law; relief was to be "confined entirely to fuel, provisions, clothing, medicine, and medical attendance." Some cash aid was reintroduced in the 1840s, but unsuccessfully. Private charities, meanwhile, also increasingly turned to relief in kind, distributing food, clothing, or medical supplies rather than cash. Indeed, of the many new charities organized in Philadelphia between 1840 and 1854, none dispensed cash.[15]

These private charities, organized in cities throughout the country, redefined the approach to poverty in the early part of the nineteenth century, anticipating many of the concerns, policies, and organizational structure of the influential Charity Organization movement of the 1870s. At issue was the growing conviction that indiscriminate alms-giving corrupted the already weak moral fiber of the poor, creating a class of indolent, dependent, and fraudulent paupers. Relief, therefore, needed to be not only parsimonious but carefully targeted. AICP societies organized a system of volunteer visitors that went into the homes of the poor, closely investigating all requests for assistance. Their central assignment, however, was not to dispense material relief but moral advice. Relief, even when determined after proper inspection of the recipients, could only be a temporary crutch in the process of moral rehabilitation and economic independence. It was best, therefore, to give "what is least susceptible to abuse"—food, clothing, or fuel, but *not* money.[16]

And, yet, despite such wariness about material aid, by the 1870s the early charities had become primarily relief-giving agencies. To the organizers of the "scientific charity" movement that began to reshape poor relief in the 1870s, the AICP societies had forsaken their original charge of moral rehabilitation of the poor. Planned relief, critics argued, had relapsed into irresponsible alms-giving. After 1855, for instance, visitors from the New York AICP could dispense cash relief without the approval of their advisory committee, and, apparently, did so increasingly.[17]

The charity societies of the 1870s were deliberately organized as coordinating and investigating agencies, not relief societies. Their "friendly visitors" were instructed in the skills of moral reconstruction; shown how "to investigate the causes of distress, and seek to remove them by friendly direction and sympathy," not direct relief. Offering "doles" would only spoil their mission. Although, in actual practice, charity-organization societies soon compromised their strictly advisory role by providing occasional petty sums of cash to the poor, their instructional handbooks expressly prohibited visitors from "giving alms on their own impulse."[18] They could, however, refer poor families to appropriate relief agencies.

Deeply suspicious of relief, the Charity Organization movement thus introduced severe restrictions in the allocation of private assistance, while it also fought unremittingly—and quite successfully—against public outdoor relief. Of course, the politics of nineteenth-century relief involved more than charity leaders; relief policies, for instance, concerned ward politicians who relied on relief to build their constituencies. And they mattered to relief businessmen, the local merchants who made money by supplying poorhouses or by filling grocery orders for public agencies or private charities.[19]

But charity workers took a leading role in reshaping late-nineteenth-century relief. Once more, monetary grants were singled out as uniquely suspect. For instance, when the Commissioners of Charities and Corrections abolished outdoor relief in New York City in December of 1875, they adopted a resolution to experiment with giving the poor the "necessities of life" instead of money (or orders on grocery stores). That year, 14,287 families had received just under $50,000 in monetary relief. One year later, only coal was distributed.[20]

By the late nineteenth century, public cash relief was rare anywhere in the country. By 1860, for instance, Philadelphia's poor received only public relief in kind. A statement on the distribution of outdoor relief in sixty-four major cities of the United States for 1897 shows only fourteen cities offering cash allowances, and in meager amounts. That same year, a survey of American poor laws noted that giving relief in kind had become an unwritten national law. Some proposed making cash aid illegal. A study of outdoor relief in Ohio, for instance, concluded that the only hope to reform the system was to amend the old statute and prohibit cash relief. Minnesota did so in 1893. The amendment to the general statutes of 1878 concerning the care of the poor now stated that "in no case shall any money be paid to any poor person."[21]

Why did money worry the charity establishment in ways that clothing or food or fuel seldom did? No doubt the uneasiness with cash resulted in part from the rapidly mounting number of poor people in American cities during the early nineteenth century. It was not, however, simply a matter of the greater cost of relieving indigence, but also of the growing anonymity of the urban poor. Worse still, in the case of immigrants, was their strangeness and their reputed intemperance. How could charity workers know how relief funds were spent; how, specifically, could they stop recipients from drinking or gambling their money away?[22]

New definitions of money further aggravated the concern with the moral incompetence of the poor. In rural American communities, legal tender had circulated along with other personalized currencies, as well as in-kind products, as acceptable payments. As one historian suggests, cash appeared to be "merely another product," of "definable qualities and particular uses." Apparently there was a saying in Ulster County in the 1790s that tradesmen accepted "wheat, rye, Indian corn, as well as cash, or *anything* that is good to eat" as legitimate payment.[23] The same may have been true with relief, which explains at least in part why late-eighteenth-century communities seemed to make fewer distinctions between cash and in-kind assistance to the poor.

As more and more workers relied on cash wages, and as cash wages became increasingly a payment for time and effort spent rather than tasks completed, it became urgent to distinguish a payment for services from unearned monies. Still echoing the 1834 English Poor Law's principle of "less eligibility"— that life on relief should remain less desirable than the lowest-paid labor—charity workers were concerned that the poor would prefer charity income to market wages. As Josephine Lowell, the leading spokeswoman for the scientific charity movement, warned, "no man can receive as a gift what he should earn by his own labor without a moral deterioration."[24]

But as the nineteenth-century state worked hard to enforce a single, anonymous, interchangeable medium of exchange, what would set the earned dollar apart from the relief dollar? The morally suspect poor, it was predicted, would be quick to treat relief as rightful income. As a speaker at the 1890 National Conference of Charities and Correction observed, "when we remember how much hard work it takes to earn one dollar . . . and then think of the reckless way in which a dollar is given here, there, and everywhere, often simply for the asking, can we wonder that many succumb to the temptation to ask?"[25]

Modern cash posed a second serious challenge to the reform-oriented charity workers. How would a morally neutral currency reshape the moral life of recipients? What could guarantee that once in the pockets of the poor, charitable cash did not turn into a corrupt currency, spent for immoral, foolish, or dangerous purposes? Opponents of outdoor relief declared it "unsafe, wasteful, and unwise to trust [the weak, the lazy, and the imposter] with money to expend in their own behalf." It was safer to keep them away from cash. Indeed, a study of unemployment relief points out that during the 1893–97 period of depression, private social agencies distributed clothing, fuel, and food more often than cash, "as it was feared money might be misspent."[26]

Distrust of the economic choices made by the poor ran deep. Indeed, their very poverty was often assumed to be the result of profligacy or financial imprudence. There would be little need for alms-giving, the Reverend S. Humphreys Gurteen maintained in his *Handbook of Charity Organization*—the key text on the principles and practices of charity organization—if only the poor were not ignorant about "the economic and provident disposition of their weekly earnings." A handbook for friendly visitors, compiled by the Charity Organization Society of

New York in 1883, explained that "the poor ... have never learned 'the power of littles.' The habit of watching where the pennies go, and of laying up against a rainy day, is generally wanting to them."[27]

If the "worthy" poor were financial incompetents, paupers were corrupt financiers, sure to spend any cash relief on "riot and intoxication."[28] The overseers of Staunton, Virginia, for instance, had made it clear in 1844 why they dispensed money only rarely, "to guard against the improvidence of paupers."[29] During most of the nineteenth century, "liquor money" was particularly suspect. Poor men, it seemed, could not avoid the lure of the saloon, spending relief dollars "in what would embitter and degrade the homes for whose benefit the money had been provided." A writer in *The Charities Review* pointedly cited an anecdote about a gift of 100,000 francs—in marked coins—given to the Paris poor by the Russian czar in a recent visit. A week later, most coins were allegedly found in taverns and wine shops.[30]

TAMING MONEY

A key challenge for charity workers thus became to regulate the economy of the poor. Since recipients of relief could not be trusted to spend money wisely or morally, charity officials would guide their expenditures or, better still, decide themselves what the poor needed. They did this in two ways: first, by providing relief in kind or creating restricted currencies, such as food orders; and, second, by intervening directly in the families' own expenditures. By making in-kind or restricted transfers, charity organizers effectively neutralized the dangers of incompetent spending. As long as no legal tender was put in the hands of the poor, their economic world was protected. But the concern with the moral risks of spending went even further, to the extent that charity workers felt entitled to appropriate money that rightfully belonged to the poor. Convinced of the inability of poor families to manage properly their "own" income, friendly visitors and settlement workers found ways to intercept part of their earnings, save the money for them, and sometimes even spend it.

Charitable workers' first technique was to *suppress legal tender*. Of course, the surest way to supervise the economic world of the poor was to institutionalize them. Indeed, since the 1820s, the almshouse had become the preferred method of poor relief. But outdoor relief persisted, both public and private. Thus, *how* to dispense assistance to poor families remained an issue of concern. Short of institutionalization, work relief was an ideologically comfortable strategy, forcing the poor to earn public or private assistance with their own labor. Yet, despite repeated experiments, work-relief projects never succeeded in becoming more than inept, token attempts to replace charity with labor.

Among other problems was the question of wages: if "charity work" was not "real" work, it could hardly be compensated with "real" wages. As a result, work-relief wages created a great deal of controversy; on the one hand, underpaying workers, officials feared, discouraged potential applicants, but, on the other hand, making relief payments equivalent to market wages risked seriously undermining the carefully established boundary between work and relief. In some cases, compensating relief work with in-kind assistance rather than cash solved the problem, by signaling concretely the difference between ordinary wages and work-relief payments. The New York Charity Organization Society, for instance, explained in its annual report for 1895 that each unskilled woman employed in their Work Rooms was paid "forty cents in groceries or clothing, and . . . given a well-cooked, hot dinner, valued at 10 cents," but, to avoid any "inducements to women to forgo regular work that might elsewhere be offered to them," the Charity Organization Society (COS) made no cash payments.[31]

More generally, by giving public or private assistance in kind rather than money, charity workers were able not only to mark a clear distinction between earned wages and relief benefits, but to shape the material and moral life of the poor more effectively, discriminating between the suitable "necessaries" of life and corrupt goods. Food, clothing, or fuel were distributed directly; or the poor received grocery orders that served as a restricted currency, limiting poor people's purchases to particular goods, sometimes in specified amounts, often obtained only in designated stores. The transaction between grocer and recipient was to be closely watched; the revised 1893 Minnesota statute on poor laws, for instance, required a "fully itemized bill of goods . . . accompanied by an acknowledgement of the same from the person receiving them," before the county treasurer paid the bill.[32] In fact, charity experts were so concerned about this that they created different categories of food orders, under varying degrees of control. In some cases, the list of groceries was determined by the charity organization or public agency, although in other cases the recipient was allowed to pick the goods, alone or in consultation with a visitor.

In-kind or restricted transfers, however, required not only administrative scrutiny but moral guidelines. If it was true that, unlike money, goods could convey a moral message, it was necessary to choose carefully what to give. Consider the dilemma faced by friendly visitors: every handbook warned them severely against providing any sort of material relief, yet gifts to the poor were acceptable, even encouraged as part of the process of moral uplift. But what turned an ordinary material good into a proper gift? The Charity Organization Society of New York was ambivalent, suggesting to its visitors "the gift of such articles as cannot pauperize, but which, on the contrary, tend to elevate and refine the tastes," like a flower or a book. It was sometimes "very puzzling," acknowledged a writer in *The Charities Review*, "to decide just what constitutes material aid—why a cast-off pair of shoes may be reckoned alms and a Thanksgiving turkey not."[33]

The social context of the exchange made the difference because different forms of bestowal signified different social relations between donor and recipient. If goods to the poor were given "as one would give to a friend equally fortunate with oneself," if goods were shaped by the "sentiment" of the giver, then the alm was transformed into a gift. Take, for instance, the Thanksgiving turkey: if the visitor "not only herself carries the dinner . . . but remains to cook the turkey," and better still, stayed for dinner, then surely the gift stood "outside the pale of alms."[34] The alchemy did not work, however, until the visitor knew the family well—and as a friend, not an almoner. "When you know your family and yourself well enough to be sure you are acting wisely," recommended the president of the Associated Charities of Boston in 1880, even money "may be added to your other gifts to your poor friends."[35]

Charity workers, however, insisted on a sharp distinction between gift and relief. For paupers, strictly the "necessaries" of life were acceptable. In Brooklyn in the 1870s, for example, flour, potatoes, or rice were legitimate items for outdoor relief, but not tea or sugar.[36] Indeed, when a study of poor relief commissioned by the town of Hartford, Connecticut, in 1891 discovered that the grocery orders distributed for "provisions for necessary support only" were being sometimes spent in "fancy groceries," "delicacies," and "fooleries," the investigators were outraged. Some of the "absolutely useless" articles purchased were "Java and Mocha mixed" coffee, cakes, "sweet crackers," and "goodies of that sort," some of which not even the committee had heard about before. As further evidence of the corrupt market of relief goods, one grocer reported that some of the poor exchanged "useful" gifts given by "benevolent" friends at Christmas "for all sorts of luxuries."

Even more disturbing, the committee found that some of the orders were being converted into cash, and used as "negotiable paper" for trade or payments of debt. If grocery orders were treated by the poor as ordinary legal tender, the regulation of relief would collapse, as "the proceeds . . . may be converted to any use which selfishness, or luxury, or idleness, or even crime may suggest." Accordingly, the committee's recommendations were to abolish grocery orders and provide the poor directly with no more than ten necessary goods from a central storeroom. Its instructions to the town's selectmen were unequivocal: "Take everything into your own hands, provisioning, clothing, burying. Examine at first; keep examining frequently thereafter." Amos Warner, in his influential study *American Charities*, published a few years later, agreed. Warner preferred relief in "goods purchased by the authorities" to the order system that allowed recipients to choose "absurdly unsuitable" or corrupt goods. In California, he warned, orders were often traded for liquor.[37]

Thus, during most of the nineteenth century, charity organizations and authorities regulated the moral economy of dependents by acting as their collective "shoppers," supplying the poor with goods or restricted currencies, but not with legal tender. Even grocery orders were suspect if they provided access to greater discretionary consumption by the poor. The profound distrust of poor people's financial wisdom blurred distinctions among their monies and led to a second area of economic control. Driven by an unrelenting commitment to transform the moral world of the poor, charity workers felt entitled to control not only relief funds but even the spending of money earned by the poor. By saving their monies, they would be saving their souls.

Charitable workers' second major technique was to *organize savings*.

> Thursday, July 22, 1890. Went to see Mrs. C to-day and let her have two dollars of her money to get another mattress for a bed.
> Saturday, April 2, 1892. I have fifteen families now that I am looking out for and drawing their pay for them and helping them about using it. Three of the men would have lost their jobs if I had not promised to take care of their wages for them, and the rest want me to take care of theirs for them . . . as I can make it go farther than they.[38]

Matter-of-factly, Mary Remington, a leading settlement-house worker at the Welcome Hall Mission in New Haven, Connecticut, recorded her tasks as self-appointed steward for the monies of her impoverished neighbors. In her daily rounds, Remington not only prayed with the poor, taught them house-keeping skills, and organized their clubs, but she also regulated their purse strings. According to her journal, neighborhood women and men, as well as children, handed their pennies over to her for safekeeping, to organize their expenses, pay their bills, and even sometimes to do the marketing.[39]

In the hands of the very poor and "easily dependent," wages, it seemed, were as morally precarious as charitable monies. Surely, they would be spent recklessly or "go for stupidness."[40] Unless of course, charity workers administered the earnings, making sure that they were properly earmarked, destined only for morally safe goods. The Charity Organization Society of New York in 1883 instructed its visitors to "urge the very poorest to lay by something, however little, in the Savings Bank, or for future supplies of fuel, flour . . . if necessary offer to go with them when they make their first payment." Likewise, in his *Handbook of Charity Organization*, Gurteen recommended that in cities without any savings institution for the very poor, the visitor should "make temporary arrangements . . . for the safe keeping and economic disbursement of any moneys that the family under his care may be able to lay by out of their weekly earnings." Even a simple word of advice, added the COS Visitors' handbook, might serve to "keep spare money out of the whiskey-seller's till, and to get it put to better use."[41]

Charity workers did much more than offer counsel. Since even the poor reportedly admitted how "easily the money slips through their fingers," it was expedient to take as much as possible out of their hands and place it into the grip of more trustworthy economic agents, such as charitable collectors "that will go directly into the homes of the poor," or to their neighborhoods, and get their monies "as soon after pay day as is possible." Unlike "friendly visitors" who referred families to relief agencies, collectors came to "take money and not to give it."[42]

After 1880, a number of institutionalized mechanisms were set up, first by charity-organization societies and then adopted by settlement workers, to collect wages from the poor and "launder" them into legitimate monies. The objective, explained Joseph Lee, the noted philanthropist and leader of the urban playgrounds movement, was to "divert the drink, tobacco, and chewing-gum fund to the purchase of the home, of furniture, of tools, of horse and wagon and stock in trade." But saving money from improper uses was not enough; the savings had to be redirected to "proper" expenses: "a cent that is laid aside does not add anything to the income, unless it be saved from an unproductive use in order that it may be well spent."[43]

The first collecting agencies went into the households of the poor with very concrete notions of how to earmark their monies. When, in 1880, the Newport, Rhode Island, Charity Organization Society noticed that some poor families were able to set money aside for the purchase of coal, while others on the same income came to them each winter for relief, the society decided to introduce a proper system of earmarking into the households of the "careless and improvident." Visitors went from house to house weekly, collecting small sums of money destined for specific and worthy purchases, such as the next winter's supply of coal or clothing, or to pay a debt. Within seven years, the Newport Savings Society had collected $10,000.[44]

Fuel funds, flour and shoe clubs, along with other special-purpose savings societies were organized by different charity organizations throughout the country to steer the earnings of "small wage-earners" toward morally safe and socially elevating purchases.[45] In many cases, the organizers did the buying themselves, often securing wholesale prices for club depositors. And collectors found ways to insure that coal pennies were not diverted into unacceptable purchases; before leaving on a summer vacation, one lady, for instance, provided toy banks for all her "savers" that were "to be opened by her on her return."[46]

The system worked well. In 1889, the Charity Organization of New York decided to go further, and organized the Penny Provident Fund, a stamp-savings bank to better safeguard the monies poor families were asking their visitors to keep. Convinced that much poverty was the result of "a waste of small sums in unnecessary expenditures," Penny Provident Fund organizers decided, as one contemporary commentator put it, "that these small sums should be got hold of." Depositors were sold stamps of various colors and denominations that were then pasted on a card. To be sure, since 1816 savings banks had been available for the working class, similarly designed to safeguard their monies away from "saloons, frivolous amusements and useless expenditures."[47] But few savings banks accepted deposits under a dollar. The Charity Organization Society's Penny Provident Fund would save cents.

More than the commodity funds, the Penny Provident Fund intended to turn depositors into true middle-class apprentices; their savings would protect "against the possible loss of work, or against accident or illness." As soon as $10 were put away, the depositor was expected to transfer the money into a regular savings account. To encourage the accumulation of their monies, Penny Provident regulations stipulated that "no sum can be withdrawn less than the amount represented by all the stamps attached."[48]

But with only pennies available, it was improbable that the poor could emulate the long-range savings habits of the middle class. Indeed, the COS observed in 1891 that the fund was "almost entirely used by those who . . . cannot leave the money long on deposit." Instead, after ten dollars or even just one dollar had accumulated, depositors usually withdrew their money for a specific purchase. By 1909, the Annual Report of the Penny Provident recognized that the fund "does not enter into competition with savings banks but seeks to help people of small means who wish to save for a given purpose, such as clothing, coal, vacations, and the necessities of life."[49]

Even if their custody was temporary, Penny Provident

agents felt it was their duty—and their right—to make sure that the money was properly spent. By winning over pennies that had been squirreled away in jugs or stockings or under mattresses, charity organizations gained a significant foothold into the economic choices of the poor. Consider the new rituals confronting depositors when they wanted their money back: they had to give at least one week's notice, and, to read the reports, paying tellers routinely questioned them on how they planned to use their funds. The "bright colored stamp," observed a collector for the Hartley House settlement in New York, "becomes but a fiction for the more effective spending of the family income." Sometimes leaflets were printed with explicit directives: "Save for a vacation, for a new dress, for coal, for a home."[50]

Clearly, all this caution was not to encourage the accumulation of interest, for Penny Provident banks paid none; and its organizers were soon aware that despite their initial expectations, most deposits would not be transferred to interest-paying savings banks. The goal, instead, was the moral safekeeping of poor people's money. More than mere custodians, charity workers became symbolic proprietors of these small deposits, for as soon as the pennies were converted into stamps, a new restricted currency was minted, under the control of the fund's managers.

And Penny Provident Fund regulations made sure that depositors did not treat stamp-pennies as freely as an ordinary cent: stamp cards were not transferable; and no local station, where savings stamps were sold, was allowed to sell detached stamps "lest they should be used for barter."[51] If Penny Provident money, or the money collected by other charitable savings funds, was allowed to become poor people's currency, then the entire effort of redirecting earmarking practices was lost. In a telling anecdote, a woman, as she withdrew her money from a savings fund to buy clothing and coal, "in tears" told the collector, "Oh, ma'am, I feel as if you had made me a present of it."[52]

By 1906, Penny Provident banks had opened 277 stations, and collected over $50,000 in deposits from almost 90,000 depositors. Funds operated in cities throughout the country, from

South Carolina and Virginia to Kentucky, Illinois, Colorado, and
Iowa, and even in Canada. Stamps were sold in numerous locations; in New York, for instance, depositors could purchase savings stamps in savings banks, churches, friendly societies, settlement houses, day nurseries, retail stores, schools, and even in a
home for ex-convicts.[53]

Who were the depositors? Aside from the fact that they
were very poor, there is little other systematic information.
Many of them were children. Poor parents, warned an expert in
savings institutions, "are often incompetent to advise their children as to how to spend their earnings, which are very likely to
be spent to the injury of the children." It became urgent, therefore, for charity organizations to take over the guardianship of
children's monies. Since 1885, school savings banks had
already assumed such a task, preventing "the wasteful expenditure of small sums." In 1894, Penny Provident stations opened
in public schools. The goal was to turn "every class-room in
every school [into] a savings bank" with "every teacher a bank
president, every girl and boy and every mother and father a
depositor with a bank account." The monetary alchemy of the
savings system would work with children, redirecting their
"candy pennies" or cigarette cash into money for books,
clothes, or other useful purposes.[54]

By 1915, Penny Provident banks closed their doors. The
institutional effort to safeguard and earmark poor people's earnings persisted, however. The effort continued in the creation of
special vacation funds for working girls or Christmas Clubs, but,
most prominently, in the opening of postal savings banks in
1911. After decades of strong opposition from commercial banks,
postal savings banks, with the enthusiastic backing of charitable
authorities, were legally authorized in 1910. Their advocates
maintained that postal savings banks would teach the new immigrants rational money management, by drawing money "out of
hoards," or, as the director of the postal savings system described
them, "queer receptacles" such as old tea kettles and stockings,
and into the banks. *Charities and the Commons* told of immi-

grants that "carry greenbacks in their boots and seldom part company with the boot even in the hours of sleep." Others kept their savings in "bedticks, holes in the wall, or down the cellar," and even in "the gob in the mines," while thousands, noted the journal, "trust the store keeper or a private banker with their spare cash." Immigrants confirmed that many of them, wary of banks, "hid their money in their socks and buried it behind the plaster of their walls." It was expected that they would respond more favorably to postal savings, a popular institution in European countries.[55]

The banks would not only safeguard foreigners' monies but redirect their uses by keeping in the United States "money that would otherwise be sent abroad." Indeed, according to one estimate, in 1907 alone about $140 million of "immigrant money" had been transferred to other countries. Postal savings currencies—postal savings-stamp cards and non-negotiable certificates—would also put out of circulation a peculiar immigrant currency; every year foreigners bought millions of dollars in money orders payable to themselves simply for savings purposes, without receiving any interest. And, echoing the nineteenth-century rhetoric, postal savings banks were expected to become an influential "enemy of dissipating and destructive spending."[56] True, the banks, as one charity worker put it, would lack the persuasive personal influence of "friendly visitors," but still they were welcome allies in the construction of "the strong type of citizen" with "resisting power against the petty immediate wants."[57] By 1916, postal savings banks had indeed become an "immigrant's bank"; 60 percent of the total number of depositors were foreign-born and they owned three quarters of all the deposits.[58]

We have seen, then, that for nineteenth-century charity workers, cash became a volatile form of relief. The morally incompetent poor, as they viewed them, would inevitably appropriate unearned charitable monies as their own rightful income and squander the funds for immoral or, at best, improvident purchases.

Accordingly, it was wiser to keep legal tender out of poor people's hands. To those who ran out of money, relief agencies gave food, fuel, clothing, or grocery orders, but as little cash as possible. And for those who subsisted on their own meager wages, charity workers made every effort to monitor how the monies were spent. Yet, by the start of the twentieth century there occurred a paradoxical turnabout: charity organizers began talking about the need to bring money *into* poor people's purses rather than keep them cashless. The next chapter will explain why.

5

With Strings Attached: The Earmarking of Charitable Cash

IN THE NEW TALES told by social workers during the early twentieth century, money was recast as the modern "white hat" of the charity saga. Consider the life story of Mrs. Czech, featured as the rhetorical centerpiece of an influential article published in *The Survey* in 1916 by Emma Winslow, home economist at the New York Charity Organization Society. Mrs. Czech was a widow who, for three years after her husband died, "was not obliged to use money in any way." A charitable society provided her and her six children with food and clothing and paid their rent and insurance. And yet, despite such "theoretically . . . perfect care," the Czechs floundered. The mother "apparently . . . had no interest in the appearance of her home or of her children." Nor did she care about their food. Soon, the children's health deteriorated, their faces becoming "sallow and pasty." At this point, the charity society decided to shift the method of relief into a weekly cash allowance, instructing Mrs. Czech "to do her own buying." Soon housekeeping "became a delight," the children's health flourished, and the formerly indolent widow turned into a "remarkable . . . domestic economist." And all because she now had the cash "to buy what she wanted when she wanted it."[1]

THE CASE FOR CASH

To Emma Winslow, the lesson was clear: the most therapeutic form of relief was to give the family a regular allowance and "permit it to do its own buying." In the revised script for charity work, in-kind relief, not money, was "unwise," destroying the "self-reliance and independence" of poor families. Many of her colleagues concurred. The "economic unity" of the home, declared the secretary of the Organized Charities Association of New Haven at the 1922 National Conference of Social Work, was possible only "when the family has been intrusted with [a rea-sonable income] and made responsible for its administration."[2]

The case for cash was not just rhetorical; between 1900 and 1920, private charities became increasingly likely to dispense money relief to the poor. Take, for instance, the United Hebrew Charities of New York (UHC); in 1895 it gave some $56,000 in "regular monthly stipends" and "occasional relief in money," and spent about $36,000 for transportation, clothing, shoes, fuel, buri-als, and other relief items. By 1909, the "cash relief" category climbed to over $277,000, while supplies and transportation fell to about $22,000. That year, the annual report noted the increas-ing frequency of assistance in cash; 55 percent of their applicants now received money grants, a quick jump from 46 percent only two years earlier. By 1922, the UHC spent almost $450,000 in cash relief, and only $52,000 on wearing apparel, furniture, material, and coal.[3]

Or consider the shifting policy of the New York Association for Improving the Condition of the Poor (AICP), that longstanding foe of cash relief. By 1896, administrators were allowed at their discretion to give cash assistance of up to $20 per family. And in 1913 the AICP started awarding monetary pensions to selected widows. The association's 1914 annual report announced that every effort would be made "to develop in the families the ability to make . . . purchases for themselves." Likewise, according to its secretary Frederic Almy, by 1917 the Buffalo Charity Organization Society had made it "almost our general rule" to give cash rather than grocery orders. And the Newark Bureau of Associated Charities reported that they were turning to cash relief after realizing that "it is better . . . for helping the housewife to retain her self-respect, that she handle her own money." By the 1920s, the New York AICP as well as the New York Charity Organization Society (NYCOS) along with, among others, the Associated Charities of Minneapolis and the Associated Charities of Cleveland, were using monetary allowances "in all cases possible."[4]

After 1911, the highly successful mothers' pension program put cash relief on the public agenda. Created to keep dependent children at home with their widowed mothers, the pensions were designed to substitute sporadic cash "doles" or inadequate in-kind relief with a regular cash income. The 1914 Report of the New York State Commission on Relief for Widowed Mothers, for instance, unequivocally declared monetary assistance as "essential," blaming the "old method" of orders for groceries or gifts of goods as "undemocratic and harmful to the character of the recipient." Money relief, on the other hand, served to rehabilitate the family by granting the mother "the responsibility of expending the income as well as the independence that comes from handling money."[5]

What had happened to that volatile nineteenth-century dollar? What accounts for the remarkable turnabout in both the statements and policies of charity-organization societies as well as in attitudes toward public relief for widows? More specifically, how were "the evils of monetary relief" transformed into modern virtues? To be sure, new twentieth-century social definitions of the causes of poverty made relief more legitimate; if the poor were not entirely to blame for their distress, society had a duty to assist them. The gradual normalization of unemployment, for instance, especially after the severe depression of the 1890s, significantly increased public responsibility for the jobless. Indeed, by 1904, about half of the charity-organization societies in the country had reversed their earlier policies and were now dispensing relief from their own funds. Material relief, explained an historian of the charity movement, had acquired "a new dignity."[6] And when it came to mothers' pensions, public subsidies were further sanctioned by the growing concern with preserving the home life of the poor. But even granting the new legitimacy of poor relief, why not continue the safer in-kind methods of dispensing assistance?

Indeed, even organizations that were moving toward cash payments moved irregularly and with many hesitations. Take, for instance, the New York Charity Organization Society's Thanksgiving policy. In November 1910 one of their donors proposed replacing the distribution of Thanksgiving dinner baskets with an alternative system that would "give the people an opportunity to purchase whatever they need most." One-dollar coupon books were to be issued to each family to be spent in designated stores that would accept the coupons "the same as cash in payment for merchandise," but valid only on Thanksgiving day, or the previous one. The NYCOS gracefully acknowledged the gift, but rejected the donor's coupon plan, explaining their concern "that the money might be used for purposes which we might not approve."[7]

The 1922 survey of private charities' methods for dispensing relief showed that while money allowances were becoming increasingly frequent, most organizations used cash in combination with grocery orders or in-kind relief. And until the 1930s, public assistance, with the exception of mothers' pensions and occasional small grants of cash, stuck firmly with in-kind methods. A 1925 report on poor relief in Pennsylvania explained the resistance to cash as a matter of tradition and "the fear that if cash is given it may be spent unwisely or . . . squandered." In Colorado, even mothers' pension legislation restricted its cash policy by adding a provision that, if necessary, the court could substitute monetary payments for "its equivalent in supplies and assistance."[8]

Yet, for leading social workers the "line of progress," as Emma Winslow put it in 1917, pointed unequivocally toward cash relief. At stake was a fundamental new challenge for poverty experts: making the poor competent participants in the twentieth-century consumer society. Recall that in the first two decades of the century the scope of rationalized consumption and its ideology expanded with dramatic rapidity. Consumerism also had a strong impact on charitable practices. Poor families, too, needed to learn how to make wise choices and "use [their] income to the best possible advantage." The social worker's task of adjusting the modern dependent family "to its economic environment," claimed one expert, now involved greater emphasis on "scientific training" in the "art of spending" than in the techniques for earning, which "today . . . does not necessarily require a great amount of skill or intelligence." "Modern methods of production," explained the expert, "have placed on the market such a wide variety of articles" that "those who spend are in constant need of exercising the most careful judgement."[9]

But without money, the task of educating consumers was impossible. "If the family is not taught how to administer its finances by experience," asked Winslow, "how else is it going to learn?"[10] The strategy of keeping money away from the poor or spending it for them became an anachronism in a society that advocated the democratic principle of free consumer choice. Professional social workers thus set out to convert dangerous cash into a modern therapeutic currency.

LIBERATING CASH

Making proper consumer choices involved more than an economic challenge. As James H. Hamilton, professor of Sociology at Syracuse University, tellingly explained in the *Quarterly Journal of Economics* in 1899, "In this day the individual discovers himself and realizes himself in the lines of expenditure." Since productive processes had become "deindividualizing," the contemporary artisan, Hamilton argued, "must unfold his character in the way in which he spends his money." That was why, theorists insisted in the 1920s, the consumer should have "the power of choice." Indeed, freedom of consumption was declared by the noted consumer-economist Hazel Kyrk to be "as well-established a principle as freedom of conscience." Even when it improved the quality of consumption, any sort of authoritative regulation, therefore, violated the basic right of "choosing the instruments of material life." Regulated consumption, Kyrk explained, degraded individualized choice into a method "analogous to the feeding, clothing, and amusing of the children of a household, of the soldiers of an army, or the inmates of a reformatory."[11]

This kind of consumerist ideology seeped into the rhetoric of charity workers. The poor, too, were entitled to become "choosers" of goods, not just passive users. Philanthropic institutions, proposed Joseph Lee as early as 1902, should "encourage people to make their expenditure an expression . . . of true personality," not the "mere unorganized dribbling away of money." More and more, the new vocabulary of social work stressed the importance of "wise choices"; the terms "extravagance" and "improvidence," or even the corrupt drinking "spree," began to sound like dusty nineteenth-century anachronisms. Avoiding sinful expenses was no longer enough; in the new consumerist terminology, the poor had to learn "the business of buying wisely."[12]

In-kind relief aborted consumer choice. To its critics, "the old-fashioned . . . bundle of half-worn clothing" necessarily stifled any independence or initiative on the part of its recipients. And while more liberal grocery orders allowed the poor some measure of discretionary buying, orders still restricted choice. The food order, Winslow claimed, was at best a "makeshift," acceptable only for emergency situations. As long as, in any way, social workers served as surrogate shoppers, the poor would remain marginalized consumers, clothed and fed with relief commodities but without access to true consumer goods. Still worse, by buying only in designated stores, they became trained in incompetent shopping, unconcerned with price, and incapable of planning their own necessities. Even thrift systems were judged by the new consumerist standards. As early as 1899, fuel or shoe clubs that purchased commodities for the poor at a discount were declared to be an inferior form of savings, encouraging depositors "not to spend [money] themselves but to have it spent for them."[13]

Only money could liberate the "charity customer" by turning her or him into an ordinary consumer. A dollar, after all, carried no visible stigma of difference nor apparent market constraints. A cash allowance made it possible for a family "to handle money, to learn its value and its buying power." "Let the family buy," Emma Winslow asserted; "the dealing with different people, the visiting of different stores, the search for the bargain, and the administering of a two-dollar-a-day income develop shrewdness, judgement and taste."[14]

Above all, money granted the power of choice, transforming the purchase of the most ordinary commodities into self-enhancing exchanges. Take clothing, for instance. If selected by the poor, clothing became a "vehicle for self-expression." Paying the rent served as an exercise in foresight; indeed, for Winslow, it was a "privilege" to be able to pay the landlord. So, too, unlike gifts of food or clothing, Christmas gifts of cash to the poor switched "the chance at self-expression" from the donor to the recipient. After all, as advocates of cash gifts explained, the "climax" of Christmas "came not with the eating of the dinner but with the buying."[15]

Money would also teach the children of the poor how to buy. Indeed, as part of their critique against institutionalizing dependent children, turn-of-the-century reformers blamed institutions for manufacturing handicapped consumers; the "institutional child," contended Edward T. Devine, the prominent social worker and general secretary of the New York Charity Organization Society, never learned the value of money "because purchases are made by steward or superintendent."[16] Only the home could train children properly. Charity experts recommended that allowances for dependent families include a few cents a week for the child's own spending money.[17]

INCOMPETENT SPENDERS

The democratic rhetoric of consumerism camouflaged a seriously limiting assumption. As much as charity experts hailed family independence and cheered freedom of choice, they still presumed the poor to be incompetent consumers, unable to make the right choices. Many of their troubles came not from the lack of money, Edward T. Devine believed, but from the "foolish use of income."[18]

What did these early-twentieth-century social workers mean by the "careless" choices of the poor? As the moral classification of poverty wavered, the financial incompetence of the poor was increasingly attributed to their technical ineptness rather than moral turpitude; the poor simply did not know how to spend, what or when to buy, where to shop, or even how or when to pay. Thus Amos Warner's early diagnosis that the poor were incapable "to judge wisely in the ordinary business affairs of life." It was less a matter of "extravagance," Warner observed, than of "pure blundering."[19]

The poor, social workers complained, were incapable even of choosing their own food properly. Listen to Mr. Frank Tucker of New York telling his colleagues at the 1901 National Conference of Charities and Correction that although he agreed with "giving material relief in the shape of money and permitting the families to expend it," his own experience with needy families suggested that the poor lacked "the faculty of saving or buying." When, for example, his agency's superintendent of relief had tried to shift from a restricted system of food orders–where the visitors specified the kind of food and the quantity required for each family—to a more discretionary arrangement whereby the families themselves selected their purchases, the families chose luxuries (tea, coffee, sugar, butter) over necessities. Confronted with such "ignorance," the agency reverted to restricted food orders. Some twenty years later, the concern with technical incompetence persisted. Consider for instance the discussion of "unwise expenditures" in John Lewis Gillin's textbook on poverty and dependency. To Gillin, a professor of Sociology at the University of Wisconsin and a former social worker, poverty was a likely result of not knowing "how to buy wisely . . . how much should be spent approximately on rent, food, clothing, amusements, etc."[20]

Such wariness with the consumer skills of the poor complicated the agenda of both public and private cash relief. Even the $23 or so monthly provided by a widow's pension, warned Carl Christian Carstens, a noted social worker and critic of the pension plan, brought "temptations . . . to spend the money recklessly or foolishly." After all, as a speaker at the 1911 National Conference on Charities and Correction put it, if the poor were incapable "to make a dollar do its full measure of work," how could they handle relief dollars? And with their domestic finances often regulated by old-time and sometimes foreign "traditions and superstitions," what would stop cash recipients from re-creating primitive, ineffective, or alien systems of earmarking monies?[21]

Much of the concern focused on poor women, especially immigrant women. If, as we observed in the use of the domestic dollar, women were appointed guardians of consumer money, they required appropriate spending skills. As the "director of consumption," the wife became responsible for making correct "market choices," experts explained, carefully diverting consumption away "from unwholesome lines." But whereas middle- and upper-class women were bred in "good living," or else could learn by reading books or attending classes, household-management experts worried that the "unwise and seldom well trained" poor homemaker, who was also a likely recipient of cash relief, had no access to information.[22]

For Florence Nesbitt, a leading social worker involved with the mothers' pension department of the Chicago Juvenile Court, Mrs. Zarmonski's experience offered a case in point. Instead of buying food, clothing, or better shelter for herself and her three children, she had spent the first month's income from her mothers' pension on white shoes, stockings, and dresses for the children. The second month, Mrs. Zarmonski purchased "an expensive bright colored rug for the sitting room." Was it any wonder that she made such poor choices, asked Nesbitt, considering there was "nothing in her experience or training to enable her to make intelligent judgements"? Clearly, an expert in charity work concluded, "there is a pressing and very definite need for some trained person to supervise the spending of money by these families."[23]

Social workers were ready to step in. Indeed, the managerial incompetence of the poor provided a perfect loophole to justify the active intervention of social workers in the domestic economy of their clients. For despite new environmental theories of poverty, it was still simpler to redo private economies than tamper with the public market. Teaching domestic finances also bolstered social workers' fledgling claims to professional status by contributing to their search for specialized casework skills. A "prudent worker," asserted a speaker at the 1911 National Conference of Charities and Correction, would show the poor how to "make a dollar do that which formerly required one and a half or two dollars to accomplish." Still more important than stretching the dollar, Devine suggested, expert advice would reshape consumption patterns, "substituting . . . a good use of income for carelessness, shiftlessness and ignorance." Even Emma Winslow, still insisting that the family "have the fun of buying," suggested that "a kind of editorial judgement" of their purchases "can be made of great assistance in adding to a family's knowledge of domestic economy."[24]

During the first few decades of the twentieth century, social workers offered much more than editorial comments as they teamed up with home economists to closely chart the monetary life of their clients. At first, charity-organization societies had relied on visiting housekeepers to assist the poor with their purchases. But, after 1910, a number of societies, for instance, NYCOS or the Cleveland Associated Charities, established separate home-economics departments, thereby formally integrating consumerist expertise into social-work practice.

Informed by standard-of-living investigations, home economists brought to scientific casework budgetary data and home-efficiency techniques designed to rehabilitate dependent families. Of course, authorities interested in the standard of living had been collecting systematic information on working-class household budgets since the last quarter of the nineteenth century. The goal of their investigations was to document, inform, and perhaps generally influence patterns of consumption, whereas home economists helped to organize direct intervention in the lives of the subjects who were studied. Statistical budget data were translated into a very concrete therapeutic program, as home economists assisted caseworkers in reshaping domestic economies, showing dependent families "how to buy as to get the most for the money, what part of the money should be spent for food, how much for clothes, how much for rent, how much for recreation and how much for savings."[25]

At first, social workers publicly and bitterly denounced mothers' pensions as an illegitimate and dangerous intrusion of the public sector into the professional domain of private relief, but by the 1920s they had been co-opted by a system that needed their casework expertise to regulate the use of public monies by mothers and their dependent children.[26] Following the 1920s, psychiatric social workers were trained to deal not only with problems of technical competence but also with the more subjective, psychological incompetence of the poor.

Incompetence, however, could not be properly treated with a fully convertible, freely circulating currency. Against the argument that "it would be better simply to turn over a weekly allowance to the family and let it assume all responsibility for spending it wisely," social workers responded that only careful casework could turn allowance dollars into "constructive" monies.[27] The challenge for modern social workers was, therefore, to craft the "right" kind of therapeutic money for their clients.

It was not an easy task. As long as they gave assistance in kind, charity workers served as surrogate "directors" of consumption for dependent families. But, now, what sort of currency could take over the critical task of transforming incompetent consumers into safe spenders?

DEFINING CHARITABLE CASH

In the new view of professional social workers, the nineteenth-century "dole" and "alm" had to be eliminated; randomly offered, such sentimental monies carried no moral markers, no lessons in spending. Nor could charitable cash be passed off as a wage, to be used without restrictions. Treating relief as ordinarily earned income would, in effect, mean recognizing the recipient's competence in spending. Edward T. Devine searched for a proper distinction; relief, he argued, was not intended as "a substitute for wages," but as "income necessary for the supply of the necessities . . . when such income cannot be earned."[28]

For Jane Addams, the influential founder of Hull House in Chicago, such cautious boundary drawing was unnecessary; the right kind of charitable money was coined simply by making "the medium of giving friendly enough." Speaking at the 1897

National Conference of Charities and Correction, Addams—with a settlement worker's typically more confident view of the poor—assured charity organizers that money, after all, was "not so different from the rest of life." As long as the donor's feeling was genuine, friendliness and kindliness would "transfigure and transform" money into as safe a donation as a pair of shoes or some soup.[29]

But traditional charity organizers were less sanguine; to them a suitable currency for the poor could be fashioned not out of sentiment, but from hard work. If relief was given "without plan or purpose," warned Mary Richmond, a leading social-work expert, "it will injure the worthiest recipient." And when Frederic Almy in 1911 suggested that monetary relief could be made as "spiritual" as "good advice," he meant "relief plus a plan." To Almy, the new cash pensions were effective only as part of a rational, educational program. Each relief dollar, agreed Devine, "should be constructive."[30]

Leaders of the mothers' pension movement were equally committed to forging a new kind of progressive currency for widows and their dependent children. Against social workers' accusations that "whatever they are called, money payments to mothers from public funds are relief-public charity," supporters countered that public pensions were much more than a new label for the old-fashioned dole. The difference, stated the report of the New York State Commission on Relief for Widowed Mothers in 1914, lay in their "new standard of constructive rehabilitation" designed to improve the home and to protect the child.[31]

Mothers' pensions were classified as a new category of honorable maternal income, much like "the payment made by the state or nation to soldiers, sailors or others who have rendered public service." Certainly, at a time when child labor was increasingly regarded as exploitative, a pension for the mother was a superior form of money than her child's wage. It was even an improvement over the privately issued "school scholarships" designed to encourage children's school attendance by replacing their income with a weekly payment to their families. But making the amount of the scholarship equivalent to a child's fore-gone income tainted the money by still defining it as the child's, not the parents', earnings.[32]

Advocates of mothers' pensions insisted that public agencies were better qualified than private charity to devise a proper income for the poor. Although in the past the state "could not even undertake the management of mints without debasing the coinage," argued William Hard, a former settlement worker who championed the cause of mothers' pensions from his column in the popular magazine, *The Delineator*, few people would still support private mints.[33] So, too, with the private production of charitable currency. Yet, ironically, despite their seemingly irreconcilable competition, public funds and private cash relief converged ultimately on a similar category of money, different from the unsystematic nineteenth-century dole, and, despite the frequent analogy between mothers' pensions and a payment for services, clearly distinct from a wage. Nor were pensions fashioned after social insurance payments; despite moving closer toward an entitlement, they remained a much more restricted currency. In fact, while recognizing the general potential of a social insurance program, Hard condemned the concept of insurance payment for its lack of proper supervision, allowing the widow to "spend her insurance stipends as she pleases."[34] Pensions—which consisted of long-term weekly or monthly regular payments of small, specified, budgeted grants of money—unlike a dole, a wage, or social insurance, were obtained only after painstaking investigation, were subject to thorough supervision, and were easily revocable if the recipient failed to meet expected standards of proper behavior.

What sort of money, then, was this new charitable cash? Rejecting the model of dole, wage, or insurance, pensions appropriated instead the forms of the middle-class domestic economy; or, more precisely, they replicated women's housekeeping currencies. Considering that most recipients of public pensions and a large number of those receiving or at least managing private cash allowances were women, charitable cash was easily transformed into a special category of domestic currency, a sort of collective pin money. Notice the vocabulary: the term "allowance" comfortably echoed the familiar income of middle-class wives. Pensions, of course, had been legitimized as a dignified payment by the enormously successful federal program of Civil War payments for veteran soldiers. But there was also a long tradition of pensions as a substitute income for husbandless women. And it was middle-class women who, for the most part, ran this feminized currency exchange; not only did women's organizations become the strongest supporters of mothers' pensions but mostly female social workers supervised both public and private forms of cash relief.[35]

This domestic model of charitable currency provided a powerful entry into the economy of poor households. Borrowing techniques developed by home efficiency experts, the cornerstone of which was the household budget, social workers turned cash relief into an elaborate apparatus for reforming earmarking systems of the poor. Paradoxically, by giving cash, social agencies gained a more thorough, profound, and long-lasting access to the spending choices of the poor.

Let us consider precisely how social workers used charitable cash to regulate the earmarking of poor people's money. There were two fundamental techniques: first, the restriction of recipients, thus making sure that cash relief circulated only among carefully selected individuals or families; and, second, systematic oversight of the uses of cash relief, both by educating the poor on the proper allocation of monies and by closely monitoring how their money was spent.

THE CASHWORTHY

The challenge of aiding victims of emergencies raised the question of whom to trust with cash. Just after the disastrous Chicago fire of 1871, the Chicago Relief and Aid Society, in an unusually explicit policy statement, explained why it was substituting its policy of relief in kind for cash. "The mass of worthy, honest, and economical poor," their Annual Report explained in 1873, "should not be treated as thieves and paupers."[36] Thirty years later, after the devastating Johnstown flood of 1899, a statewide Flood Relief Commission proposed a long-term plan to assist survivors with provisions of clothing and food but no money; but local community leaders strongly objected, forcing the commission to reconsider its policy and distribute instead half a million dollars in cash, with no strings attached. According to Edward T. Devine's account, the Johnstown representatives recognized the "absurdity of applying to skilled mechanics and prosperous tradespeople conclusions based upon experiences with applicants for ordinary relief." The Johnstown elders were convinced that their impoverished neighbors were fully competent to spend cash relief properly.

What made it safer to offer money to the suddenly destitute than to the ordinary poor? It was a matter of character, Devine explained; industrious and thrifty emergency victims could be trusted to use their money competently, without "any pauperizing or demoralizing influence."[37] Their misfortune was temporary and certainly involuntary. Some experts disagreed, insisting that even in the case of emergency victims, relief "should never be in money, but always in its equivalent"; but Devine maintained that the decision should depend on "the character of the proposed beneficiaries."[38] The key was not to confuse the cashworthy with the corrupt or undeserving poor.

A similar criterion of sufficient moral competency justified, during the nineteenth century, giving occasional private or even public cash pensions to other categories of worthy recipients—most notably, Civil War veterans, but also selected widows, elderly women, the ill, the blind, and, during periods of Depression, a few unemployed men. In all these cases, donors were prepared to assume that, as integrated members of the community, recipients generally possessed moral competence for proper spending. The same was true of the American Red Cross's cash-relief policy for enlisted men's families during the First World War. In cases of need, its Home Service Division provided cash grants for emergencies or regular allowances to the relatives of soldiers, sailors, and men in other branches of service. The Red Cross Manual of Home Service explained that, except for occasional untrustworthy recipients who should be assisted with food and clothing, cash was a "safe form of help" for enlisted men's families. "When a family has always paid its bills," according to the Home Service Manual, "it should not be exposed to the humiliation of having to present relief orders to local tradesmen." Most important, these families had a "moral claim" to support, having "spared their breadwinners and protectors to the service of our country."[39]

But as the consumerist definition of relief took over in the early twentieth century, cashworthiness became not just a matter of moral fiber but of practical competence. Without consumer skills, not even the morally righteous could know how to handle cash properly. Moreover, unlike moral character, consumer competence could be built *with* money; indeed, the new therapeutic conception of material assistance implied that, if properly dispensed, cash rehabilitated the poor. Spending money, one expert asserted, could aid in developing "thrift, foresight, and initiative."[40]

Even so, cash was not allowed to circulate freely. The New York Charity Organization Society, for example, selected an "allowance family" only after careful screening, and, especially in the case of immigrant families, only if "the family standards are sufficiently high, or can be sufficiently raised . . . so that the money will really be expended for the purposes designed."[41] A key criterion for identifying trainable recipients was the mother's spending skills. The United Charities of Chicago, for instance, gave cash only when a woman "is wise in her expenditures or can be trained into discretion." If, on the other hand, the mother was "of such low mentality" that she could not be "trained to buy," experts recommended relief in kind.[42]

Mothers' pensions were equally selective. While it is true,

as historians have shown, that public pensions significantly improved the welfare of many mothers, the program still carefully discriminated between the cashworthy and untrustworthy widow. Most recipients were indeed widows rather than deserted, divorced, or single mothers, and most were white; two states restricted benefits to American citizens.[43] And, as with private relief, mothers had to prove an "entry-level" spending ability in order to become eligible for a cash pension. A major study of mothers' pension administration in Illinois explained that the program admitted only those women "who can be trusted to make reasonably wise expenditures." One way to test the cashworthiness of widows was to require those who had received insurance benefits to account for their expenditure. The Illinois report conceded that "it is not easy for any one who has spent money foolishly to tell about it," and, indeed, many women complained that such accounting was "a needless prying into their private affairs"; yet, the investigating committee required the information to "form a judgement concerning [a woman's] ability to spend money wisely."[44]

The new cashworthy poor were thus selected partly on the basis of sufficient consumer "disposition"; cash relief would then serve to transform them into fully competent spenders. If carefully regulated, the pension was expected to make a widow as competent as the Johnstown flood survivor. Not that moral character became suddenly irrelevant; in fact to become eligible for a widow's pension a mother had to be "a proper person, physically, mentally and morally fit to bring up her children."[45] Competence in spending was thus still tinged with moral concerns; buying skillfully also meant choosing morally correct goods. It was true, reported a New York AICP study in 1914 of their pension program, that a mother's "ability to spend . . . wisely" depended greatly on having the necessary information: "love without knowledge . . . feeds children on buns, pickles and coffee." But knowledge without moral competence could not guarantee safe spending; some mothers, the report suggested, "might be tempted to cut down the amount allowed for food for the sake of spending more on dress or amusements." In the case of the public mothers' pensions, investigators checked if applicants spent money to buy "intoxicating liquors" or tobacco. If a mother failed to maintain proper household standards, the pension could be withdrawn.[46]

Turning cash into an effective tool for consumer training, however, required time. Reversing the long-standing preference for making cash relief temporary and therefore less likely to encourage dependence, experts now explicitly recommended monetary aid for cases that "will require long time assistance." With consistent guidance, cash therapy would create an independent, skillful consumer. In an ironic twist, the less instructional food order was now demoted to an "emergency measure."[47]

Time alone, however, could not correct what caseworkers called "defects in expenditure." Recipients needed personalized, sustained, and pervasive instruction to become consumer competent. Only the "carefully supervised cash allowance," maintained Colcord, offered adequate training in "household management and individual budget planning."[48] How, then, did social workers use cash relief to shape the earmarking of poor people's monies?

TEACHING HOW TO SPEND

In 1916, the New York Charity Organization Society launched a novel "educational campaign" to teach poor families how to use their monies properly. A special household account book prepared by the Committee on Budgets of the American Home Economics Association was distributed by the agency to each family receiving a regular allowance. By keeping a detailed weekly inventory of the different household expenses, the housewife would discover "just how much money she is paying for each item in her budget" and learn, with the help of a social worker, how to improve her spending habits.[49]

If cash relief was going to turn ignorant spenders into competent consumers, charitable monies had to be steered toward proper middle-class consumer choices. Poor families, stated a 1913 report on widows' pensions, "need not only money, but also advice as to how to spend the money." Social workers recognized the task was difficult: "expenditure habits" were well entrenched, and money, after all, was more fungible and, therefore, less subject to control than food or clothing. Yet experts soon understood that charitable cash, if properly supervised, presented a serendipitous "educational opportunity" to replace "careless" choice with "real values."[50]

The household budget became the pivot of the consumer rehabilitation program. To Emma Winslow, home economist at the New York Charity Organization Society and a forceful advocate of the new accounting system, the budget worked as an "active dynamic force in improving expenditures," not only by revealing defects in spending but "pointing the way toward remedial effort." Budget planning, maintained Winslow, was indispensable "for any educational work which involves readjustment in expenditure habits."[51] Accordingly, social caseworkers, advised by home economists, set up an elaborate monetary accounting system modeled after middle-class domestic efficiency techniques. As part of the budget plan, families receiving cash relief were required to keep detailed records of their daily or weekly expenses. Social workers then used the information to prepare a workable long-term budget that would guide the family's purchases while also providing a "peg upon which to hang further instruction."[52] Decisions had to be made concerning what items to include in the budget, how much money to apportion to different needs, and, sometimes, even how to determine the proper timing for the various purchases.

True, nineteenth-century "friendly visitors" as well as Penny Provident collectors had also often advised the poor on money management. But starting around 1910, the social workers' budget method formalized and bureaucratized personal counseling into printed documents that registered in greater detail than ever before the monetary life of the poor. Whether in a simple piece of paper or in a printed account form, usually reported in English but occasionally in the family's native language, mostly jotted down by the mother but sometimes by her husband or her child, recipients of cash relief were expected to account for every dollar, from the money spent to buy food to the postage for sending a letter abroad. By providing their visitors with "a definite idea of the way in which the money grants are being expended," a New York AICP report explained in 1914, household budgets made it possible to "constantly . . . suggest to the families ways of improvement in buying."[53]

As private agencies shifted from in-kind to cash relief, they became more likely to adopt the budget system. So were the administrators of mothers' pensions who relied on budget estimates and accounts to shape an adequate relief policy. In Cook County, Illinois, for example, the juvenile court judge formally instructed new recipients to "keep full and accurate accounts" of their expenditures. Such bookkeeping, explained the official form handed to the mother, was not merely to account for the money spent but to direct the recipient toward "the most intelligent use of the funds." In Allegheny County, Pennsylvania, all mothers were required to keep "itemized monthly household-expense accounts either on loose slips of paper or on blanks provided by the State office."[54] Here, too, as in other jurisdictions, it was expected that the records would serve to improve the women's domestic and consumer skills.

But was the enthusiasm for budgets justified only by their educational potential? Experts in domestic economics were certainly convinced that for all social classes, "normal" family life depended on "sound household economics." And budgets provided the fail-safe key to rational domestic management. "Any attempt to teach women how to spend to the best advantage," concluded a survey of methods used for supervising the spending of cash relief, "involves the use of a budget." Yet, when it came to budgeting cash relief, the accounting of expenses did more than teach the poor how to spend money; the budget verified whether recipients of relief were in fact earmarking the money for officially approved expenses. "The requirement that the family make accounting . . . of a given week's or month's allowance," noted one prominent supporter of cash relief, "can usually be relied upon to prevent any attempt to bank or save money given for quite other purposes." What better way was there than the account, as Florence Nesbitt pointed out, to obtain "uncolored facts" about "what has been secured" by the money?[55]

Administrators of mothers' pensions were equally concerned with assuring that a widow's public money allowance "may serve the purpose to which it is appropriated." Despite advocates' claims that unlike private charities, public pensions would concentrate on instruction, not supervision, most jurisdictions regularly sent investigators to check up on the mothers. True, in some localities, families were visited only a few times a year; but in many cases there were monthly or even weekly visits. Supervising officers in Cook County, Illinois, for instance, visited pensioned families about once a month, checking that the "best possible use be made of the pension income."[56] And although mothers were reassured that the account "was not a form of espionage," the supervision of their monies was far-reaching, sometimes extending even to unbudgeted gifts of Christmas money.

The matter of holiday cash for the poor, in fact, created a parallel yet distinct set of problems from the gifting of money in households or in business. As the old-fashioned charitable dole—much like the housewife's dole—was replaced by a rationalized currency more akin to an entitlement than a voluntary bestowal, the place of monetary gifts was questionable. Social workers certainly recognized the significance of holiday gift-giving for the poor, not only by marking their Christmas offerings apart from ordinary relief but going as far as occasionally providing mothers with their own cash to buy their children gifts. And donors tried hard to personalize their Christmas gifts to the poor, shopping for a particular family, choosing a desirable item, delivering the gift in person, or sending a personalized gift certificate. Some agencies even arranged Christmas parties to distribute gifts of cash or objects to poor families, hoping that the families "looked upon this entertainment [as] given by friends to friends, and the gifts they received were never considered as charity, but as Christmas gifts in the best sense of the word."[57]

But personalization did not quite work in relationships that were so obviously unequal and ultimately impersonal. In some cases, gifts delivered to a poor family's home deeply embarrassed the recipients by publicly disclosing their need. As social agencies recognized the failure of personalizing gifts to the poor, they tried to make the transfer increasingly anonymous, for instance, by refusing—despite a great deal of resistance—to release names of recipients, and also by encouraging gifts of money rather than the more restricted in-kind gifts of food or clothing.[58]

But just as the Christmas bonus or the tip never did qualify as an intimate personal gift, charitable Christmas money was still earmarked as a special currency, never fully a free gift. However, while the bonus or the tip moved closer to a payment, Christmas money for the poor remained an unequal bestowal. Notice what happened to the Berks County, Pennsylvania, mothers who were allowed by a mothers' pension agency to become their children's Santa Claus. Each mother received $10 to spend "as she saw fit"; yet after the holidays they dutifully reported how the money was spent. When another private agency decided to give each of the children a dollar to buy a present for his or her mother, a visitor accompanied them to make the purchase. The assistant general secretary of the Minneapolis Welfare Association, which encouraged holiday gifts of cash to the poor, explained how "care was exercised" that the money "should be used for very special things." For example, a sixteen-year-old messenger boy, the only support of his invalid and widowed mother, needed a watch; his mother was given the money to repair a "fine watch" that had belonged to the boy's father.[59] Thus, the approach of charity officials to gift money remained ambivalent, balancing the preferred intimacy, equality, and spontaneity of personal gifts against the inequality, surveillance, and control of administered budgets.

By itemizing expenses in extraordinary detail, household budgets allowed private charities as well as public pension supervisors to step into the domestic economy of poor families more deeply than the charity worker who distributed in-kind relief or grocery orders. Indeed, experts insisted on the importance of multiplying budget headings "to give necessary detail concerning the amount and nature of the various expenditures."[60] A typical budget sheet used by the New York Charity Organization Society, for example, included columns for rent, fuel, clothing, and food, and also for household supplies, lunch money, carfare, insurance, and recreation. Still more inclusive, the monthly household account form often used for mothers' pensions required information about such items as sewing supplies, shoe mending, toilet articles, or gifts received. There was even a "good times" entry, where mothers were urged to report money spent for "pleasure and fun."[61]

Consider also the sort of investigatory data required to prepare a "constructive" budget. It was critical, urged Emma Winslow, to secure as much information as possible on "previous and present habits of expenditure in each family"—not only general food expenditures, but detailed information on what sorts of foods were consumed by the family, how the food was cooked, where it was purchased, and whether it was bought on credit. Or take clothing. Itemizing what the family owned was just the start. The caseworker was instructed also to investigate other issues: Was it necessary "to develop in the family a greater appreciation of the importance of suitable dress at home and outside the home?" Was there sufficient "knowledge concerning relative values in clothing selection . . . under American living conditions?"[62] Recreational expenditures were also closely examined: Were newspapers purchased daily? And did the family contribute money to the church, pay union dues, or provide aid to their relatives?

Even the internal division of family monies came under surveillance. Private social workers were asked to observe whether working members of the family turned over all their earnings, or if anybody kept some for himself or herself. Would changing established practices develop "better family relationships" or "cause a more equable use of the total family income?" Administrators of mothers' pensions were greatly preoccupied with the proper economic ties between the mother and her children. Would a pension destroy a child's sense of domestic responsibility or would working children still contribute their earnings to the family purse? At a time when the economic role of children was being redefined, the issue of their contributions was admittedly "a matter of most delicate adjustment" where "no hard and fast rule can be made." In some localities, arrangements "were not interfered with if they were reasonable," but it was the "expectation of the court" that "a good mother would get all the money the children earned up to the age of sixteen years" and at her discretion give the children some spending money. In other jurisdictions, however, the amount of a child's spending allowance was specified by pension administrators, as was the payment expected by children over sixteen. In King County, Washington, for instance, older children were expected to pay their board, amounting to at least half of their earnings.[63]

This thorough financial X ray of pensioned families was considered an essential part of their economic rehabilitation. A well-constructed household budget served as the best tool to shape competent consumers, by revealing defective spending patterns and pointing the way to "desirable" spending practices. Properly supervised cash relief, maintained one expert, should awaken "the desire for better things."[64] The concern with "wise spending" even made traditional thrift somewhat suspect; home economists worried about families who saved their money instead of consuming properly.

Sometimes, the effort to assure the proper earmarking of monies became remarkably concrete. The New York Charity Organization Society, for instance, borrowing the techniques of independent families, proposed the use of budget envelopes to help clients in "apportioning their income." Each envelope would be illustrated with a picture "relating to the purpose for which it is to be used," and would be expected to guide the families in spending their money "in accordance with our budget plans." Similarly, at the 1928 New York State Conference on Social Work, a thrift specialist recommended to family caseworkers the use of coin banks "opened only by the banker who furnishes them," as well as the "special object clubs like Christmas, insurance and tax clubs" as ways to direct the spending of dependent families.[65]

When it came to the poor, the rhetoric of consumption thus took a peculiar turn. To be sure, unlike nineteenth-century charity workers who assisted the needy with clothing, fuel, or food but kept them penniless, modern social workers were ready to put cash into the pocketbooks of the poor. If consumer competence was a teachable skill, how could the lessons be taught effectively without money? With proper coaching, advocates of cash relief argued, money would give dependent families full access to the new consumer society. But cash relief never circulated as the currency of an ordinary consumer. Whether given by private charities or dispensed by the mothers' pension program, charitable cash was marked as tutorial money for dependents, modeled after the highly regulated middle-class domestic currency, confined to a very limited and carefully selected group of recipients, apportioned parsimoniously, and monitored closely.

Following the 1920s, psychiatric social workers attached new psychological significance to the instructional mission of cash relief: with careful management, money could also work as an effective "casework tool" in the treatment of emotional dependency. Rather than approaching cash as a "simple economic issue," it was, therefore, necessary to sort out the client's unspoken emotional and symbolic connections to money. In an influential study of family casework practice made for NYCOS in the late 1920s, Grace Marcus cautioned that a caseworker's failure to recognize these emotional values could defeat any attempts to educate the client in the constructive uses of money. On the other hand, if properly handled, monetary relief created an "excellent entrée into the confidence and good will of the clients," laying the groundwork for emotional as well as financial independence.[66]

Next to the itemization of material needs, Gordon Hamilton, another expert in casework practice observed years later, a "psychologized" version of the budget would need to "sort out objective reality from emotional demands," distinguishing "neurotic" requests for relief from real deprivation. Thus, as social work stepped up its psychological assessment of relief methods, cash grants took on the additional task of training an emotionally adjusted consumer; therapeutic money grants, in the new psychological vocabulary, served to "constructively support ego strengths."[67] Caseworkers now had access not only to the pocketbooks of the poor, but to their psyches.

Twentieth-century consumerism reshaped welfare practices. Social-work experts became increasingly willing to put money into poor people's hands and let them do the buying. But despite a rhetoric that praised freedom of consumer choice for dependent families, social workers remained ambivalent. They gave cash, but with strings attached. In the end, paradoxically, the supervision of relief may have intensified as agencies dispensed an allegedly free currency instead of commodities. True, cash did offer the poor a wider range of consumer choices compared to the in-kind gifts of soup or a second-hand coat. But it was still an officially defined currency, budgeted by strangers and therefore never entirely their own. However, charity workers did not always have their way. For, in fact, the poor had their own ideas about how to earmark monies. And, sometimes, in the contest between social workers and their clients over how, where, and when to spend money, social workers lost.

6

Contested Monies

WHEN A BERKS COUNTY, Pennsylvania, mothers'-pension visitor inspected the F family's monthly expense account during the 1920s, she was bemused by a daily entrance for "milk, 6 cents" under the "good times" column earmarked for recreational expenses. Fifteen-year-old Thaddeus, the family's sole breadwinner and record-keeper, explained: "Since we have the money I can buy a pint of milk every day at the factory, so that is a 'good time' for me."[1]

THE STRUGGLE FOR CONTROL

Disagreements between social workers and recipients of relief were not always as benign as the one occasioned by Thaddeus' choice of a pint of milk. They involved both struggles over competing systems of earmarking and clashes over defining the relationship between authorities and the poor. Recall the contest for household monies among wives, husbands, and children, or the disputes between donors and recipients of tips and year-end bonuses, each group struggling to earmark either part of the household monies or a monetary gift according to their own system. In the case at hand, donors and recipients of charity frequently had incompatible systems of earmarking, but also disagreed about the extent to which the charity constituted a free gift among equals, an entitlement merely expedited by the charitable agent, sympathetic help to a dependent, or something else. For instance, did the social workers' bestowal of money involve the right to tell families how to spend? Or did charitable income, once it entered the households of the poor, become their property?

The poor, too, had their own systems for earmarking household monies, not just for good times, but for a whole range of expenses; rent money was not the same as food money, and insurance money was kept apart from a church donation. Even personal monies were differentiated; a son's personal-spending allowance was treated quite differently from his sister's, or from their father's saloon money or his carfare. When poor families could afford it, they often set money aside for fraternal organizations or other mutual-aid societies, or, in the case of immigrants, earmarked certain monies to be sent to their families abroad. Indeed, many poor housewives would have probably agreed with the ninety immigrant women who told Sophonisba Breckinridge that what they needed most was not expert training on how to spend money, but simply "getting the wherewithal to pay."[2]

Official budgets therefore encountered unwritten, yet still powerful, alternate accounting systems. And despite social workers' deliberate and elaborate arrangements to retain control over relief funds, needy families routinely managed to overcome bureaucratic restrictions, finding ways to make charitable monies as much "theirs" as possible. Recall how Penny Provident depositors reshaped the savings system conceived by charitable societies. At first, poor families were suspicious of the attempts to take hold of their monies; as Mary Remington, the settlement worker, noted in her diary, "they are all afraid of [the Penny Savings Bank], as some one tells them that we want to get their money away from them."[3] But poor families were resourceful. Whereas organizers had planned to "save" their pennies until there was enough money to be transferred into a regular savings account, poor families turned the Penny Provident banks into short-term, consumer-oriented deposits. Women, children, and men saved for their own specific purposes: buying spring clothes, paying for a summer vacation, and very often for an Easter present or a Christmas gift.[4]

To be sure, relief money was not the same as a Penny Provident depositor's wages. Middle-class observers may have been upset or impatient with a whole range of working-class expenditures, as they were with money spent treating friends to a drink in a saloon, or what one charity worker referred to as the "pernicious 5 and 10 cent theatres," or the "foolish Sunday treats for the children in bags of cheap candy, popcorn, ice cream cones, bottles of pop"; but beyond moralizing, there was little they could do about it, as long as members of the household earned the money they spent.[5] Charitable monies, on the other hand, gave social workers license to intervene directly in the domestic spending of the poor.

Yet even with regulated monies, the poor managed to impose their own systems of control. They did so with a broad range of charitable allocations, and sometimes in simple ways, as did the needy women who refused the gift of a fashionable upper-class green coat, until it had been dyed and remodeled "in order to blend with the styles in vogue among the families of two-dollar-a-day incomes."[6] Or consider the many strategies devised by families to modify food orders to suit their own dietary preferences, negotiating with grocers, neighbors, or relatives to convert orders to cash or to exchange them for different goods than those allowed. Observe, for instance, how Mrs. C, the Italian immigrant widow described in chapter 4, managed to persuade her assigned grocer (who had known the family in better times) to let her buy bread at an Italian bakery and have him pay her weekly bill, transferring the amount to the grocery order. The arrangement broke down only when Mrs. C went too far, adding macaroni and Italian cheese to the bakery purchases. In fact, the strategy extended beyond food. Recall how the poor of Hartford, Connecticut, reshaped charitable currencies by using coal orders to pay debts or converting food orders into rent money.[7]

The poor also found ways to appropriate cash relief. It may have been merely symbolic, as with the Italian housewives who, on instructional shopping expeditions with domestic visitors, insisted on carrying the money and paying for the purchases themselves; or it may have been as overtly confrontational as fourteen-year-old Carl Pularski who, when asked by the social worker to keep his mother's accounts (she could not write English), responded that "he would rather starve than let anyone know what the family ate." A Minneapolis woman considered "too independent" by her Family Welfare Association (FWA) caseworker told them, according to the social worker's notes, that "if they did not want to help her without telling her just how the money should be spent [then] FWA could keep away from there [her house]. She was getting tired of having to acc[oun]t for every cent."[8]

Often, the assertions of control were subtle but poignant. Witness how Mrs. Rutsiki, a Bohemian widow, upset the charity worker when, without consulting her, she spent a few secretly kept dollars, saved while she still worked, to buy a pair of patent-leather shoes for her ten-year-old Bennie. Why, wondered the visitor, had the mother spent her "treasured reserve" for goods that, like most of the family's clothing and household supplies, would have been provided by the agency? Mrs. Rutsiki explained:

"You buy everything for the children. If I don't buy them something, sometimes they will not think of me when they are big. They will think that I have never done anything for them."[9]

Most notably in the case of burial money, the contest between social workers and the poor sometimes involved a long-standing and uncompromising economic, social, and moral controversy. This chapter examines the contest over charitable monies, exploring poor people's attempts to regulate charitable income as well as social workers' persistent ambivalence toward a consumerist ideology that supported freedom of consumption for the poor and their belief that the poor could not be trusted to spend well. By 1935 public authorities will seem to have finally recognized, via the Social Security Act, the autonomy of poor people's earmarking systems. Restricted charitable cash could at last be put out of circulation, and the poor would be allowed to handle legal tender and spend as they wished. But the new monetary policy did not last long. Relief workers and other authorities, including the courts, soon found ways to once again confront, contest, and regulate the financial choices made by recipients of relief. New charitable currencies once again were being coined to distinguish the monetary world of the putatively incompetent poor.

POOR PEOPLE'S MONEY VERSUS OFFICIAL EARMARKS

Social-work experts, during the early part of the century, recognized that the orderly columns of their expertly drawn account books and budget ledgers did not neatly or easily contain the domestic economies of the poor. Purely on a practical level, they knew that keeping records was hard work, so that persuading housewives to register every expense was not always an easy task, let alone making sure the record was accurate. Caseworkers were warned that account books were often semifictional documents, in which some families registered fantasized expenditures, a few invented expenses simply to please the visitor, and still others concealed inappropriate purchases. The difficulties of budgeteers, however, went beyond the relative precision of their clients' records. Social workers were also aware that the "expenditure habits" of the poor were in many cases "firmly fixed," rooted in distinct "racial and community customs" as well as religious beliefs.[10]

Nevertheless, different systems of consumer choice were typically dismissed as the mistaken prejudices of ignorant or incompetent people, at best trivialized as mere foolishness or a foreigner's quaint customs, at worst attacked as morally corrupt economies, perpetually on the brink of alcoholism or gambling. Ironically, charity workers were most upset when poor people expressed the sort of freedom of consumer choice celebrated by twentieth-century experts, spending their small sums "for that which is not bread."[11] Consider, for instance, the "horror" of a Penny Provident officer when a poor man with a large family withdrew the $50 saved in the fund and, instead of putting the money in a bank as he had been repeatedly urged to do, spent it on a "Kodak." Or take Edward T. Devine's concern with the "starving family" that divided the four dollars of assistance received during a snowstorm into a dollar for food, a dollar for drink, and two dollars, as the father explained, for buying "a pup for de kids to play wid."[12]

Turn-of-the-century charity experts such as Mary Willcox Brown were certain that the poor were too easily dazzled by peddlers or shopkeepers into buying "knicknacks" or similarly "useless articles." Some two decades later, leading social workers such as Sophonisba Breckinridge still worried about the fiscal incompetence of immigrant Bohemian women who bought "recklessly," spending on jewelry and "all sorts of things they see for sale in neighborhood stores." Or, like Florence Nesbitt, experts called attention to the effort often involved in convincing recipients of mothers' aid to forgo some self-indulgent "pet extravagance" such as puffed rice or boiled ham in order to purchase a healthier diet of vegetables or fruit for their families.[13]

At issue is not whether the dietary choices of domestic experts were in fact healthier than the meals prepared by poor housewives, or whether or not their clothing budgets or general spending schedules were more adequate, but that the experts' notions of a more rational, efficient, and scientific budget obscured the viability or legitimacy of alternative systems for earmarking monies. Indeed, as historian Daniel Horowitz has pointed out, the very categories used by early-twentieth-century budget studies of poor and working-class families often failed to reflect the real experience of their subjects. Robert C. Chapin's influential 1909 study of workingmen's families in New York City, for instance, classified their contributions to volunteer societies under insurance as well as recreation, although Chapin acknowledged that "expenditure for recreation is sometimes not differentiated from dues and payments to the society." Alcohol consumed at home was listed as food, although in fact it often served medicinal or recreational purposes, while candy, soda water, and ice cream were labeled luxuries, a classification that, as Horowitz suggests, would probably have been contested by "children living in cramped tenements during the summer's heat."[14]

To be sure, the two systems of earmarking did not always conflict. Penny Provident banks reported with pride not only when one of their depositors had actually met the society's goal of opening a savings account or had bought a home, but also when depositors used their money for socially "uplifting" consumer goods: for example, the boy who, after discovering the penny bank, was encouraged to earn some money by running errands until he saved enough to buy a new suit of clothes and found regular work "that he never could get . . . before because he was so ragged." Or they pointed to the child who, after a "fresh air" summer vacation, was so impressed with the "clean bed and soft pillows" that her mother saved enough to purchase a bed, "thus taking one long step in a much needed reform in our tenement-houses."[15] Penny Provident organizers also boasted of the many families who had "avoided being dispossessed by discovering the children's money on the stamp card." Or they spoke of the altruism inspired by the savings system, as in the case of two brothers, eight and ten years old, who explained that they would not spend money on themselves until they had saved enough to buy their mother some teeth; she only had five left.[16]

In essence, Penny Provident leaders, along with other charity experts, approved when the poor spent their money on "useful," educational, or socially and morally uplifting purchases or activities—supporting the family economy by paying for fuel or for rent, buying shoes, hats, books or medicines, and sometimes making contributions to the church. By the 1920s, probably reflecting the growing prestige and popularity of pianos and phonographs among working-class families, both items were included, by administrators of mothers' pensions, within the array of legitimate consumer goods for the poor, albeit with certain qualifications. In Wayne County, Michigan, for instance, the purchase of "cheap phonographs" was encouraged as "a means of promoting family unity"; payments for pianos, on the other hand, "were not forbidden if they were already nearly paid for." Some jurisdictions encouraged the purchase of "inexpensive instruments . . . as a means of home entertainment," but only if the money came out of a working child's income. Increasingly, too, mothers'-pension leaders spent funds to subsidize "summer outings," sending mothers and children for a week or two to summer vacation camps.[17]

In their effort to shape the household economy, poverty workers often became the poor housewife's collaborators. Consider how nineteenth-century charity workers regularly sided with the wife against husbands who presumably drank or gambled away their family's income. Friendly visitors were specifically instructed to ascertain whether in fact husbands kept back "an undue share of their earnings."[18] It is also possible that women themselves found official earmarking systems useful in their struggles against husbands over the allocation and control of household monies.

Recall the many strategies used by women to secure control over some portion of their husband's wages, from stealing change from men's trousers to concealing purchases or earnings. The nineteenth-century special-purpose savings funds, the Penny Provident bank, or, later, the Christmas Club account and even the caseworker's budget, regardless of their restrictions, offered housewives an alternative mechanism for segregating monies for various expenses—something for the home, new clothes, a Christmas gift, or a donation to the church. It was women, after all, who met with the savings-fund collectors who came to their homes, and it was usually the women who negotiated the social worker's budget. Indeed, the postmaster general explicitly advertised as one of the virtues of postal savings banks that "a married woman may open an account free from interference by her husband."[19] Even mothers' pensions, despite the meager sums awarded and the supervision involved, allowed women a new measure of discretion over domestic money. And at least one study suggests that pensions may have in fact provided some widowed women with a larger income than their late husband's wages.[20]

A PROPER DEATH

When it came to spending money for burial insurance and other preparations for death, however, the lines between social workers and the poor were clear-cut, regardless of gender. In fact, it was usually the housewife who, despite the opposition of charity workers, managed to set aside a few cents from the household money to pay the insurance agent in his weekly round of house-to-house calls. Insurance money, charity experts recognized, was an undisputed priority in the budgets of poor people. "However distasteful the idea of burial insurance may be to those who are in more comfortable circumstances," Edward T. Devine observed, "it is possible that if the items for which provision must be made were arranged in the order of their importance to the majority of the poor in the great cities, among the unexpected features of such a table would be that in advance of both food and shelter would appear provision for burial."[21]

Early twentieth-century studies of working-class budgets confirmed that providing for a proper burial had become such an "essential part of the American standard of living" that even the poorest working-class families were willing to be "dispossessed or to go without food or clothing or fuel in order to keep up the insurance." Indeed, a study of some 3,000 working-class Chicago families conducted in 1918 by the Illinois Health Insurance Commission found that almost 82 percent of the families carried some form of life insurance.[22]

Certainly by the late nineteenth century, middle-class men also routinely insured their own lives to protect the welfare of their wives and children. But the poor bought insurance to pay for a proper burial, not to subsidize their survivors. Starting in 1875, industrial insurance companies revolutionized the industry by sending their agents into the homes of the poor, offering affordable insurance not only for husbands, but also for their wives and children. Fraternal societies and mutual aid groups also provided death protection; but their methods were unsound, resulting in frequent failures and limited assistance for bereaved families. For five to ten cents a week, an industrial policy guaranteed a decent funeral. And there were plenty of customers eager to pay; by 1895, $268 million of insurance were in force in the United States.

Charity workers resented the "phenomenal success" of insurance agents; they decried the salesmen's aggressive intrusion into the domestic economies of the poor, particularly since many of the insured were allegedly paying for their funeral while living off relief.[23] Stories were told of families depending on charities for "daily bread" who, after a death, "suddenly indulge in a funeral display which their benefactors would probably consider too costly for themselves." What could justify, charity experts asked, the perverse budgeting of parents who relied on relief organizations to feed and clothe their children, yet found sufficient money to insure the children's lives? By persuading families to earmark their money for a proper burial, insurance agents were dangerously sabotaging the financial rehabilitation of the poor. With their "insidious stories," complained charity workers, agents were "a steady drain on the resources of the family."[24]

Insurance sales were the dark double of friendly visiting; while friendly visitors or Penny Provident "bank ladies" used their personal influence to rehabilitate the domestic economies of poor dependents, insurance agents corrupted their economic choices, turning living monies into a useless death currency. Charity workers pointed to the telling reminder to "cut down any and every expense, but keep up your insurance" that was inscribed on the envelope holding the insurance receipt book, which the mother was instructed to tack to the wall "so as to be always in view."[25] To the industry's protestations that they, too, were "saving" poor people's money by diverting into a policy what would otherwise go "for beer or ribbons," charity experts countered with poignant domestic scenarios of insurance money "seen on a shelf awaiting [the agent] when not a crumb of food is in the house." Or they told of the family who skipped breakfast on a particular day each week "because the agent called on that day and the breakfast money must be given to him." Charity workers also reported cases of children sent to beg for money to pay the insurance premiums; of families living "in the filthiest and most unwholesome" conditions but with sufficient insurance to afford an elaborate funeral for one of their members.[26]

To be sure, charity officials at the turn of the century were well aware that insurance agents were not their only competitors. Saloon-keepers, chattel mortgage "sharks," pawnbrokers, as well as installment-plan businesses, were similarly branded as "insidious foes" of the poor, soliciting their few pennies for misguided or improper expenses.[27] Insurance, charity workers recognized, at least encouraged thrift, reducing dependence on publicly subsidized burials. And saving for a proper death was surely more uplifting than spending on drink, or for some useless knicknack. Indeed, Penny Provident banks admiringly reported when one of their depositors put money away to fix a father's grave, or when, after the death of a child, parents saved to buy tombstones or keep the grave in order.

Why, then, the battle against industrial insurance? It was partly a matter of control; insurance monies escaped the monitoring web of charity workers. By paying their premiums, the poor purchased the right to subsidize their own version of a "good death," spending in ways that often violated middle-class notions of a proper funeral. To the dismay of charity workers, insurance premiums were directly and almost exclusively converted into funeral fees, paying not only for a "costly casket" but also, in some cases, for an "imposing cortege" of carriages (including a special one to display flowers) and sometimes a band to head the procession. If any money was left, it went for mourning garments.[28]

Indeed, some charity workers observed a "strong sentimental prejudice," particularly among Germans, Irish, and Italians, against using insurance money for anything but funeral expenses. Spending this "blood money," as it was sometimes called, for the family's ordinary expenses was apparently considered as "heartless" as to "pick pennies from the dead one's eyes." Among Orthodox Jews, the earmarking of insurance money was somewhat modified by ritual laws that dictated a simple funeral; less was spent on the burial, and, according to a New York settlement worker, some widows saved the balance of the insurance as a dowry for a second marriage.[29] Still, as Irving Howe describes it, among poor immigrant Jews during the late nineteenth century the funeral was "rapid, explosive, and with a large residue of bills." As late as 1911, the United Hebrew Charities were sufficiently concerned with the misuses of insurance money (including benefits collected from fraternal organizations and mutual aid societies) that a special committee was formed to provide widows with financial advice.[30]

For middle-class observers, death monies subsidized an incomprehensible form of consumerism, debasing a sacred expense into a sacrilegious extravagance. Indeed, what could make a greater mockery of the charities' rational budgeting efforts than these purely symbolic burial monies, earmarked exclusively for social and ritual display? Not only were useful monies squandered away for an apparently useless expense but, still worse, after the funeral was over the bereaved were often forced to seek charitable assistance.

It is not that charity workers were indifferent to the singular significance of a proper burial among the poor. Jane Addams observed how, after a child's death, a mother's "social standing" with the other neighborhood women depended on mourning of a "certain kind and quality." A county burial, therefore, "forever ostracizes a family from their midst" by breaking its "last strand of respectability." That was why, explained a handbook for friendly visitors, the dread of a pauper burial among the poor was much greater than "dread of either dependence or privation."[31]

A study of a tenement-house district on the West Side of New York City in the early 1900s spoke of Irish and German families' "fear of a plain pine box and cheap shroud and rest on Harts' Island," making life insurance "a necessity." The "funeral display," concluded the investigator, was such a critical measure of social status that "all things are sacrificed in order to avoid a pauper burial." A mother, she was told, wants to "'bury her dead boy as good as any rich man's son.'" Even in the case of a wife who did not think her husband deserved it, the insurance money went for a "big funeral," since "the neighbors would talk if she didn't give him a 'fine layout.'"[32]

When there was no insurance money to pay for a private burial, the very poor found strategies to minimize the indignity of a publicly subsidized funeral. Hartford's 1891 report on out-door relief, for instance, discovered that few of their "pauper" burials were "genuine" town-authorized funerals, restricted to the maximum $13 allowance; friends or relatives paid the difference not only for a better coffin but in some cases to subsidize carriages, flowers, entertainment, and religious services. Likewise, in Chicago, where "tardy and cruel" county burials cost a little more than a dollar, friends often provided funerals for their destitute kin. "If the neighbors hear that there is going to be a pauper burial," reported the study of tenement families in New York, "one of them goes round for a subscription and the required sum is soon raised."[33]

When it came to death, charitable monies were not only insufficient but more deeply humiliating than private monies. Thomas and Znaniecki point to the Polish immigrant's "unmitigated aversion" to a municipal burial; the Judziewicz woman, they tell us, "prefers to beg for money for her child's funeral rather than let the burial be performed by an institution." Charitable assistance may have been acceptable for living expenses but not for death; not only did a charity burial brand the respectable poor as paupers but, Thomas and Znaniecki explain, it did so publicly, becoming "the object of general gossip." Insurance money thus substituted for the morally tainted charity payments. Tellingly, a report from the representative of the Cleveland Associated Charities in 1919 suggested that, in many cases, relatives of poor families who were unwilling to help their needy kin in any way "can be persuaded to be responsible for [insurance] premiums."[34]

But while they recognized the social significance of death monies for the poor, charity workers remained convinced that with proper instruction it was possible to alter the irrational bookkeeping that put sentimental death expenses ahead of pressing daily needs. "Whether the poor are to have expensive or modest burials," commented an editorial in *The Charities Review*, "is perhaps primarily an educational problem." Part of the task was to protect their clients against the skillful salesmanship of insurance agents as well as entrepreneurial undertakers. Charity workers were urged to undercut insurance agents' business by turning the industry's methods of personal solicitation against them, persuading the poor to drop their insurance and "use that mite for life, instead of giving it to the agent for burial."

Although by 1909 a leading insurance spokesman offered the industry's collaboration in educating the poor "to the desirability of lack of extravagance and the absence of show and pomp in the burial of their near and dear ones," the charity establishment remained as convinced as ever that industrial insurance promoted "extravagance and useless display in funerals."[35]

But, as we've seen, charity experts also understood that "extravagant" funerals were not just a marketing invention but the product of a "strongly developed sentiment." It was therefore indispensable, argued Jane Addams, to "break through" deeply held "social ideals" and "notions of propriety." And who better than charity workers to "enlighten the poor on the subject of burials"? Since they assumed that the insured were not as competent to judge their budgeting as those who "from disinterested motives, are trying to regulate their expenses," charity workers could rightfully show them how to reallocate their monies more sensibly.[36] The poor had to be taught to provide first "for the claims that are not posthumous," such as "the need of fresh air in the summer . . . of more nourishing food in time of sickness." They had to understand that the "false pride to appear to advantage in a neighborhood" should not make them "deny a little one, a living child," any of its present needs in order to afford "a befitting funeral." And the poor needed to see that there was nothing "beautiful" about an almshouse pauper "who can draw out an insurance book taken in better days and say, 'I won't have to be buried by the city,'" nor about a family that "receives outdoor relief . . . while it is meeting the weekly demands of the collector." Above all, as one speaker at the 1909 National Conference of Charities and Correction put it, it was necessary to "set the example of a decent burial, which means no indecent display."[37]

How successful were these efforts of charity workers to rationalize the burial expenses of the poor? By 1914 a report issued by the New York Association for Improving the Condition of the Poor noted that the payment of insurance premiums for pensioned widows had become a problem "concerning which there is much difference of opinion." For its own part, the AICP, although it discouraged children's insurance, did continue to pay the family's policies. As the supervisor of its Home Economy division explained some years later, "it was found . . . that the people cling so tenaciously to the certainty of a decent burial" that "no one had the heart" to stop the payments. At the 1919 National Conference of Charities and Correction, the dilemma of whether to pay insurance premiums for relief families or force them to drop the insurance was still being debated. The Associated Charities of Milwaukee decided to include insurance in their family budgets "as it is felt the families would pay insurance even if they go without food." Mothers' pensions likewise varied in their insurance allowances, with only some states including premiums in their budgets.[38]

By the 1920s, however, the claims to burial insurance gained unexpected legitimacy. Although some experts still maintained that insurance was more of a "fetish worship" than a "constructive social habit," other leading social workers made a strong case for including insurance premiums in the budgets of relief families. Building on the consumerist rationale for cash relief, one of its advocates explained that insurance payments were necessary to minimize differences between dependent families and their neighbors. And clearly, there was a "neighborhood standard in funerals which must be approximated unless our families are to be humiliated and to 'lose face.'"[39]

In the same vein, a national study of private cash relief recommended that dependent families "be given a sum sufficient to insure them against . . . death." However costly to the society, the expenditure was justified by considering the significance of a "decent burial" for poor families and "the effect it has on their pride and morals to have one of the family buried by the public." Tellingly, Mrs. C, the Italian widow discussed earlier, allotted $5.25 of her monthly charitable income to pay for burial insurance for herself and her six children. By 1933, the *Social Work Year Book* still reported considerable variation in social agency policies regarding the insurance of dependent families. However, one major study of some 6,000 families showed that life insurance was carried by a large proportion of the clients of family welfare agencies.[40]

Clearly, the mission to regulate the economies of the poor was not a simple process of imposing middle-class budgetary standards. Poor people did in fact adopt some of the charity worker's notions of proper spending, but they also tenaciously, and sometimes defiantly, persevered in retaining some control over their own purse strings, even when the money was not their own. When it came to a proper death, poor families resisted the instructions of social workers and found ways to subsidize their meaningful rituals. Their insistence paid off; by the 1920s the social worker's household budget often took death monies as seriously as living expenses.

THE CONTEST CONTINUES

Poor people may have won the contest over burial money. Nevertheless, by the late 1920s social workers felt increasingly confident that the charitable agencies' strategy of "supervised cash relief" was successfully reshaping the domestic economies of their clients, "awakening the desire for better things."[41] It was only a matter of time, leading social workers hoped, before cash relief would be broadly adopted by public agencies as well.[42]

But the Depression abruptly bankrupted social workers' consumerist welfare enterprise; as applications for relief multiplied, breadlines, soup kitchens, commissaries, and grocery orders proliferated while cash relief quickly dried up. Private agencies ran out not only of funds but of time to properly supervise their clients' budgetary decisions or even to assess their "willingness to spend money judiciously." For the social agency, in-kind relief, a social worker explained in 1932, "became an indirect substitute for education in home economics and knowledge of clients."⁴³ When Harry Hopkins, a progressive social worker, was appointed in 1933 as the administrator of the Federal Emergency Relief Administration (FERA), social work professionals anticipated a possible return to cash relief. And indeed, under Hopkins's leadership, cash grants did replace grocery orders and commissaries in many communities around the country. But FERA also got involved in the nation's largest effort of surplus commodity distribution, making in-kind assistance a visible, massive—and to its critics—publicly degrading form of relief.⁴⁴

Social workers, however, did not give up. In fact, their advocacy of cash relief seemed radicalized by the Depression. Consider, for example, Dorothy Kahn's "ardent appeal" for cash assistance at the 1933 National Conference of Social Work. Money, argued Kahn, the director of the Philadelphia County Relief Board, allowed relief recipients "discretion in providing for the fundamentals of existence for their families." Even if the money was a gift, it offered independent "purchasing power." By replacing choice with constraint, on the other hand, relief goods debilitated the otherwise competent consumer. "If you are a vast relief organization," Kahn continued, "these things you give me [a basket of food, or a pair of shoes, or a dress] are leaden with the weight of your power, your choice, your restrictions." Worse still, in-kind relief bred a corrupt form of consumerism, as the poor were forced to "connive" with the grocer, to write "three loaves of bread on the grocery order in lieu of the fifteen cents in cash he has given me to take my crippled child to the hospital."⁴⁵

Not much later, as a matter of fact, the social scientist E. Wight Bakke's study of recipients of relief during the Depression provided a detailed look at household patterns of barter and bargaining that converted in-kind relief into cash or into goods the families wanted. Grocers, for instance, were persuaded to substitute expensive cheese or cigarettes for permitted food items. Or else relief clients sold their groceries to neighbors, like the ingenious Italian housewife who, in order to get cash, used all her grocery orders to get macaroni and tomato sauce that she then sold to her neighbors. People, Bakke concluded, got around a relief system that deprived them of such "normal functions" as spending money, as they searched for ways to "spend as they please."[46]

It was better, argued social workers, to let them have the cash directly. In her *Cash Relief*, Joanna Colcord, one of the most forceful and persistent advocates of monetary assistance, provided a glowing account of pilot programs in cash relief started in 1934–35 by state emergency relief administrations in nine cities across the nation. To be sure, Colcord admitted, a few recipients still misspent the money, like the New York woman "who half starved herself" but used her first check to get a permanent wave and a henna shampoo, or the Pittsburgh man who used rent money to insure his entire family. But Colcord offered compelling evidence that, for the most part, cash grants subsidized household needs far more effectively than did grocery orders or commissaries. In New York, where cash relief was adopted in 1934 in order to restore the "normal function of choice and planning" to dependent families, the Emergency Home Relief Bureau found that many of their clients, "by employing ingenuity and planning ability," were able to "obtain more food for their money by cash" than with food orders, as well as satisfying what the agency referred to as "racial food tastes and habits." Colcord reported recipients' own celebration of the discretion provided by cash. "Even when it is not earned," observed a client of the Philadelphia County Relief Board, cash "gives nerve and ambition." For some clients cash offered the pleasure to "spend foolishly once in a while," but for most it meant purchasing choices: "we can buy what we want, and feel more independent." For one recipient in Cook County, Illinois, the relief check meant not only buying "twice as much groceries . . . that I could get on a grocery order," but also having a spare "nickel or a dime" to put each Sunday into his church's collection box.[47]

To be sure, social workers drew more confidence for their ardent lobbying for cash from the certifiable "cashworthiness" of the Depression's new poor. These were not, they argued, the pre-1930s charity cases but "ordinary citizens whose only social problem is lack of a job." Certainly, the past history of the new poor as safe spenders made them reliable recipients of monetary assistance. Cash relief, noted a 1933 report on unemployment relief in San Francisco, is "merely a minimum maintenance wage . . . presenting exactly the same problems of expenditure which [the recipients] have met during their entire economic lives."[48]

SOCIAL SECURITY ERASES EARMARKS

The 1935 Social Security Act took the monetization of welfare one step further. Not only were recipients of the new categorical public assistance programs (old-age assistance, aid to dependent children, and aid to the blind) to receive "money payments" rather than in-kind relief or vouchers, but, more significantly, federal cash was termed an "unconditional and unrestricted" currency. The Bureau of Public Assistance explicitly warned that federal assistance payments, administered by the states, were to be spent as the recipient wished, without any kind of "direction or control" by the state agency.[49]

The new businesslike terminology was not accidental. Social Security "monetary payments" were intended to upgrade even the most liberal versions of cash relief. As long as the money could only "be spent for purposes approved by the agency," explained Jane M. Hoey, director of the Bureau of Public Assistance, cash allowances were not a true payment but an "indulgence," much like "the allowance given by a parent to a child."[50] Indeed, despite the strong consumerist rhetoric of social-work advocates, many cash-relief programs in the 1930s still required recipients to show receipts for their expenditures.

Visitors were instructed to provide a written statement of items covered by the relief check, urging their clients "to spend the money according to the budget items."[51]

These cash allowances, or "conditioned tender," were declared illegal by the Social Security Agency. By definition "monetary payments," explained the agency's assistant general counsel, implied a "valid and legal tender," thereby excluding "the tender of goods and services." What is more, when a state agency awarded a recipient "a certain sum of money upon the express or implied condition ... that such money ... be expended for the purchase of certain designated goods or services," the action, the counsel argued, was "legally equivalent" to the direct provision of such goods and services to the recipient. For the Bureau of Public Assistance, therefore, restricted cash payments did not qualify as legal tender, and thus violated the Social Security Act's requirement of "monetary payment." Only when a recipient of federal assistance was assured "the free and unrestricted use, in any manner he sees fit, of the money payments made to him," advised the agency's counsel, could it be said "that 'financial assistance' has been rendered."[52]

The Bureau of Public Assistance thus proposed a revolutionary reinterpretation of the consumer sovereignty of poor people; and they were ready to back it up by putting conventional charitable cash out of circulation. The needy, a bureau circular declared, should be treated as ordinary consumers, with the same "freedom to carry on activities through the normal channels of exchange" as their "friends, neighbors and other members of the community." Specifically, there should be no difference between a recipient's relationship to merchants and suppliers and that of other purchasers. Poverty, stated the bureau's report, need not handicap consumer competence; the bureau recognized that poor people's "skill in handling money often surpasses that of the agency in handling money for them." Why, then, should they be limited by a restricted currency? Supervised monies unjustifiably hampered a recipient's free "choice of the goods and services he requires."[53]

To be sure, these "liberated" federal monies were designed to circulate only among certain categories of traditionally "cash-worthy" recipients, the elderly, children, and the blind. General state relief in cash also increased, but without displacing in-kind assistance or grocery orders. By December 1937, cash assistance predominated or was used exclusively in eleven states and the District of Columbia, while seventeen states gave relief both in cash and in kind, and twenty states were still distributing only in-kind assistance.[54]

In its effort to construct a single national medium of exchange, the government was now willing to turn federal relief currencies into what it defined as perfectly fungible money. If there was to be only one official currency, any distinctions between assistance money and other income, including restrictions in the uses of relief payments, became anachronistic. Consequently, the recipient had the right to use his payment "with the same freedom as do persons who receive their income from other sources," including wages. Significantly, the Assistant General Counsel for the Federal Security Agency explicitly insisted on this point by citing the analogy of constitutional and legislative provisions requiring the payment of wages in legal tender rather than in a company's more restricted scrip. In the same way as the courts guaranteed that a worker's wages "constitute property which he is entitled to deal with as he pleases," declaring the employer's incompetence "to abridge this right," the Social Security Act assured the unrestricted expenditure of relief payments.[55]

This was not mere rhetoric. The Bureau of Public Assistance intended to put these principles of money payment into practice. Public-assistance administrators were closely instructed on how to treat charitable monies as an unrestricted monetary payment. Take, for instance, an agency's methods for notifying recipients of its assistance policies. The bureau differentiated between acceptable informational material and inappropriate "directive" statements; whereas the agency was expected to inform the recipient how need was established and how it computed the amount of the payment, it could not suggest in any way that "the payment is made with the understanding that it will be used for a specific item," or that the recipient "will suffer any loss because of his failure to use the payment or any part of it for a specific purpose."[56] Neither could any receipts be required to show how the payment had been used.

Tellingly, assistance agencies were also strongly warned against any collaboration with vendors, such as grocers or landlords. Such collaboration, as for example making direct payments to vendors, or intervening between a recipient and a creditor, might interfere with a recipient's use of his payment. Agencies were discouraged as well from the apparently common practice of requiring the recipient to endorse the check, returning part or all of the money to the agency, which then paid the recipient's bills. The bureau's recommendations were backed by sanctions. A state agency might unilaterally decide to distribute goods and services rather than cash or in any other way "abridge the recipient's right to the unrestricted use of the payment," but it could do so with its own monies; it would automatically lose federal funds. The Social Security Board, according to the agency's counsel, "is unauthorized to match with Federal funds either the cost of goods and services or anything which is their substantial equivalent"; any violation of the "unrestricted and unconditioned grants of funds," the counsel concluded, constituted a "perversion" of the Social Security Act.[57]

It seemed, then, that Social Security gave complete victory to unrestricted cash payments; the contest appeared to be over. Restricted payments, recognized the Bureau of Public Assistance, had remained the "agency's money, in that the agency directs the use of it." Presumably, at least with categorical public assistance programs, poor people's own system of earmarking could now prevail. The new bureaucratic guidelines were unequivocal: the recipient was to spend public assistance money "as he, not the agency, determines what will best meet his need."[58] The new monetary transfers would have no strings attached.

RECOINING CHARITABLE CURRENCIES

The welfare system was not quite ready to untie its purse strings; the earmarking of charitable cash proved indelible. It soon foiled the bureau's attempt to erase distinctions between assistance payments and other forms of income. Indeed, framers of the Social Security Act themselves drew a clear ideological and practical boundary between the more legitimate social insurance benefits and public assistance payments. True, both were paid in cash, but social insurance payments ranked close to a payment for services, whereas assistance monies remained a more undignified "gratuity." Consider the insistence on an individual means-test requirement that made assistance monies dependent on an extensive and intrusive investigation of the recipient's financial life. The Social Security Board strongly and repeatedly resisted any move by individual states toward a flat, undiscriminating system of grants to the poor. So strong was the resistance that when the California legislature in the early 1940s enacted a guaranteed-income plan for its aged, the Social Security Board, lacking legal authority to ban outright the new policy, used a subterfuge—alleged "serious deficiencies" in California's administrative structure—to justify a serious curtailment of federal funds to the state.[59]

When it came to the actual uses of assistance monies, the Bureau of Public Assistance recognized that state agencies found it difficult to develop policies, standards, and procedures to protect "a recipient's right to the unrestricted use of assistance payments." State welfare administrators, often pressured by grocers or landlords protesting the occasional nonpayment of a recipient's bill, repeatedly violated the intent to erase earmarks, sometimes by making payments directly to vendors or else restricting in other ways the recipient's use of his or her money. Take, for instance, the case of a public-assistance agency, in the early 1940s, that required recipients to use a designated portion of their payments to purchase food stamps. Those people who failed to do so found their grants accordingly reduced.[60]

The effort to make Social Security cash an unmarked monetary payment thus ironically evolved into the invention of *new* forms of earmarking monies for the poor, ranging from "vendor payments" made directly to the provider of goods or services; to "protective payments," where the money is sent to another, more competent recipient; and including two-party payments, where checks are mailed to the recipient but become negotiable only by the additional endorsement of the person furnishing particular goods, services, or items.

As long as poor people's consumer competence remained suspect, it was justifiable to keep coining restricted assistance monies. Indeed, underlying the new democratic discourse, which insisted that a recipient of assistance had the same right and responsibility to "direct his affairs, manage his money . . . as does any other citizen," still lingered the traditional suspicion that the poor did not know how to use money properly. By 1962, an amendment to the Social Security Act federalized the new restricted currencies. In order to protect the interests of children, for instance, in cases where a child's caretaker "is so incapable of managing funds," Aid to Families with Dependent Children (AFDC) protective payments could now be issued to third parties "interested in the welfare of the child."[61]

Echoing the home-economics instructors of the 1920s, the new rules also required a state agency to rehabilitate the incompetent adult, making "special efforts to develop greater ability on the part of the relative to manage funds in such manner as to protect the welfare of the family."[62] Although, at first, protective payments were limited to 5 percent of all families receiving assistance in the state, the total was raised to 10 percent, and then to 20 percent in 1977. By 1981, Congress eliminated any federal cap, allowing the state to decide on the number of restricted payments. Thus, although by federal law a state still may not "designate AFDC funds to be spent in a particular manner," in practice the "mismanagement" provision justifies the restriction of monies for the incompetent poor. By 1982, all but eight states relied on the "mismanagement" clause to regulate AFDC funds, taking control of the money away from the parent. Significantly, while protective and vendor payments to landlords and other creditors are increasingly used for AFDC recipients, they are forbidden in nonpublic assistance programs, such as Social Security and veterans' benefits.[63]

Restricted charitable monies also multiplied outside of the Social Security categorical assistance programs. Between 1939 and 1943, for instance, new food stamps were created to distribute surplus food products to the needy; specially engraved orange stamps were used for regular food items and blue stamps for surplus foods. New monies were also invented to give recipients of food stamps their change; since grocers were not allowed to give out U.S. coins as change, they issued scrip, tokens, or handwritten IOUs that were required to indicate the color of the stamps used for payment.[64]

Following the 1960s, restricted in-kind assistance to the poor—primarily in food, housing, and medical care—increased dramatically, while cash payments fell. More specifically, by the 1980s, only three out of every ten welfare dollars were being transferred as cash. Consider, for instance, the food-stamp program, which began in the mid-1960s and in 1991 had twice the number of recipients as did AFDC. In 1993, a record-breaking 26.6 million people—more than 10 percent of the population— bought their food with coupons.[65] But not any food: Under U.S. Department of Agriculture regulations, food stamps cannot buy, among other things, alcoholic beverages and tobacco, hot foods ready to eat, lunch-counter items, vitamins or medicines, pet food, or any nonfood items. Neither can food stamps be traded for cash. The restrictions are upheld in court; a retailer, for instance, who accepted food stamps as payment for Ajax Cleaner, baby powder, shampoo, and other "ineligible" products was suspended from participating in the food-stamp program for six months.[66] Also in general assistance programs, protective and vendor payments, particularly to landlords, are common, again limiting the discretion of recipients.

*   *   *

The contest between official charitable monies and poor people's earmarking has thus never ended. True, unrestricted cash payments to the poor have gained new allies, namely economists who invoke the principle of consumer sovereignty to argue against the government's inefficient attempt to "distort individual consumption decisions" by providing aid in kind.[67] Many of them support a negative income tax system that would provide a unified cash-only welfare system. Economists find themselves in an unlikely alignment with welfare-rights activists who also strongly endorse the unrestricted money payment—not for the sake of economic efficiency, but in order to protect poor people's "freedom to control" their income. Especially in the case of housing, they argue that vendor payments further pauperize needy recipients by depriving them of any bargaining power with landlords, such as the option to withhold rent in order to force property improvements, or the option to use housing funds for self-help. For instance, in the case of some New York tenants who were refused heat by the landlord, rent monies were used by relief recipients to survive the bitter winter by paying for space heaters or winter clothing, or to run their ovens continuously.[68]

Distrust of poor people's competence, however, has overridden the claims of unrestricted-cash advocates. Even some economists admit that, granted the variability of consumer competence, "simple efficiency" may require "constraining family management inefficiencies with in-kind aid." The economist Lester Thurow, for instance, proposes a possible "continuum of transfers ranging from cash, cash with advice, vouchers, in-kind provision, and, finally, compulsion."[69]

Authorities, for their part, have worked hard to preserve or create separate, identifiable, controllable currencies for the poor, either coining new monies, such as food stamps, or regulating the uses of legal tender, as with protective payments. Currently, the food-stamp program is computerizing its earmarking system; an experimental electronic benefits transfer system replaces paper coupons with more anonymous computerized cards, thus bringing food stamps closer to ordinary money. But electronic transfers still supervise purchases, restricting a recipient's food purchases to designated items. Meanwhile, even private groups invent new restricted currencies for the poor. In Berkeley, California, for example, merchants and charitable organizations in 1991 devised vouchers to encourage "good panhandling" by making their coupon-currency redeemable only for food, bus fares, or other essentials, but not for alcohol, cigarettes, or illegal drugs.[70]

Still, poor people contest official earmarks, finding ways to convert assistance monies into their own systems. Food stamps, much like the nineteenth-century grocery orders, are traded on the black market for cash, or the food bought with stamps is then sold for cash. Tellingly, burial monies persist in poor people's budgets. In the midst of deep poverty, some welfare mothers—especially in high-risk inner-city housing projects—still find ways to earmark a portion of their monies to buy burial insurance for their children. While, at the turn of the last century, mothers were afraid of a pauper burial for a dying sick child, at the turn of this century, welfare mothers buy burial insurance against their child's probable violent death.[71]

For more than a century, professional charity workers have been struggling over the definition and disposition of poor people's money. Doles, grocery orders, fuel funds, flour and shoe clubs, Penny Provident savings, money gifts, postal savings banks, family allowances, mothers' pensions, burial monies, food stamps, vendor payments, protective payments—all raise questions about who should define the proper spending not only of relief funds but also of money earned by the poor. Despite phases of consumerism and even legal standardization of relief, charitable workers continued their efforts to impose their own systems of earmarks, based on the assumption that poor people frequently lacked the competence to spend money on their own.

For their part, recipients insisted on their own earmarking practices. In fact, in recent years, the poor have taken the struggle to earmark their own monies all the way to court. Consider Annie Mae Roberts's challenge to the Connecticut practice of vendor payments. When Ms. Roberts, an AFDC recipient, did not receive her welfare check on January 1, 1970, she promptly notified the landlord that the rent payment would be delayed until a duplicate check arrived. But the landlord requested and obtained from the state welfare department a vendor payment for Ms. Roberts's rent. As stipulated by the law, the landlord would continue to be paid by the welfare department until the plaintiff's tenancy would end. Ms. Roberts contended that by being deprived of her "right to receive welfare assistance in the form of direct money payments," she had also lost her "right to dignity" and independence.

But the court ruled that Annie Mae Roberts had no protectable legal right to direct money payments: as long as vendor payments had not deprived her "of the means to subsist," any loss of "dignity" or independence was declared irrelevant. The motion was denied and the action dismissed.[72] Like Mrs. C, the Italian immigrant widow discussed earlier in this account of charitable monies, Annie Mae Roberts' assistance payments were not considered legal tender but only a restricted charitable currency. Whereas Mrs. C's domestic economy had been closely supervised by social workers, Ms. Roberts's monies were regulated not only by the welfare agency and by her landlord, but restricted also by the legal system.

7

What Does Money Mean?

IN *Funes the Memory-Keeper* Jorge Luis Borges gave us one of his most fantastic characters. Bedridden after an equestrian accident, Funes developed his own whimsical system of enumeration during sleepless nights:

> Instead of seven thousand thirteen, he said (for instance) *Máximo Perez;* instead of seven thousand fourteen, *The Train;* other numbers were . . . *sulphur, clubs, whale, gas, cauldron, Napoleon, Agustin de Vedia.* Instead of five hundred, he said *nine.* Each word had a particular sign, a sort of marker. . . . I tried to explain that this rhapsody of disconnected voices was precisely the opposite of a system of enumeration. I told him that to say 365 meant three hundreds, six tens, five ones—an impossible analysis with the "numbers" *Dark Timothy* or *meat blanket.* Funes did not understand or did not want to understand.[1]

If money turns the modern world into a "huge arithmetical problem," as Georg Simmel put it in *The Philosophy of Money*, are social monies no more than an insomniac's fancy? If money is essentially a numerical phenomenon, are we as mad as Funes when we call certain monies dirty or clean, domestic or charitable, tips or wages? To classical theorists the "mathematical character" of money filled social life with "measuring and weighing," with an "ideal of numerical calculability," which necessarily blunted personal, social, and moral distinctiveness.[2] So, too, historians tell us how Americans in the late nineteenth century responded to social upheaval with a "quantitative ethic" that became "the hallmark of their crisis in values." For "lack of anything that made better sense of their world," Robert Wiebe observes, "people everywhere weighed, counted, and measured it."[3] The graying of the world promoted by the money economy left room for only objective, quantitative calculations; anonymous numbers inexorably erased personal markers.

Yet Funes may have been on to something. For, as we have seen, people constantly deploy a social lexicon of monies, creating phrases, sentences, paragraphs, whole books as they manipulate their currencies, earmarking certain monies for particular uses, distinguishing others by how they were earned, designating special users for particular exchanges, inventing new names for distinct uses of official currencies, or converting nonmonetary objects into media of exchange. Of course, quantity makes a difference; people care about how much money is involved in their transactions. But *what kind* of money it is and *whose* money also matter greatly.

Nor are these distinctions erratic, romantic, or isolated exceptions to a dominant rational monetary system in which earmarking does not exist. Social differentiation of money is pervasive; not only in the dark exotic corners of the economy but everywhere we look, different kinds of social relations and values reshape monies. Not just individuals but organizations and even the government distinguish among forms of legal tender or other monies. Multiple monies are thus not curious residuals of a primitive life in which, as Simmel put it, money still retained "sacred dignity" or "the quality of an exceptional value," but a central feature of advanced capitalist economies.[4]

EARMARKING IN THE FACE OF MONETIZATION

Indeed, between the 1870s and 1930s, people invented increasingly elaborate and extensive systems of earmarking, precisely as a national market system was being consolidated in America, as industrial capitalism flourished, as consumerism boomed, and as the government worked hard to achieve a centralized, uniform legal tender. The modern consumer society turned the spending of money not only into a central economic practice but into a dynamic, complex cultural and social activity. What *should* money buy, when, and how often? Did the source of the money matter? Who could spend properly and freely and who needed guidelines, supervision, and restrictions?

Whereas contemporary social observers were right to predict that money would enter ever more social and commercial exchanges, they were wrong in their assessment of the consequences. Suffering from a sort of intellectual color blindness, Simmel's brilliant analysis of money failed to capture the rich new social hues emerging in a monetary economy as people improvised different ways to personalize and differentiate monies. Where the color blind see only shades of gray, people of normal vision see the whole rainbow. But money-marking people go one better: they create their own spectra in place of those provided by governments and banks.

The earmarking of monies took place even in the most vulnerable areas of social life, those relationships and exchanges supposedly peculiarly susceptible to the dollar's rationalization: domestic transactions, the bestowing of gifts, and charity, both public and private. Money concerns increasingly permeated the

American household, from gift exchanges to charitable donations. Here, of all places, we should have found the standardizing, depersonalizing effects of state-homogenized money.

Instead, we have uncovered a complex social economy. As
money entered the household, gift exchanges, and charitable
donations, individuals and organizations invented an extensive
array of currencies, ranging from housekeeping allowances, pin
money, and spending money to money gifts, gift certificates,
remittances, tips, Penny Provident savings, mothers' pensions,
and food stamps. They sorted ostensibly homogeneous legal tender into distinct categories, and they created other currencies
that lacked backing from the state.

Within households, families carefully and sometimes passionately differentiated and segregated their monies, setting food
money apart from rent money, school money, or charity money,
as well as funds for burial, weddings, Christmas, or recreation.
Wives, husbands, and children did not always agree on earmarking arrangements, as family members struggled over how to
define, allocate, and regulate their monies. We've seen how a
wife's money differed fundamentally from her husband's or her
child's, not only in quantity but in how it was obtained, how
often and how it was used, even where it was kept. Disputes
were not always settled cordially: women, men, and children
often lied, stole, or deceived each other in order to protect their
separate currencies. Families thus constructed distinct forms of
monies, shaped by a powerful domestic culture and by changing
social relations between husbands and wives, parents and children. They were also influenced by class: middle- and working-
class domestic dollars were not exact equivalents.

Families, intimate friends, and businesses likewise
reshaped money into its supposedly most alien form, that of a
sentimental gift, expressing care and affection. It mattered who
gave gift money and who received it, when it was given, how it
was offered, and how it was spent. Defying all notions of
money as neutral, impersonal, and interchangeable, gift money
circulated as a meaningful, deeply subjective, nonfungible cur-

rency, closely regulated by social conventions. At Christmas, weddings, christenings, or other religious and secular events, cash was turned into a dignified, welcome gift, almost unrecognizable as market money and clearly distinguished from other domestic currencies.

Gift givers and gift receivers often disputed the earmarking of money gifts. Especially when it came to exchanges between strangers, money gifts became controversial currencies, symbolizing the inequality of particular social relations. The tip, for instance, was a strongly contested category of money, partly payment, partly gift, sometimes defined as a token of appreciation but other times rejected as an insulting dole. Again, money given to poor people balanced precariously between gift, tip, rightful benefit, and payment for services. Whether a given transfer counted as a payment for services, lawful entitlement, or a discretionary gift concerned the parties so much that they erected visible boundaries among the categories, and fought over the locations of those boundaries.

When authorities intervened in the earmarking of monies, a different category of currencies emerged. Concerned with ostensibly incompetent consumers, a number of institutions and organizations during the early twentieth century entered earmarking systems of dependent populations. In the case of the poor, public and private welfare authorities became deeply involved in creating charitable currencies designed to teach their clients the proper uses of money. What social workers did with the poor resembled the efforts of other institutions to regulate spending patterns, as in the case of prisons, reformatories, or orphan asylums, as well as a range of workplaces; company towns, or even the Ford Motor Company. Ford's notable 1914 innovation, the Five-Dollar-Day and Profit-Sharing Plan, distinguished between workers' regular wages and a conditional supplement based on the company's profits. That arrangement made a worker's share of the profit contingent on an upright lifestyle, including proper use of the additional income.[5]

Where extensive evidence concerning authorities' imposition of currencies exists, we invariably find counterearmarking and contest. We therefore have reason to expect resistance and alternative currencies in other settings as well. When it came to charitable currencies, after all, the poor retained their own systems of differentiating monies, making cash relief a controversial, contested, and complex monetary exchange.

Family life, gift exchanges, and charities hardly stand at the periphery of modern economic life. They are vital, creative centers, actively and continually involved in the earmarking of monies. In fact, innovation and differentiation of monies are particularly energetic, elaborate, and visible in these areas of delicate social interactions. People invest a great deal of effort in creating monies designed to manage complex social relations that express intimacy but also inequality, love but also power, care but also control, solidarity but also conflict. The point is *not* that these areas of social life valiantly resisted commodification. On the contrary, they readily absorbed monies, transforming them to fit a variety of values and social relations.

We have seen most notably the gendering of currencies, as women in all social classes increasingly handled important aspects of both domestic and gift economies. Similarly, there have been deep changes in the marking of money by gender in courtship practices. But gender cuts across many other social settings: offices, schools, churches, casual social encounters, and more. In each of these settings, we have reasons to expect the designation of monetary forms and practices as male or female. Obviously, we need to understand better the work of gender. In a parallel way, we must explore how age, race, and ethnicity shape the uses, meanings, and allocation of monies.

THE SOCIAL BASIS OF MARKET MONEY

What about market money? Is it true that at least market money roamed freely as the homogeneous, colorless currency described by classic theorists? Is there perhaps a black-and-white money map of the world? Yes and no.

Surely from the eighteenth to the twentieth century in significant areas of market settings, people invented monetary arrangements, such as checks, the one-price store, money orders, automatic transfers, or the enormous variety of credit cards, to regularize and routinize interaction, and reduce the difficulty of social relations in the economy. Simmel may have been color blind but he still could see: the monetization of economic life did facilitate the expansion of commercial relations, extending markets in time and space.

The problem, however, is that classical thinkers focused so much on standardized market routines that they made two fundamental errors. First, they failed to recognize the difficult social process involved in the invention of market money. Earmarking market money was not the automatic, irrepressible outcome of modern market economies. Instead, as the American case demonstrates, the creation of a centralized, homogeneous, uniform legal tender took enormous and sustained governmental effort.

Second, by assuming its inevitability, classic thinkers absolutized market money. Persuaded that only market money existed, they did not look at the invention of new monies or recognize the wide varieties of currencies in modern society. They did not capture a growing paradox: as the physical forms and legal status of money became more standardized, the use of legal tender in many areas of life turned into a more delicate social process, making cultural and social differentiation increasingly elaborate.

Recall what happened when social workers or home economists earnestly tried to do Simmel's work, shaping rational consumers, defining domestic monies or cash relief as no different from a wage, to be spent as anonymously and freely as an ordinary payment. Their project failed as invariably a different sort of currency was created, as market money went bankrupt in an alien set of social relations. Treating domestic money as a wage, for instance, was defined not only as an indignity but as a direct threat to family solidarity.

"Free" cash relief, on the other hand, did not fit the established social relations between social workers and their clients. That is why, despite the rhetoric of market freedom, social workers continued to restrict and guide the earmarking systems of their clients. But the homogenization of money also failed because the people who were the objects of these efforts had their own ideas about earmarking monies.

Let me be clear: money multiplies everywhere, including within competitive markets. Indeed, Arthur Nussbaum, a legal historian, has noted Americans' "extraordinary aptitude" for monetary experimentation. Today, the Federal Reserve recognizes as part of the national money supply not only cash, currency, demand deposits, and travelers checks, but also, among other financial assets, overnight repurchase agreements, Eurodollars, money market mutual-fund shares, savings bonds, commercial paper, bankers' acceptances, and liquid treasury obligations. In fact, as economist Joel Kurtzman points out, in the recent past a whole series of monies and "near" monies have come into existence, such as the billions of dollars in privately issued credit-card money, home-equity lines of credit, or the money lent to individuals and businesses by the "so-called non-banking financial institutions" such as General Electric Credit Corporation. "It becomes clear," Kurtzman observes, "that calculating how much money exists is nearly impossible."[6]

Certain market exchanges, however, have developed sets of routinized transactions, so that in fact electronic money transfers, direct bank deposits, computerized home shopping, or automated telephone purchases are clearly regulated, involving little or no personal contact between payer and payee. In a "cashless society" the sociologist James Coleman points out, where most people pay by credit cards, interpersonal ties and trust in specific others become irrelevant as sellers no longer depend on buyers but on an impersonal, central, electronic clearinghouse of debts.[7] These important transactions correspond in many ways to the classic sociological theory of monetization. But in areas of more complex, less routinized social interaction—both market and nonmarket—innovation, bargaining, and contest over types of monies are the rule. In any case, all participants in these complex systems rely on a generalized trust of the unknown agents with whom they are interacting.

Indeed, the argument in this book has implications for the broader analysis of variation among different types of markets. Recently, social scientists have challenged neoclassical models of a single, autonomous, self-sustaining market by arguing that market activity, as the sociologist Harrison White puts it, is "intensely social—as social as kinship networks or feudal armies."[8] Socially variable markets not only differ in price but are shaped by historically changing social relations between buyers and producers as well as by diverse cultural contexts. Thus, while certain markets achieve some degree of standardization, new markets are continually being created and other markets redefined.

Even within the apparently narrow range of the professional theater market, as White points out, there is a subset of markets—Broadway musicals or drama, dinner theaters, off- and off-off-Broadway plays, repertory companies—each with particular, distinctive characteristics. Many forms of theater, for example, only survive through their appeal to highly specialized clienteles or their support by wealthy patrons. Likewise, conventional economists find they must differentiate between external and internal, professional and nonprofessional, labor markets; and many go on to distinguish among segments of labor markets shaped by race, ethnicity, and gender.[9]

Recent changes in Eastern Europe underscore the prevalence and significance of market innovation. Take, for instance, the anthropologist Caroline Humphrey's analysis of the former Soviet Union's economic fragmentation, which extends not just to its constituent republics, but to regions, localities, and individual establishments. Far from moving toward the formation of a single, connected market, the new local economic structures, Humphrey demonstrates, are regulated by local bosses and conducted by barter or with a variety of restricted coupons, food cards, and orders, issued not centrally but by regional, local, and even workplace organizations. The exchange relations are fragmentary and particularizing; food cards, for instance, are for specific products, issued only to residents of a particular town or region, and exclude any visitors; coupons are even more limited, distributed to certain categories of people—workers at a factory, war veterans, mothers of young children—for the purchase of specified products, sometimes limited to a specific store.[10] Indeed, the ad hoc creation of credits among firms—clearly a new monetary form—has severely threatened all governmental attempts to control inflation.

In Eastern Europe and elsewhere, what passes for straightforward expansion of the market is actually a much more complex economic transformation, one that involves the creation of multiple monies. A proper sociological understanding of this type of transformation should eventually challenge and renew explanations of large-scale economic change and variation. It should also illuminate such economic phenomena as income redistribution, rates of saving, response to inflation, aggregate expenditures on consumer variables, and a wide range of other phenomena in which individual consumer actions make a great macroeconomic difference. Of course, this book has not come close to providing a theoretical statement on macroeconomics. Yet by focusing on small-scale counterparts of large-scale processes, it has shown how differentiation, innovation, and contest are integral parts of the process by which spending and saving take place. Earmarking, in short, lies at the heart of economic processes.

HOW AND WHY PEOPLE EARMARK

How does earmarking work? How do people set apart multiple monies? We've seen that techniques vary widely. Monies are sometimes *physically earmarked*, as in the case of the nineteenth-century engraved love tokens or housewives' artful creations of gift monies. People also segregate monies *spatially*, using all sorts of domestic containers—labeled envelopes, colored jars, stockings, piggy banks—or designated institutional accounts, such as Christmas Clubs or vacation funds. At the extreme, monies are set apart simply by keeping them out of circulation, as, for example, the dollar bills tacked to the wall or the counter of a new store, usually inscribed with a friend's cheerful good-luck message, or as a collector's item.

Monies are commonly earmarked by constraining their *uses:* a child's income is designated for specific appropriate purchases, to be spent only for the child's entertainment or clothing; gift monies are usually intended for specified objects or activities; cash relief is often restricted to budgeted expenses approved by social workers. Monies are also distinguished by designating particular *users* for specified currencies: a weekly allowance is for children, not adults; pin money is a female, not a male, currency; tips are acceptable for waiters, not for lawyers. Or monies are set apart by linking certain *sources* of money to selected uses: income earned by the wife may be reserved for her children's education while her husband's income pays the mortgage; inherited monies may be spent differently from earned income or a windfall profit. Currencies are further distinguished by creating different *systems of allocation:* the calculation and distribution of household income, gift monies, or cash relief, for instance, are based on contrasting domestic principles, affective guidelines, and welfare philosophies. Finally, people not only earmark legal tender but, in some instances, either transform selected material objects into currencies (cigarettes, subway tokens) or create new restricted currencies (gift certificates, food stamps).

How persistent are earmarks? When does a dollar stop being an allowance to become a gift, or how long does it take for a charitable currency to turn into domestic money? The duration of a particular form of earmarking is directly tied to a particular money's cultural and social context. Some types of earmarking are in fact routinized, lasting over long periods of time (for example, token currencies in institutions); some earmarks are so deeply imprinted with moral or sentimental meanings that the monies involved can never be used differently or by different people (for example, an inheritance); yet other earmarks are volatile and short-lived (lottery winnings). Particularly in areas of delicate social interactions, innovation is constant as people create new monies to define difficult or changing social ties.

Is all this cultural and social diversity ultimately a form of sentimental self-deception? Is monetary creativity and experimentation no more than a naive illusion, camouflaging the fundamentally uniform, calculative, and corrosive reality of money? Or is earmarking at most a luxury of the affluent that disappears in the desperate economies of the very poor? After all, it is difficult to reconcile the creativity of social relations with the existence of power and social inequality, of widespread economic distress.

The evidence speaks otherwise. Surely money serves as a powerful instrument of inequality. The accounts of domestic, gift, and charitable monies leave no doubt that separate currencies have repeatedly served to enforce the dependency of women, children, and the poor. The forms of monetary transfers mark the equality or inequality of the parties just as they mark their degree of intimacy and the durability of their relationship. But the histories of these currencies also demonstrate that people, however powerless, find ways to contest dominant systems of earmarking, redirecting the uses of their limited funds in ways that define, maintain, and sometimes transform their social lives. Recall the battle over burial insurance: welfare clients insisted, despite the criticism and limitations set by social workers, that the earmarking of death monies was a fundamental, non-negotiable economic decision.

Indeed, people in all economic situations care so deeply about the proper differentiation of their monies that they struggle to maintain or change earmarking systems. It matters that domestic money differs from a payment for service, or that a welfare check is distinct from a prison stipend. That is why defining domestic, gift, and charitable currencies often led to heated public debates, carried on not only within the privacy of households or the confines of welfare offices but argued in the popular press, newspaper editorials, and magazine articles.

Multiple monies matter as powerful, visible symbols of particular types of social relations and meanings. But they are more than that; they directly affect social practices. People not only think or feel differently about their various monies, but they spend them, save them, or give them for different purposes and to different people. What's more, some groups—as in the case of welfare workers—erect entire programs of reform intended to spread a particular system of earmarking monies.

IS MONEY UNIQUE?

The earmarking of monies is not a unique social process, whether we restrict it to the uses of legal tender or include the invention or conversion of other objects that serve as media of exchange. People differentiate, mark, and segregate all sorts of objects and events—time, space, food, art, fashion, literature, language—thereby defining particular categories of social relations and expressing different symbolic systems. A vibrant new literature on consumption, for instance, has recently shown that far from standardizing tastes and practices, consumerism created novel ways to endow social and personal life with multiple modern meanings.[11] As mass-produced goods multiplied at the beginning of the twentieth century, Americans were not reduced to a nation of interchangeable consumers. Instead, people turned their new material possessions—such as cars, radios, washing machines, clothes, or cosmetics—into socially meaningful objects, integrating mass-marketed products into personalized networks.

Moving away from a utilitarian, atomistic model of consumption, where goods are simply chosen for their quality and price, consumer theorists ranging from Veblen to Bourdieu examine commodities as clues to the changing symbolic world of social groups.

Their best documented analyses examine the acquisition of goods as cultural markers of class position, including what the sociologist Pierre Bourdieu identifies as people's "cultural capital." Historians document this active, complex, and meaningful differentiation of consumer goods. The "defenseless" consumer, as the sociologist Michael Schudson puts it, is being recast as a creative participant in the making of consumer culture, not the alienated victim of a mass commercial invasion.[12] The point is more general. Repeatedly, people employ goods simultaneously as markers of their social rank, as indicators of other shared collective identities, and as signals of their individuality.

Consider some concrete instances of how people turn purchased goods into meaningful possessions. Take, for example, the case of East European Jewish immigrants at the turn of the century. Buying a new suit of clothes, or a piano, or choosing a famous brand-named product, or paying for a summer vacation were not merely economic transactions; but, as Andrew Heinze's study of Jewish immigrants on the Lower East Side of New York City during the decades before World War I documents, these luxury goods and activities became central to these Jewish immigrants' symbolic construction of their new American identity. It is not, however, a straightforward tale of Americanization but an involved cultural process that created a Jewish style of Americanism, in which mass-marketed goods were often integrated into the celebration of traditional ritual events, such as the Sabbath, Hanukkah, or Passover.

The active efforts of American Jews to forge, as Heinze puts it, "a meaningful life with new products" was not only complex but contested.[13] Material goods held different symbolic meanings for upper-class German Jews, for instance, than for their East European counterparts. Jenna Weissman Joselit's vivid account of Jewish domestic culture in New York between 1880 and 1950 shows, for instance, that while affluent German Jewish domestic reformers at the turn of the century advised poor housekeepers about the importance of austere, neatly organized home furnishings, tenement dwellers "preferred the 'plush colors,' the 'scroll work and gorgon hands' of late Victorian parlor suites." The "severity of Mission-style furniture," Joselit observes, "had little appeal to the immigrant consumer who wanted his or her couch and English oak-finished sideboard to have heft, color, and strong lines . . . to be an object of substance."[14]

Consider also the historian Lizabeth Cohen's report of the varied ethnic responses of industrial workers to mass culture in Chicago during the 1920s. Although the working class had only limited discretionary income to spend on consumer items or activities, their small purchases were clearly marked by particularized concerns. Italians in Chicago, for instance, played Caruso or popular Italian songs on their newly purchased Victrola phonographs, keeping the sounds of Italian culture vibrant within their homes. Ethnic workers shopped in their local grocery stores, where Italian women found escarole, dandelion leaves, and many varieties of pasta, while Jewish women could purchase kosher meat or challah bread. Even when they went to the movies, ethnicity colored their experience as "the language of the yelling and jeering that routinely gave sound to silent movies" reflected the community's ethnic character. Neighborhood stores and theaters, Cohen observes, harmonized "standardized products with local, particularly ethnic, culture." So did radio listening, as different groups used stations to broadcast ethnic news and information.[15]

The earmarking of consumer goods by different ethnic and religious groups, by class, by gender, and by age runs parallel to the differentiation of monies, documenting the pervasiveness of earmarking as people make sense of their individual and collective lives by personalizing material possessions and activities. In that respect, the specialized uses of money in marriage ceremonies, gift giving, or household expenditure are examples of the general differentiation of consumption and exchange by class, race, age, religion, gender, or region.

Yet the case of money *is* unique. In accounts of the instrumentalization and rationalization of modern life, it takes center stage; classical social theorists invariably single out money as the leading edge in the tragic dissolution of a formerly cohesive social life. Money seems to operate in a separate realm, a free zone independent from any meaningful influences or restrictions. Tellingly, even analysts of consumer culture stop at money, as if socially differentiated goods were inevitably purchased with a neutral, standardized currency.

Aside from theoretical constructs, money is in fact different from other social goods: more fungible, remarkably mobile, and highly transferable, connecting people over great distances and multiple time zones. It is unquestionably more difficult to personalize money than other objects. Therefore, if the rationalization of modern life were universal, it should be happening precisely with money. Instead, the constant, vigorous, and pervasive differentiation of modern monies provides the most powerful evidence *against* a homogenized, instrumental model of social life.

FUTURE CURRENCIES

Have we reached these conclusions when it no longer matters? One can hear Simmel's ghost whispering: "So you found a few ripples. The current is still running strongly in my direction. Just wait, and money will disenchant the world. Haven't you noticed the way electronic transfers of money are converting all monies into a single, global, invisible 'megabyte money'?[16] Haven't you heard that by 1999 the European Community plans to introduce the European Currency Unit (ECU), a single European currency to replace all national currencies? Money is becoming not only increasingly homogeneous but also unstoppable. Simply look around you: money is turning all aspects of social life into marketable commodities—blood, babies, organs, courtship, funerals."

Contemporary social observers echo Simmel's ghost, warning us about what the sociologist Robert Bellah and his collaborators describe as the growing "tyranny of the market." In the past two decades, argues Alan Wolfe, the logic of the marketplace has increasingly penetrated our most intimate social relations of family and community. While areas of solidarity, altruism, and affection do persist in American life, Wolfe greatly worries that in recent years the boundaries between civil society and the market have been progressively weakened, as "in a way unprecedented in the American experience the market has become attractive not only in the economic sphere, but in the moral and social spheres as well."[17]

To be sure, the forms of legal tender have changed and the uses of money multiplied. Yet there is no sign that people are choosing to relinquish the earmarking of their multiple monies. True, banks now rely on automatic transfers, but special "club accounts" persist; Christmas, Hanukkah, or vacation monies are automatically set apart weekly or monthly by computerized transfers. Even the welfare system is experimenting with electronic welfare payments, but without abandoning its restrictions. Computerized earmarking actually makes it increasingly possible to regulate, supervise, and differentiate benefits. With new internationalized currencies, the scope of earmarking may increase and techniques for earmarking will vary, but differentiation persists. Indeed, with the explosion of personal computers, people's capacity to create and segregate new currencies is expanding even faster than any standardization of international money. If this book's analysis is correct, people will take advantage of that capacity with an extraordinary variety of monetary innovations.[18]

The vision of society fully transformed into a commodity market is no more than a mirage. Money has not become the free, neutral, and dangerous destroyer of social relations. As the world becomes more complex, some things do, of course, standardize and globalize; but as long-distance connections proliferate, for individuals everywhere life and its choices become more, rather than less, intricate. Earmarking currencies is one of the ways in which people make sense of their complicated and sometimes chaotic social ties, bringing different meanings to their varied exchanges. That is why we can expect new forms of earmarking to multiply with social change. To the extent that money does become more prominent in social life, people will segregate, differentiate, label, decorate, and personalize it to meet their complex social needs. Like Funes and his particularized numbers, we will keep coining new names, as well as defining new uses and designating separate users, for our multiple currencies.

NOTES

CHAPTER 1 THE MARKING OF MONEY

1. Georg Simmel, *The Sociology of Georg Simmel*, ed. Kurt H. Wolf (Glencoe, Ill.: Free Press, [1908] 1950), p. 414; Georg Simmel, *The Philosophy of Money*, trans. Tom Bottomore and David Frisby (London: Routledge & Kegan Paul, [1900] 1978), p. 259; Gertrude Stein, "Money," *Saturday Evening Post*, 208 (July 13, 1936): 88. In order to reduce the number of footnotes, I have generally itemized references at the end of each paragraph in the order of their appearance in the text.

2. Cecilie Hoigard and Liv Finstad, *Backstreets: Prostitution, Money and Love* (Cambridge: Polity Press, 1992), p. 49.

3. Carl Husemoller Nightingale, *On the Edge: A History of Poor Black Children and Their American Dreams* (New York: Basic Books, 1993), p. 36.

4. Randall Collins, review of *The Bankers* by Martin Mayer, *American Journal of Sociology* 85 (1979): 190; Francois Simiand, "La monnaie, réalité sociale," *Annales Sociologiques*, ser. D (1934): 1–86; Pitirim A. Sorokin, *Sociocultural Causality, Space, Time* (Durham, N.C.: Duke University Press, 1943). For attempts to examine the moral economy of distinctions in other domains, see Pierre Bourdieu, *Distinction* (Cambridge: Harvard University Press, 1984); Eviatar Zerubavel, *Hidden Rhythms* (Berkeley: University of California Press, 1985) and *The Fine Line* (New York: Free Press, 1991); Michele Lamont, *Money, Morals, and Manners* (Chicago: University of Chicago Press, 1992). To be sure, sociologists have recognized the symbolic and social meanings of money in various empirical settings but only in an ad hoc way. For instance, in his classic study of Boston's West End, William F. Whyte shows that gang leaders consistently spent more on their followers than they received in return. "The financial relations must be explained in social terms," Whyte comments. *Street Corner Society* (Chicago: University of Chicago Press, [1943] 1967), p. 258. But he takes the example no further. For more general treatments of money, see for example, Simon Smelt, "Money's Place in Society,"

British Journal of Sociology 31 (1980): 205–23; Bryan S. Turner, "Simmel, Rationalisation and the Sociology of Money," *The Sociological Review* 34 (1986): 93–114; Heiner Gansmann, "Money—A Symbolically Generalized Medium of Communication? On the Concept of Money in Recent Sociology," *Economy and Society* 17 (August 1988): 285–316; Wayne Baker, "What Is Money? A Social Structural Interpretation," in *Intercorporate Relations*, ed. Mark S. Mizruchi and Michael Schwartz (New York: Cambridge University Press, 1987), pp. 109–144; Wayne Baker and Jason B. Jimerson, "The Sociology of Money," *American Behavioral Scientist* 35 (July/August 1992): 678–93; Mark S. Mizruchi and Linda Brewster Stearns, "Money, Banking, and Financial Markets," *Handbook of Economic Sociology*, ed. Neil Smelser and Richard Swedberg (Princeton, N.J.: Princeton University Press and New York: Russell Sage Foundation, forthcoming). On links between religion and money, see Robert Wuthnow, "Pious Materialism: How Americans View Faith and Money," *The Christian Century*, March 3, 1993, 238–42; and *God and Mammon in America* (New York: Free Press, forthcoming). For a provocative, historically grounded alternative to utilitarian conceptions of money, see William Reddy, *Money and Liberty in Modern Europe* (New York: Cambridge University Press, 1987). For an interdisciplinary discussion of the meanings of money, "The Meanings of Money," ed. Kenneth O. Doyle, *American Behavioral Scientist* 35 (July/August 1992). For an original interpretation of literary treatments of money, see Marc Shell, *Money, Language, and Thought* (Berkeley: University of California Press, 1982).

5. Thorstein Veblen, *The Theory of the Leisure Class* (New York: Mentor, [1899] 1953). On the cultural, social, and historical aspects of consumption, see Talcott Parsons and Neil Smelser, *Economy and Society* (New York: Free Press, 1956); Bernard Barber, *Social Stratification* (New York: Harcourt, Brace & World, 1957), chap. 7; Lee Rainwater, *What Money Buys* (New York: Basic Books, 1975); Mary Douglas and Baron Isherwood, *The World of Goods* (New York: Norton, 1979); Richard W. Fox and T. J. Jackson Lears, eds., *The Culture of Consumption* (New York: Pantheon, 1983); Michael Schudson, *Advertising, The Uneasy Persuasion* (New York: Basic Books, 1984); Pierre Bourdieu, *Distinction* (Cambridge: Harvard University Press, 1984); Daniel Horowitz, *The Morality of Spending* (Baltimore, Md.: Johns Hopkins University Press, 1985); Arjun Appadurai, ed., *The Social Life of Things* (New York: Cambridge University Press, 1986); Daniel Miller, *Material Culture and Mass Consumption* (Oxford: Blackwell, 1987); Simon Bronner, ed. *Consuming Visions* (New York: Norton, 1989); Susan Strasser, *Satisfaction Guaranteed: The Making of the American Mass Market* (New York: Pantheon, 1989); Martha L. Olney, *Buy Now, Pay Later* (Chapel Hill: University of North Carolina Press, 1991); Thomas J. Schlereth, *Victorian America: Transformations in Everyday Life, 1876–1915*, chap. 4 (New York: HarperCollins, 1991); Vincent Vinikas, *Soft Soap, Hard Sell: American Hygiene in an*

Age of Advertisement (Ames: Iowa State University Press, 1992); Stanley Lebergott, *Pursuing Happiness: American Consumers in the Twentieth Century* (Princeton, N.J.: Princeton University Press, 1993).

6. Lee Rainwater, Richard P. Coleman, and Gerald Handel, *Workingman's Wife* (New York: Oceana Publications, 1959), pp. 154–67; E. Wright Bakke, *The Unemployed Worker* (Hamden, Conn.: Archon Books, [1940] 1969), pp. 142–3; Jean Lave, *Cognition in Practice* (Cambridge, Eng.: Cambridge University Press, 1988), pp. 132–3.

7. See Albert O. Hirschman, *The Passions and the Interests* (Princeton, N.J.: Princeton University Press, 1977); Allan Silver, "Friendship in Commercial Society: Eighteenth-Century Social Theory and Modern Sociology," *American Journal of Sociology* 95 (May 1990): 1474–504.

8. Max Weber, "Religious Rejections of the World and their Directions," in *From Max Weber: Essays in Sociology*, ed. H. H. Gerth and C. Wright Mills, (New York: Oxford University Press, [1946] 1971), p. 331; Simmel, *The Sociology of Georg Simmel*, p. 412. On sociologists' longstanding "obsessive concern" with the social consequences of the "cash nexus," see Bruce Mazlish, *A New Science* (New York: Oxford University Press, 1989).

9. Simmel, *The Philosophy of Money*, p. 346. Since its first translation in 1978, Simmel's book has received increasing international attention; see David Frisby's preface to the second edition (New York: Routledge, 1990), pp. xv–xli; David Frisby, *Simmel and Since: Essays on Georg Simmel's Social Theory* (New York: Routledge, 1992), chap. 5; Gianfranco Poggi, *Georg Simmel's Philosophy of Money* (Berkeley: University of California Press, 1993); *A propos de "Philosophie de l'Argent" de Georg Simmel*, ed. Jeans-Yves Grenier et al. (Paris: L'Harmattan, 1993).

10. Simmel, *The Philosophy of Money*, pp. 211, 280, 279, 444.

11. Ibid., pp. 373, 128, 441, 427, 125.

12. Ibid., pp. 441, 444.

13. Karl Marx, "The Power of Money in Bourgeois Society," *The Economic and Philosophic Manuscripts of 1844* (New York: International Publishers, [1844] 1964), p. 169; *Grundrisse* (New York: Vintage, [1858–59] 1973), p. 221.

14. Marx, *Grundrisse*, p. 222; Karl Marx, *Capital*, vol. 1, ed. Friedrich Engels (New York: International, [1867] 1984), pp. 96, 103, 111, 132, 105; Karl Marx, *A Contribution to the Critique of Political Economy*, ed. Maurice Dobb (New York: International, [1858] 1972), p. 49. See also "Money," in *A Dictionary of Marxist Thought*, ed. Tom Bottomore (Cambridge, Mass.: Harvard University Press, 1983), pp. 337–40.

15. Marx, *Capital*, p. 132; *Grundrisse*, p. 163; Simmel, *The Sociology of Georg Simmel*, p. 414; *The Philosophy of Money*, p. 377; Weber, *Religious Rejections*, p. 331.

16. Albert O. Hirschman, *Rival Views of Market Society* (New York: Viking, 1986); Charles H. Cooley, "The Sphere of Pecuniary Valuation," *American Journal of Sociology* 19 (September, 1913): 202, 191, 203. In another paper, "The Institutional Character of Pecuniary Valuation"

(*American Journal of Sociology* 18 [January 1913]: 543–55), Charles H. Cooley stressed the institutional setting of monetary valuation.

17. Alfred Marshall, "The Present Position of Economics (1885)," in *Memorials of Alfred Marshall*, ed. A. C. Pigou (London: Macmillan and Co., 1925), p. 158.

18. Wesley C. Mitchell, "The Role of Money in Economic Theory (1916)," *The Backward Art of Spending Money and Other Essays* (New York: Augustus M. Keeley, 1950), p. 170; Mitchell, "The Backward Art of Spending Money (1912)," in *The Backward Art of Spending Money*, p. 13.

19. Joseph A. Schumpeter, *Capitalism, Socialism and Democracy* (New York: Harper and Row, [1942] 1962), pp. 123–4, 129; "Money and Currency," *Social Research* (Fall 1991): 521–22.

20. James Coleman, *Foundations of Social Theory* (Cambridge, Mass.: Harvard University Press, 1990), pp. 119–31; Talcott Parsons, "Higher Education as a Theoretical Focus," in *Institutions and Social Exchange*, ed. Herman Turk and Richard L. Simpson (New York: Bobbs-Merrill, 1971), p. 241; "Levels of Organization and the Mediation of Social Interaction," in ibid., pp. 26–27; "On the Concept of Influence," *Sociological Theory and Modern Society* (New York: Free Press, 1967), p. 358; Marx, *Grundrisse*, p. 222.

21. Anthony Giddens, *The Consequences of Modernity* (Stanford, Calif.: Stanford University Press, 1990), pp. 22, 25, 21; Jürgen Habermas, *The Theory of Communicative Action*, vol. 2 (Boston: Beacon Press, 1989), p. 327. For a different critique of Habermas, as well as Parsons's and Luhmann's treatment of money, in particular for ignoring power and inequality, see Gansmann, "Money—A Symbolically Generalized Medium of Communication?" For other statements on the social dangers of unrestricted monetization, see Richard M. Titmuss, *The Gift Relationship* (New York: Vintage, 1971); Fred Hirsch, *Social Limits to Growth* (Cambridge, Mass.: Harvard University Press, 1978); Michael Walzer, *Spheres of Justice* (New York: Basic Books, 1983); Eugene Rochberg-Halton, *Meaning and Modernity* (Chicago: University of Chicago Press, 1986), chap. 10.

22. Simmel, *Philosophy of Money*, p. 440.

23. See James R. Beniger, *The Control Revolution* (Cambridge, Mass.: Harvard University Press, 1986), pp. 329, 331; Thomas J. Schlereth, "Country Stores, County Fairs, and Mail-Order Catalogues," in *Consuming Visions*, ed. Simon J. Bronner (New York: Norton, 1989), p. 364; Lewis Mandell, *The Credit Card Industry* (Boston: Twayne Publishers, 1990).

24. Bray Hammond, *Banks and Politics in America* (Princeton, N.J.: Princeton University Press, [1957] 1967), pp. 702–3. The heterogeneity of state notes went beyond their diverse economic values; banks also frequently personalized notes with elaborate designs of individuals or scenes meaningful for their locality. For an excellent collection of bank-note illustrations, see *Important Early American Bank Notes, 1810–1874, from the Archives of the American Bank Note Company*

(New York: Christie's, 1990). For evidence of the diversity of American currencies in the eighteenth century, see Alice Hanson Jones's thorough analysis of probate inventories in the thirteen colonies around 1774, *Wealth of a Nation to Be* (New York: Columbia University Press, 1980), pp. 8, 132–3. According to Jones, financial assets ranged from bonds and notes to gold and silver coins, the local paper money issued by each particular province, English pound sterling notes, as well as the "Joe"s or Johannes, a Portuguese gold coin, or the "piece of eight," a Spanish dollar. People often used in-kind payments at accepted valuations in local money; in Maryland and Virginia, for instance, taxes and other debts were settled in pounds of tobacco.

25. Milton Friedman and Anna J. Schwartz, *A Monetary History of the United States, 1867–1960* (Princeton, N.J.: Princeton University Press, 1971), pp. 15–25.

26. On the various circulating monies, see ibid., pp. 20–29. For other cases of restricted receivability, see S. P. Breckinridge, *Legal Tender* (Chicago: University of Chicago Press, 1903), pp. 124–26; Arthur Kemp, *The Legal Qualities of Money* (New York: Pageant Press, 1956), pp. 59–93. Richard F. Bensel, in *Yankee Leviathan* (New York: Cambridge University Press, 1990), sees the nationalization of currency as further evidence of the general centralization of state activities during and after the Civil War. Southern currency, however, remained in a state of "unbelievable chaos," since all sorts of paper currencies were being issued not only by the Confederacy but also by its states and municipalities as well as by state banks. Arthur Nussbaum, *A History of the Dollar* (New York: Columbia University Press, 1964), p. 123.

27. John A. James, *Money and Capital Markets in Postbellum America* (Princeton, N.J.: Princeton University Press, 1978), pp. 22–27; Walter T. K. Nugent, *Money and American Society, 1865–1880* (New York: Free Press, 1968). See also Bruce G. Carruthers and Sarah Babb, "The Color of Money and the Nature of Value: Greenbacks and Gold in Postbellum America," paper presented at the annual meeting of the American Sociological Association (1993, Miami).

28. "The Field for 'Money'," *Money* 1 (May 1897): 9; Nugent, *Money and American Society*, p. 167.

29. Nussbaum, *A History of the Dollar*, p. 181. Nussbaum points to the decrease in litigation over specific money as another measure of growing monetary uniformity. See Arthur Nussbaum, *Money in the Law* (Chicago: Foundation Press, 1939), pp. 59–60. Indeed, Bensel explains how "by making the greenback a 'legal tender' for public and private debts, the Union in effect made the acceptance of paper currency mandatory in all contracts and transactions in which money changed hands if those obligations were to be enforceable in court"; *Yankee Leviathan*, p. 162 *n*141. There were exceptions. As late as 1864, California and Nevada still upheld "specie contracts" allowing for payment of a specific kind of currency. See Breckinridge, *Legal Tender*, pp. 126, 158–60, and Wesley Clair Mitchell, *A History of the*

Greenbacks (Chicago: University of Chicago Press, 1903), pp. 142–44.

30. On church money, see Nussbaum, *A History of the Dollar*, p. 42; *New York Times*, September 10, 1989. On the brass-check system used by brothels, "Wage-Earning Pittsburgh," *The Pittsburgh Survey* (New York: Russell Sage Foundation, 1914), p. 360. For other examples of eighteenth-century private coins and tokens, see Thomas Wilson, *The Power "To Coin" Money: The Exercise of Monetary Powers by the Congress* (New York: M. E. Sharpe, 1992), pp. 72–73; Sylvester S. Crosby, *The Early Coins of America* (Lawrence, Mass.: Quarterman Publications, Inc. [1873] 1974).

31. Neil Carothers, *Fractional Money* (New York: John Wiley & Sons, 1930); rept. Bower and Merena Galleries (Wolfeboro, New Hampshire, 1988), p. 166, and Mitchell, *History of the Greenbacks*, pp. 160–61. See also Lyman Haynes Low, *Hard Time Tokens* (San Jose, Calif.: Globe Printing Co., [1900] 1935); Roland P. Falkner, "The Private Issue of Token Coins," *Political Science Quarterly* 16 (June 1901): 303–27; B. W. Barnard, "The Use of Private Tokens for Money in the United States," *Quarterly Journal of Economics* 31 (1917): 600–34. On the private issue of gold coins, see Carothers, *Fractional Money*, p. 128; Wilson, *The Power "To Coin" Money*, p. 124.

32. Carothers, *Fractional Currency*, pp. 195, 171, 341. Mitchell, in *History of the Greenbacks*, p. 162, notes that the postage currency law did not prevent the circulation of town and city notes.

33. Carothers, *Fractional Money*, pp. 195, 343; *Statutes at Large*, vol. 35, pt. 1 (Washington, D.C.: Government Printing Office, 1909), sec. 167, p. 1120.

34. *Hancock et al. v. Yaden*, 366 Supreme Court of Indiana at 371 (1889); Lillian P. Clark, *Federal Textbook on Citizenship Training*, Pt. 3: "Our Nation" U.S. Department of Labor, Bureau of Naturalization (Washington, D.C.: Government Printing Office, 1926), p. 64. On scrip wages, see Knoxville Iron Co. v. Harbison, 183 U.S. 13 (1901). Whereas the courts did not suppress competing currencies, the law required that wages be paid in money if the wage earner so elected. There was opposition; some courts held that "truck laws" violated the constitutional liberty of the laborer by interfering with his freedom of contract. See Ernst Freund, *The Police Power* (Chicago: Callaghan & Company, 1905), pp. 307–8.

35. *Hancock et al. v. Yaden*, 366 Supreme Court of Indiana at 372. The Secret Service was founded in 1865 in great measure to control counterfeiting. For some general accounts of counterfeiting, see Laurence Dwight Smith, *Counterfeiting: Crime against the People* (New York: Norton, 1944); Murray Teigh Bloom, *Money Of Their Own* (New York: Charles Scribner's Sons, 1957). In *After the Hunt: William Harnett and Other American Still-Life Painters, 1870–1900* (Berkeley: University of California Press, 1969), pp. 82–83, Alfred Frankenstein tells about Harnett's encounter with the Secret Service for his paintings of United States Treasury notes. For specific legislation, see "Offenses against the Currency, Coinage, etc.," *Statutes at*

Large, vol. 35, pt. 1 (Washington, D.C.: Government Printing Office, 1909), chap. 7, pp. 1115–22. The Secret Service is still concerned with artistic representations of currency, as in the highly publicized case of J. S. G. Boggs, who has "spent" over $250,000 of his hand-drawn bills by persuading merchants to accept his personalized renditions of legal tender in exchange for their goods or services. See Lawrence Weschler, "Money Changes Everything," *The New Yorker*, January 16, 1993, pp. 38–41; *New York Times*, December 6, 1992, p. 42. On love tokens and other jewelry coins, see *New York Times*, January 10, 1910; "Modern Use of Old Coins," *American Journal of Numismatics* 16 (April 1882): 88–89; Louise M. Campbell, "Love Tokens," *Mana Journal* 16 (1972): 4–17; Dudley L. McClure, "Love Token Collecting Offers Romantic Glimpse of History," *Numismatic News Weekly* (February 14, 1976): 14, 20, 22; Lloyd L. Entenmann, *Love Tokens as Engraved Coins* (Audubon, N.J.: Lloyd L. Entenmann, 1991).

36. *Congressional Record*, 60th Cong., 1st sess., 1908, 42, 4: 3387, 3389. The religious inscription had been authorized in 1864. Roosevelt argued that the motto came "dangerously close to sacrilege." *New York Times*, November 14, 1907, p. 1. Some religious leaders agreed. See Edward Emerson, *Money and Mottoes* (1908), on file at the New York Public Library. Emerson, a Methodist minister, sent copies of his pamphlet to Roosevelt ("the fearless President") and members of Congress strongly supporting the decision to remove the inscription from coins. Most religious organizations, however, passed resolutions condemning President Roosevelt's ruling; see the *New York Times*, November 14–16, 1907. Even the government earmarked monies, authorizing for instance commemorative coins—the first in 1892 for the Columbian Exposition in Chicago—or "patriotic" currencies such as the extraordinarily successful Liberty Bonds during the First World War. Private issue of scrip was tolerated through the Great Depression as emergency substitutes for official money. About $1 billion in scrip were issued in the 1930s depression. See Wilson, *The Power "To Coin,"* pp. 218–21.

37. On prisons, see Samuel J. Barrows, "Prisoner's Earnings," *Charities* 13 (November 26, 1904): 186–87; Isabel C. Barrows, "When Wardens Differ Who Shall Decide?" *The Survey* 28 (July 20, 1912): 577; Shelby M. Harrison, "A Cash-Nexus for Crime," *The Survey* 27 (January 6, 1912): 1549–50; "Should Not Convict Labor Support the Convict's Innocent Dependents?" *Charities* 14 (September 9, 1905): 1089–90; Frank L. Randall, "Possible Development of Schemes for Payment of Prisoners on the Basis of the Services which They Render," *Proceedings of the Forty-Second Annual National Conference of Charities and Correction* (May 1915), pp. 392–96; on tips, see chap. 3. On orphanages and foster-care policies, see Franklin Thomas, "The Place of the Institution in a Child-Welfare Program," *Twenty-Seventh New York State Conference of Charities* (1926), p. 120; Viviana A. Zelizer, *Pricing the Priceless Child: The Changing Social Value of Children* (New

York: Basic Books, 1985), pp. 182–84. On coupons, trading stamps, and premiums, see Strasser, *Satisfaction Guaranteed.*
38. Simmel, *The Philosophy of Money*, pp. 273, 406; Jonathan Rabinovitz, "The Math of Giving: Some Use Formulas to Aid the Neediest," *New York Times*, February 5, 1991; Schlereth, *Victorian America*, pp. 79–85. On French compensation cases, see Henri Mazeaud, Léon Mazeaud, and Amdré Tunc, *Traité théorique et pratique de la responsabilité civile délictuelle et contractuelle*, 5th ed. (Paris: Editions Montchrestien, 1957). For an example of the connection between quantity of money and its social and symbolic meaning, see Clifford Geertz, "Deep Play: Notes on the Balinese Cockfight," in *The Interpretation of Cultures*, ed. Clifford Geertz (New York: Basic Books, 1973), pp. 425–42.
39. For instance, see Stephen E. G. Lea, Roger Tarpy, and Paul Webley, *The Individual in the Economy* (New York: Cambridge University Press, 1987), pp. 450–76, on the introduction of therapeutic or behavior-modifying token monies—metal or plastic chips, personalized stamps, printed paper—in mental hospitals, schools, and industry. For examples of prison money, see Jerry Zara and Bob Lemke, "The Media of Exchange of our 'Penal Institutions,'" *TAMS Journal* 21 (April 1981): 1–6; David B. Kalinich, *The Inmate Economy* (Lexington, Mass.: Lexington Books, 1980). At Club Med resorts where everything is prepaid or can be charged, plastic bead necklaces are used as currency to purchase bar drinks; see Nicole Woolsey Biggart, "Labor and Leisure," *Handbook of Economic Sociology*, ed. Neil Smelser and Richard Swedberg (Princeton, N.J.: Princeton University Press and New York: Russell Sage Foundation, forthcoming).
40. On the invention of new currencies, see R. A. Radford's classic case of the creation of the "bully mark" paper currency at a prisoner-of-war camp, "The Economic Organization of a P.O.W. Camp," *Economica*, New Series, vol. 12 (November 1945): 189–201. On cigarette currency within institutions, see Radford, "The Economic Organization"; Erving Goffman, *Asylums* (Garden City, N.Y.: Anchor Books, 1961), pp. 270–73. *The Baltimore Sun*, June 22, 1993, reports the recent circulation of dollar bills inscribed with the words "gay money" or a pink triangle, apparently as efforts to dramatize gay economic power.
41. Karl Polanyi, "The Economy as an Instituted Process" in *Trade and Market in the Early Empires*, ed. Karl Polanyi, Conrad M. Arensberg, an Harry W. Pearson (Glencoe, Ill.: Free Press, 1957), pp. 264–66. See also Paul Bohannan, "The Impact of Money on an African Subsistence Economy," *Journal of Economic History* 19 (1959): 491–503; Lorraine Baric, "Some Aspects of Credit, Saving and Investment in a Non-Monetary Economy (Rossel Island)," in *Capital, Saving, and Credit in Peasant Societies*, ed. Raymond Firth and B. S. Yamey (Chicago: Aldine, 1964), pp. 422–23; William Graham Sumner, *Folkways* (New York: Mentor [1906] 1940), p. 140; Orlando Patterson, *Slavery and Social Death* (Cambridge, Mass.: Harvard University Press, 1982), pp. 167–71. Defining precisely what constitutes primi-

tive money, however, has been a source of much dispute in anthropology; see, for example, Marcel Mauss, *The Gift* (New York: Norton, [1950] 1990), pp. 100–102 n. 29; Marshall Sahlins, *Stone Age Economics* (Hawthorne, N.Y.: Aldine, 1981), pp. 226, 230.

42. W. I. Thomas and Florian Znaniecki, *The Polish Peasant in Europe and America* (New York: Dover [1918–20] 1958), pp. 164–66.
43. Mary Douglas, "Primitive Rationing," in *Themes in Economic Anthropology*, ed. Raymond Firth (London: Tavistock, 1967), pp. 119–47; Thomas Crump, *The Phenomenon of Money* (London: Routledge & Kegan Paul, 1981), p. 19.
44. Douglas, "Primitive Rationing," p. 139.
45. Ibid, pp. 138, 140. Crump, *The Phenomenon of Money,* pp. 125–30. See also Jacques Melitz, "The Polanyi School of Anthropology on Money: An Economist's View," *American Anthropologist* 72 (1970): 1020–40. For another current in the anthropological study of money that has aimed instead at the psychological interpretation of behavior, see Joachim Schacht, *Anthropologie culturelle de l'argent* (Paris: Payot, 1973).
46. J. Parry and M. Bloch, *Money & the Morality of Exchange* (Cambridge, Eng.: Cambridge University Press, 1989); Parker Shipton, *Bitter Money* (Washington: American Anthropological Association, 1989). See also Michael Taussig, *The Devil and Commodity Fetishism in South America* (Chapel Hill: University of North Carolina Press, 1980) and Rena Lederman, "Pearlshells *in* and *as* Mendi History," paper presented at the annual meeting of the American Anthropological Association, Phoenix, Arizona, November 1988.
47. Lave, *Cognition in Practice*, pp. 133, 141. Another very suggestive essay is Russell W. Belk and Melanie Wallendorf, "The Sacred Meanings of Money," *Journal of Economic Psychology* 11 (1990): 35–67. For evidence of earmarking practices among diverse households in France, see Colette Pétonnet, *On est tous dans le brouillard* (Paris: Editions Galilée, 1983), and Jean-Francois Le and Numa Murard, *L'Argent des Pauvres* (Paris: Editions Du Seuil, 1985).
48. See Lea, Tarpy, and Webley, *The Individual in the Economy,* Daniel Kahneman and Amos Tversky, "The Psychology of Preferences," *Scientific American* 246 (January 1982): 160–73; Richard Thaler, "Anomalies: Saving, Fungibility, and Mental Accounts," *Journal of Economic Perspectives* 4 (1990): 193–205 and *Quasi Rational Economics* (New York: Russell Sage Foundation, 1991); Robert Lane, *The Market Experience* (New York: Cambridge University Press, 1991). For a different, more interpretative version, see Martin Gorin, "Argents-contes et comptes" (Ph.D. diss., École des Hautes Études en Sciences Sociales, 1985). In his *Life against Death* (Middletown, Conn.: Wesleyan University Press, 1959), Norman O. Brown offered a psychoanalytical critique of the rational model of money.
49. Marcel Mauss, "Les origines de la notion de monnaie," *Institut Français d'Anthropologie,* Compte rendu des séances, vol. 2 (1914): 14–19.

50. Alice Kessler-Harris, *A Woman's Wage* (Lexington: The University Press of Kentucky, 1990), pp. 17, 19–20.

51. On the link between modes of payment and systems of control over workers, see Mark Granovetter and Charles Tilly, "Inequality and Labor Processes," in *Handbook of Sociology*, ed. Neil Smelser (Newbury Park, Calif.: Sage Publications, 1988), pp. 201–7. Legislating the timing of payment has been the subject of considerable constitutional argument; see, for example, Freund, *The Police Power*, pp. 304–8.

52. For an excellent discussion of some of the social structural determinants of variation in market money, see Wayne Baker, "What Is Money? A Social Structural Interpretation." Max Weber developed his own typology of legal tender, distinguishing "free" or "market" money from "limited" or "administrative" money, and "regulated" money; see *Economy and Society*, ed. Guenther Roth and Claus Wittich (New York: Bedminster Press, 1968), vol. I. p. 77.

53. Daniel T. Rodgers, *The Work Ethic in Industrial America, 1850–1920* (Chicago: University of Chicago Press, 1979), pp. 30–44, shows the controversial nineteenth-century construction of the wage. In a society where self-employment was a "moral norm," wage payment symbolized dependence and degradation.

54. On children's wrongful-death settlements, see Zelizer, *Pricing the Priceless Child*, pp. 162–63; on widows' monies, Life Underwriter Training Council and Life Insurance Agency Management Association, *The Widows Study*, vol. 2, "Adjustment to Widowhood" (Hartford, Conn.: Life Insurance Agency Management Association, 1971).

55. See John F. Padgett, "Hierarchy and Ecological Control in Federal Budgetary Decision Making," *American Journal of Sociology* 87 (July 1981): 75–129.

56. U.S. Department of Commerce, Bureau of the Census, *Historical Statistics of the United States, Colonial Times to 1970* (Washington, D.C.: Government Printing Office, 1975), Pt. 1, pp. 164–65. To be precise, real annual earnings of *nonfarm* employees rose from $375 (1914 equivalents) in 1870 to $573 in 1900 (an increase of 53 percent), while real annual earnings of *all* employees went from $496 in 1900 to $834 in 1930, a further increase of 68 percent; since farm workers comprised about 18 percent of the labor force in 1900 and 9 percent in 1930, the estimated 122 percent increase for 1870 to 1930 must be close to the mark. For an insightful discussion and bibliography of the emergence of modern patterns of consumption, see Horowitz, *The Morality of Spending*, pp. xxiv–vii, 187–201.

57. Lebergott, *Pursuing Happiness*, p. 36.

58. Hazel Kyrk, *A Theory of Consumption* (Boston: Houghton Mifflin, 1923), p. 9; Mitchell, "The Backward Art of Spending Money," pp. 4, 13. For an early statement of the limits of consumers' sovereignty, see W. H. Hutt, *Economists and the Public* (London: Jonathan Cape, 1936), pp. 273–281.

59. Kyrk, *A Theory of Consumption*, p. 86.

60. Benjamin R. Andrews, *Economics of the Household* (New York: Macmillan Co., 1924), p. 129; Kyrk, *A Theory of Consumption*, p. 271.

61. U.S. Department of Labor, Bureau of Naturalization, *Federal Textbook on Citizenship Training* (Washington, D.C.: Government Printing Office, 1924), pt. 1 "Our Language" (Conversational And Language Lessons For Use In The Public Schools By The Candidate For Citizenship Learning To Speak English), pp. 113–14; Henry H. Goldberger, *America for Coming Citizens* (New York: Charles Scribner's Sons, 1922), p. 187.

62. Horowitz, *The Morality of Spending*, pp. 61, 118, 121–22. To be sure, the discretionary income of the very poor remained restricted. On differences within the working class with respect to income and consumption, see Mark J. Stern, *Society and Family Strategy* (Albany: State University of New York Press, 1987), pp. 403.

CHAPTER 2
THE DOMESTIC PRODUCTION OF MONIES

1. Guy Bolton, "Chicken Feed" ("Wages for Wives"), in *The Best Plays of 1923–24*, ed. Burns Mantle (Boston: Small, Maynard and Company, 1924), pp. 240–41, 243, 260.

2. Clarence Budington Kelland, "Wives are Either Tightwads or Spendthrifts," *American Magazine* 106 (1928): 12.

3. See Elaine Tyler May, *Great Expectations* (Chicago: University of Chicago Press, 1928), p. 137; Robert S. Lynd and Helen Merrell Lynd, *Middletown* (New York: Harcourt Brace Jovanovich, 1956), p. 126.

4. Christine Stansell, *City of Women* (New York: Knopf, 1986), p. 29 and personal communication; Catherine E. Beecher, *A Treatise on Domestic Economy* (Boston: Marsh, Capen, Lyon, and Webb, 1841), p. 176; Mary P. Ryan, *Cradle of the Middle Class* (New York: Cambridge University Press, 1984), p. 33. See also Mary Beth Norton, "Eighteenth-Century American Women in Peace and War," in *A Heritage of Her Own*, ed. Nancy F. Cott and Elizabeth Pleck (New York: Simon and Schuster, 1979), p. 145; Ruth S. Cowan, *More Work for Mother* (New York: Basic Books, 1983), pp. 81–82; Jeanne Boydston, *Home $ Work* (New York: Oxford University Press, 1990), p. 103. On the "cult of domesticity" see Barbara Welter, "The Cult of True Womanhood: 1820–1860," *American Quarterly* (1966) 18: 151–74; Nancy F. Cott, *The Bonds of Womanhood* (New Haven, Conn.: Yale University Press, 1977).

5. Benjamin R. Andrews, *Economics of the Household* (New York: Macmillan, 1924), p. 34. On the home-economics movement, see Hazel T. Craig, *The History of Home Economics* (New York: Practical Home Economics, 1945); Emma Seifrit Weigley, "It Might Have Been Euthenics: The Lake Placid Conferences and the Home Economics Movement," *American Quarterly* 26 (March 1974): 79–96; Susan Strasser, *Never Done: A History of American Housework* (New York: Pantheon, 1982), chap. 11; and "The Business of Housekeeping: The

Ideology of the Household at the Turn of the Twentieth Century," *The Insurgent Sociologist* 8 (Fall 1978): 147–63; Glenna Matthews, *"Just A Housewife": The Rise and Fall of Domesticity in America* (New York: Oxford University Press, 1987), chap. 6.

6. Alice Bradley, *Fifty Family Budgets* (New York: Woman's Home Companion, 1923), p. 7; T. D. MacGregor, *The Book of Thrift* (New York: Funk & Wagnalls, 1915), pp. 145, 151. Jewish housewives also kept a number of domestic "tsedokeh pushkes," or charity boxes, where they and their children kept small sums of money earmarked for various charities; see Ewa Morawska, "Small Town, Slow Pace: Transformations of the Religious Life in the Jewish Community of Johnstown, Pennsylvania (1920–1940)," *Comparative Social Research* 13 (1991): 147. On the economic significance of immigrant remittances, see Dino Cinel, *The National Integration of Italian Return Migration, 1870–1929* (New York: Cambridge University Press, 1991).

7. From his English evidence, Paul Johnson concludes that working-class savings are more likely to be short-term and designated for a specific purpose than middle-class savings; see *Saving and Spending* (Oxford: Clarendon Press, 1985), p. 99.

8. Mary Alden Hopkins, "Understanding Money," *The Woman Citizen* 8 (January 12, 1924): 17.

9. Robert S. Lynd, "Family Members as Consumers," *Annals of the American Academy of Political and Social Science* 160 (1932): 90; *Thrift by Household Accounting and Weekly Cash Record Forms* (Baltimore: Committee on Household Budgets, American Home Economics Association, 1916), p. 4.

10. "Substitution Facts," *The Delineator* 68 (November 1906): 911; "Women and Money Spending," *Harper's Bazar* 39 (December 1905): 1144.

11. *New York Times*, December 23, 1900, p. 10. On the importance of wives' frugality in the eighteenth and early nineteenth centuries, see Mrs. Child, *The American Frugal Housewife* (Boston: Carter, Hendee, and Co., 1832); Beecher, *A Treatise on Domestic Economy*, pp. 175–86; Joan M. Jensen, *Loosening the Bonds* (New Haven, Conn.: Yale University Press), pp. 119–28.

12. Lucy M. Salmon, "The Economics of Spending," *Outlook* 91 (1909): 889. The term "Mrs. Consumer" is from Christine Frederick, *Selling Mrs. Consumer* (New York: Business Course, 1929).

13. For an excellent analysis of the public, private, and academic construction of the nineteenth-century "unproductive" housewife, see Nancy Folbre, "The Unproductive Housewife: Her Evolution in Nineteenth-Century Economic Thought," *Signs* 16 (Spring 1991): 463–84; see also Boydston, *Home and Work.*

14. Amartya Sen, "Economics and the Family," *Asian Development Review* 1 (1983): 14–26; Michael Young, "Distribution of Income within the Family," *British Journal of Sociology* 3 (1952): 305. See also Heidi Hartmann, "The Family as the Locus of Gender, Class, and Political Struggle: The Example of Housework," *Signs* 6 (1981): 366–94; Diana

Wong, "The Limits of Using the Household as a Unit of Analysis," in *Households and the World-Economy*, ed. Joan Smith, Immanuel Wallerstein, and Hans-Dieter Evans (Beverly Hills, Calif.: Sage, 1984), pp. 56–63; Christine Delphy and Diana Leonard, "Class Analysis, Gender Analysis and the Family," in *Gender and Stratification*, ed. Rosemary Crompton and Michael Mann (Oxford: Polity, 1986), pp. 57–73.

15. Blanche Crozier, "Marital Support," *Boston University Law Review* 15 (1935): 33.

16. Margaret E. Sangster, "Shall Wives Earn Money?" *Woman's Home Companion* 32 (April 1905): 32.

17. *New York Times*, December 16, 1914, p. 22.

18. "The Family Pocketbook," *Good Housekeeping* 51 (1910): 15.

19. Letters to the Editor, *Good Housekeeping* 51 (February 1910): 246.

20. Alice Ives, "The Domestic Purse Strings," *Forum* 10 (1890): 106, 111; Elsa G. Herzfeld, *Family Monographs* (New York: James Kempster Printing Co., 1905), p. 50. On immigrant women, see "If It's Only a Page, It's Five Cents," in *Grandma Never Lived in America: The New Journalism of Abraham Cahan*, ed. Moses Rischin (Bloomington, Indiana, 1985), p. 308.

21. 3 *Bench and Bar* 1905: 6; *New York Times*, July 14, 1921. Mrs. Marabella's conviction was reversed and she was discharged. The *Times* reported she had reconciled with her husband.

22. Salmon, "The Economics of Spending," p. 889; Alice Ives, "The Domestic Purse Strings," p. 110.

23. Salmon, "The Economics of Spending," p. 889; Elia W. Peattie, "Your Wife's Pocketbook," *The Delineator* 77 (June 1911): 466; "Story of a French Dressmaker, in *The Life Stories of [Undistinguished] Americans*, ed. Hamilton Holt (New York: Routledge, [1906] 1990), p. 75; Etsu Inagaki Sugimoto, *A Daughter of the Samurai* (New York: Doubleday, 1936), p. 176. Sugimoto was puzzled by this "strange" American custom that departed so radically from the Japanese arrangement in which, regardless of class, wives controlled the purse strings. I thank Sarane Boocock for this reference. Lack of access to cash may have led some women to shoplifting, according to Elaine S. Abelson, *When Ladies Go A-Thieving* (New York: Oxford University Press, 1989), p. 167.

24. Cochran Wilson, "Women and Wage-Spending," *Outlook* 84 (October 13, 1906): 374; Edward Bok, "The Wife and Her Money," *Ladies' Home Journal* (March 1901): 16. On the sales strategies of department stores aimed at an almost entirely female middle-class clientele, 1890–1940, see Susan Porter Benson, *Counter Cultures* (Champaign: University of Illinois Press, 1986). See also William R. Leach, "Transformations in a Culture of Consumption: Women and Department Stores, 1890–1925," *Journal of American History* 71 (September 1984): 319–42. On the commercialization of the beauty industry in the early twentieth century, see Lois W. Banner, *American Beauty* (Chicago: University of Chicago Press, 1983), pp. 202–25.

25. "Adventures in Economic Independence," *Harper's Weekly* 61 (December 25, 1915): 610; Letters to the Editor, *Good Housekeeping*

50 (December 1909): 50; Maude C. Cooke, *Social Etiquette* (Boston, 1896), p. 139.

26. Bok, "The Wife and Her Money," p. 16; "The Money Question Between Husband and Wife as it Has Been Worked Out in Several Homes," *Ladies' Home Journal* 26 (April 1909): 24.

27. Margaret E. Sangster, "Shall Wives Earn Money?," p. 32. Marion Harland, a prolific nineteenth-century novelist and author of "advise" literature, deplored little girls' aptitude for making "prettiness a draft payable at sight," with "Papa's pocket" as their bank; see *Eve's Daughters, or Common Sense for Maid, Wife, and Mother* (New York: Dabor Social Science Publications, [1882] 1978), p. 73. Joan Jacobs Brumberg brought this reference to my attention.

28. Dorothy Dix, "Woman and Her Money," *Good Housekeeping* 58 (March 1914): 408–9; Salmon, "The Economics of Spending," p. 889; Hugh Black, "Money and Marriage," *Delineator* 98 (June 1921): 58.

29. See Lenore J. Weitzman, *The Marriage Contract* (New York: Free Press, 1981); Marylynn Salmon, *Women and the Law of Property* (Chapel Hill: University of North Carolina Press, 1986); Homer H. Clark, Jr., *The Law of Domestic Relations in the United States* (St. Paul, Minn.: West, 1968). On the concern with "extravagant" wives, see Ryan v. Wanamaker 116 Misc. 91; 190 N.Y.S. 250 (1921); Saks et. al. v. Huddleston 36 F. (2d) 537 (1929); and W.A.S., "Charge It to My Husband," *Law Notes* 26 (1922): 26–8.

30. Rheta Childe Dorr, *A Woman of Fifty* (New York: Funk and Wagnalls, 1924), p. 13. I thank Michael Schudson for this reference. The nursery rhyme is cited by Mary W. Abel, *Successful Family Life on Moderate Income* (Philadelphia: J. B. Lippincott Co., 1921), p. 60.

31. "The Family Pocketbook," (1910), p. 15; Charles Zueblin, "The Effect on Woman of Economic Dependence," *American Journal of Sociology* 14 (March 1909): 609; "Domestic Relations and Small Change," 15 *Bench and Bar* (October 1908): 10.

32. C. S. Messinger, et. al., "Shall Our Daughters Have Dowries?" *North American Review* 151 (December 1890): 746–69; "Family Pocketbook," *Good Housekeeping* (1910): 9–15; "Adventures in Economic Independence," *Harper's Weekly* 61 (December 25, 1915): 610.

33. Maude Parker Child, "Her Weight in Gold," *Saturday Evening Post* 198 (January 1926): 125; *New York Times*, October 11, 1926; Abel, *Successful Family Life*, p. 69.

34. *New York Times*, January 29 and January 30, 1923; Emily Post, "Kelland Doesn't Know What He Is Talking About," *American Magazine* 106 (1928): 110.

35. G. V. Hamilton and Kenneth MacGowan, "Marriage and Money," *Harper's Monthly* 157 (September 1928): 434–44. As described by *Harper's*, this survey of financial arrangements was part of a larger study of different aspects of married life conducted under the auspices of the Bureau of Social Hygiene. Using a prepared set of questions, the two hundred respondents were interviewed individually over a period of two years.

36. Dorothy Dix, "Woman and Her Money," *Good Housekeeping* 58 (March 1914): 409; Henry F. Pringle, "What Do the Women of America Think About Money?" *Ladies' Home Journal* 55 (1938): 102.

37. Letters to the Editor, *Good Housekeeping* 51 (February 1910): 517; A Mere Man, "The Domestic Blunders of Women" (New York: Funk and Wagnalls, 1900), p. 33.

38. Coleman v. Burr, 93 N.Y. 17, 45 Am. Rep. 160 (1883); *New York Times*, November 7 and 8, 1926.

39. "Business Contracts in Family Life," *Living Age* 264 (January 1, 1910): 54; Ives, "The Domestic Purse Strings," p. 113; Bok, "The Wife and Her Money."

40. *New York Times*, January 30, 1923.

41. *New York Times*, March 2 and 3, 1925.

42. Christine Frederick, *Household Engineering* (Chicago: American School of Home Economics, 1919), p. 269; Andrews, *Economics of the Household*, p. 398.

43. Hazel Kyrk, *Economic Problems of the Family* (New York: Harper and Brothers, 1933), pp. 182–83; H. I. Phillips, "My Adventures as a Bold, Bad Budgeteer," *American Magazine* 97 (January 1924): 64.

44. Alice Ames Winter, "The Family Purse," *Ladies' Home Journal* 42 (May 1925): 185; Mata R. Friend, *Earning and Spending Family Income* (New York: Appleton, 1930), p. 112; Andrews, *Economics of the Household*, p. 554.

45. Hamilton and MacGowan, "Marriage and Money," p. 440; Robert S. Lynd and Helen Merrell Lynd, *Middletown* (New York: Harcourt Brace Jovanovich, 1956), p. 127, n24; John R. Seeley, R. Alexander Sim, and Elizabeth W. Loosley, *Crestwood Heights* (New York: Wiley, 1956), pp. 184–85; W. M. McNally, "A New Monologue on Marriage," *McNally's Bulletin: Periodical of Sketches and Jokes*, No. 8, 1922, p. 4.

46. Abel, *Successful Family Life on Moderate Income*, p. 5; Mary K. Simkhovitch, *The City Worker's World in America* (New York: Macmillan Co., 1917); Margaret E. Byington, *Homestead* (New York: Charities Publication Committee, 1910), p. 10. The available evidence suggests that a similar domestic financial arrangement applied to different ethnic groups. See, for example, Ruth S. True, *The Neglected Girl* (New York: Survey, 1914); Micaela di Leonardo, *The Varieties of Ethnic Experience* (Ithaca, N.Y.: Cornell University Press, 1984); John Bodnar, *The Transplanted* (Bloomington: Indiana University Press, 1987); research material from Ewa Morawska, 1985 (personal communication). However, Louise Lamphere, in "From Working Daughters to Working Mothers: Production and Reproduction in an Industrial Community," *American Ethnologist* 13 (1986): 118–30, suggests possible ethnic variations. On Jewish families, see Andrew R. Heinze, *Adapting to Abundance* (New York: Columbia University Press, 1990), chap. 6. Further research should better illuminate the impact of ethnicity as well as race on domestic money.

47. Louise Bolard More, *Wage-Earner's Budgets* (New York: Henry Holt and Company, 1907); True, *The Neglected Girl*, p. 48; Leslie W.

Tentler, *Wage-Earning Women* (New York: Oxford University Press, 1982), p. 177; *New York Times*, January 30, 1923.

48. See Daniel Horowitz, *The Morality of Spending* (Baltimore: Johns Hopkins University Press, 1985), p. 60. Determining the impact of a particular household financial arrangement on the relative power of family members is a difficult task. Not only can power be measured in a number of ways, but each dimension of monetary power within the family—whether consuming, saving, investment, or managing—has very special meanings that are culturally and socially constructed. More research is needed to define and understand the relative degree of power of the "cashier" working-class wife.

49. Katherine Anthony, *Mothers Who Must Earn* (New York: Survey Associates, 1914), pp. 135–36; Louise C. Odencrantz, *Italian Women in Industry* (New York: Russell Sage, 1919), p. 176; Elsa Herzfeld, *Family Monographs* (New York: James Kempster Printing Co., 1905), p. 50.

50. Leila Houghteling, *Income and Standard of Living of Unskilled Laborers in Chicago* (Chicago: University of Chicago Press, 1927), p. 37.

51. David Nasaw, *Children of the City* (New York: Anchor, 1985), pp. 131–32; *Boyhood and Lawlessness* (New York: Survey, 1914), p. 69; True, *The Neglected Girl*, p. 49. See also Viviana A. Zelizer, *Pricing the Priceless Child: The Changing Social Value of Children* (New York: Basic Books, 1987), pp. 97–112. On the increased individualization of children's income, especially after the 1920s, see Judith E. Smith, *Family Connections* (Albany: State University of New York Press, 1985); Elizabeth Ewen, *Immigrant Women in the Land of Dollars* (New York: Monthly Review, 1985).

52. Kathy Peiss, *Cheap Amusements* (Philadelphia: Temple University Press, 1986), pp. 23–24; Tamara K. Hareven and Randolph Langenbach, *Amoskeag* (New York: Pantheon, 1978), p. 258.

53. "Industrial Home Work of Children," U.S. Department of Labor, Children's Bureau Publication no. 100 (Washington, D.C.: Government Printing Office, 1924), p. 22. On women's alternative sources of income, see Kathryn M. Neckerman, "The Emergence of 'Underclass' Family Patterns, 1900–1940," in *The "Underclass" Debate*, ed. Michael B. Katz (Princeton: Princeton University Press, 1993), pp. 202–3; Ellen Ross, "'Fierce Questions and Taunts': Married Life in Working-Class London, 1870–1914," *Feminist Studies* 8 (Fall 1982): 590; Melanie Tebbutt, *Making Ends Meet: Pawnbroking and Working-Class Credit* (New York: St. Martin's, 1983); Pat Ayers and Jan Lambertz, "Marriage Relations, Money, and Domestic Violence in Working-Class Liverpool, 1919–39," in *Labour & Love: Women's Experiences of Home and Family, 1850–1940*, ed. Jane Lewis (Oxford: Blackwell, 1986), pp. 203–4.

54. John Dos Passos, *The 42nd Parallel* (New York: New American Library, [1930] 1979), pp. 140–41.

55. Anzia Yezierska, *Bread Givers* (New York: Persea Books, [1925] 1975), pp. 89–90.

56. Lynd and Lynd, *Middletown*, p. 127 n. 24. Henry F. Pringle, "What Do

the Women of America Think about Money?" *Ladies' Home Journal* 55 (April 1938): 102. See also Friend, *Earning and Spending Family Income*, p. 108. On English families, see Laura Oren, "The Welfare of Women in Laboring Families: England, 1860–1950," *Feminist Studies* 1 (Winter–Spring 1973): 115; Peter N. Stearns, "Working-Class Women in Britain, 1890–1914," in *Suffer and Be Still*, ed. Martha Vicinus (Bloomington: Indiana University Press, 1972), p. 116; Jan Pahl, "Patterns of Money Management Within Marriage," *Journal of Social Policy* 9 (1980): 332–33.

57. Joan M. Jensen, "Cloth, Butter, and Boarders: Women's Household Production for the Market," *Review of Radical Political Economics* 12 (1980): 14–24; Laurel Thatcher Ulrich, *Good Wives* (New York: Oxford University Press, 1983), pp. 45–47; Ewa Morawska, *For Bread with Butter* (New York: Cambridge University Press, 1985), pp. 134–35.

58. W. W. Thornton, "Personal Services Rendered by Wife to Husband under Contract," *Central Law Journal* 183 (1900); Helen Z. M. Rodgers, "Married Women's Earnings," 64 *Albany Law Journal* 384 (1902); Joseph Warren, "Husband's Right to Wife's Services," 38 *Harvard Law Review* 421 (1925). Starting in the mid-nineteenth century, Married Women's Property Acts granted wives the right to own and control their property but focused primarily on inherited property. Married women's right to their earnings were excluded by the acts and were incorporated only slowly and with much resistance by amendments or later statutes. See Percy Edwards, "Is the Husband Entitled to His Wife's Earnings?" *Canadian Law Times* 13 (1893): 159–76; Rodgers, "Married Women's Earnings"; Warren, "Husband's Right to Wife's Services"; Crozier, "Marital Support," pp. 37–41; Carole Shammas, Marylynn Salmon, and Michael Dahlin, *Inheritance in America* (New Brunswick, N.J.: Rutgers University Press, 1987), pp. 88–89, 96–97, 163.

59. Priscilla Leonard, "Pin Money versus Moral Obligations," *Harper's Bazar* 37 (November 1903): 1060. On England, see Lawrence Stone, *The Family, Sex, and Marriage* (New York: Harper and Row, 1977), p. 244, and Susan Staves, "Pin Money," in *Studies in Eighteenth-Century Culture* 14, ed. O. M. Brack, Jr. (Madison: University of Wisconsin Press, 1985), pp. 47–77. See also Catherine Gore, *Pin-Money* (Boston: Allen and Ticknor, 1834), a popular early-nineteenth-century British "silver-fork" novel.

60. John Modell, "Patterns of Consumption, Acculturation, and Family Income: Strategies in Late Nineteenth-Century America," ed. Tamara K. Hareven and Maris A. Vinovskis (Princeton, New Jersey: Princeton University Press, 1978), p. 225; Joan M. Jensen, "Cloth, Butter, and Boarders: Women's Household Production for the Market," *Review of Radical Political Economics* 12 (1980): 14–24; "Story of a Farmer's Wife," in Holt, *The Life Stories*, p. 99; Sangster, "Shall Wives Earn Money?," p. 32. See also Thornton, "Personal Services Rendered by Wife," p. 188; Mary M. Atkeson, "Women in Farm Life and Rural

Economy," *Annals of the American Academy of Political and Social Science* 143 (1929): 188–94; Ann Whitehead, "'I'm Hungry, Mum,'" in *Of Marriage and the Market*, ed. Kate Young, Carol Wolkowitz, and Roslyn McCullagh (London: Routledge and Kegan Paul, 1984), p. 112. An investigation by the U.S. Department of Agriculture reported extensive conflict between farm wives and their husbands over the earmarking of monies. "Economic Needs of Farm Women," Report No. 106 (Washington, D.C.: Government Printing Office, 1915). For this reference I am grateful to Kathleen R. Babbitt, whose forthcoming doctoral dissertation at SUNY Binghamton deals with this issue in greater detail. The relative importance of gender versus source of income in distinguishing between the two kinds of money remains unclear. For instance, W. I. Thomas and Florian Znaniecki, in *The Polish Peasant in Europe and America* (New York: Dover [1918–20] 1958), p. 165, suggested that the qualitative difference between the money a peasant got from selling a cow and the money his wife obtained from selling eggs and milk was not marked by gender but by the "different sort of value" represented by each type of money: the cow was property, while eggs and milk were income. Each type of money was set aside for different types of expenses. However, since property, within the peasant economy, belonged to a "higher economic class" than income, it is clear that gender did intervene in the social marking of the two monies; lower-value money was assigned to women.

61. Helena Huntington Smith, "Husbands, Wives, and Pocketbooks," *Outlook* (March 28, 1928): 500; Mary Beynon Ray, "It's Not Always the Woman Who Pays," *Saturday Evening Post* 205 (September 3, 1932): 11.

62. Laura Oren, "The Welfare of Women in Laboring Families: England, 1860–1950," *Feminist Studies* 1 (1973): 110; Hilary Land, "Inequalities in Large Families: More of the Same or Different?" in *Equalities and Inequalities in Family Life*, ed. Robert Chester and John Peel (New York: Academic Press, 1977), pp. 163–176.

63. Mary Anderson, *United States Daily*, September 23, 1929. Cited in editorial, *Journal of Home Economics* 21 (December 1929): 921. See also Alice Kessler-Harris, *Out of Work* (New York: Oxford University Press, 1982), pp. 100–101.

64. Ironically, Max Weber's own family provided evidence against his rational conception of money. According to Marianne Weber, in *Max Weber: A Biography* (New York: Wiley, 1975), p. 141, Weber's father "was typical of the husbands of the time [1860s] . . . who needed to determine by themselves how the family income was to be used and left their wives and children in the dark as to how high the income was." Helene, Weber's mother, had no housekeeping allowance "nor a special fund for her personal needs." I thank Cecilia Marta Gil-Swedberg for this reference.

65. Elwood Lloyd IV, *How to Finance Home Life* (New York: B.C. Forbes Publishing Co., 1927), p. 82. For an extended discussion of the emer-

gence of the allowance, see Zelizer, *Pricing the Priceless Child*, 1987.

66. Karl Marx and Friedrich Engels, *The Communist Manifesto* (New York: International, [1848] 1971), p. 11; Philips, "My Adventures as a Bold, Bad Budgeter," p. 15.

67. There is, however, an emerging interdisciplinary and cross-national literature—by sociologists, historians, economists, and anthropologists—that is contesting traditional unified models of domestic economies. For sociological critiques, see, for example, Philip Blumstein and Pepper Schwartz, *American Couples* (New York: Pocket Books, 1985); David Cheal, "Strategies of Resource Management in Household Economies: Moral Economy or Political Economy?" in *The Household Economy: Reconsidering the Domestic Mode of Production*, ed. Richard R. Wilk (Boulder: Westview, 1989), pp. 11–22; *Gender, Family, and Economy: The Triple Overlap*, ed. Rae Lesser Blumberg (Newbury Park: Sage, 1991); Marcia Millman, *Warm Hearts & Cold Cash: The Intimate Dynamics of Families and Money* (New York: Free Press, 1991). For the position of economists, see Robert A. Pollak, "A Transaction Cost Approach to Families and Households," *Journal of Economic Literature* 23 (June 1985): 581–608; Nancy Folbre, "The Black Four of Hearts: Toward a New Paradigm of Household Economics," in *A Home Divided: Women and Income in the Third World*, ed. Daisy Dwyer and Judith Bruce (Stanford: Stanford University Press, 1988), pp. 248–62; Edward P. Lazear and Robert T. Michael, *Allocation of Income Within the Household* (Chicago: University of Chicago Press, 1988). For anthropological studies see Daisy Dwyer, ed. *A Home Divided*; Marilyn Strathern, "Self-interest and the social good: Some implications of Hagen gender imagery," in *Sexual Meanings: The Cultural Construction of Gender and Sexuality*, ed. Sherry B. Ortner and Harriet Whitehead (Cambridge, Eng.: Cambridge University Press, 1981), pp. 166–91; R. L. Stirrat, "Money, Men, and Women," and Janet Carsten, "Cooking Money: Gender and the Symbolic Transformation of Means of Exchange in a Malay Fishing Community," in *Money & the Morality of Exchange*, ed. J. Parry and M. Bloch (Cambridge, Eng: Cambridge University Press, 1989), pp. 94–116; 117–41; Marion Benedict and Burton Benedict, *Men, Women, and Money in Seychelles* (Berkeley: University of California Press, 1982). For cross-national contemporary and historical studies of intrafamily accounting systems in English households, see Ross, "'Fierce Questions and Taunts'"; Laura Oren, "The Welfare of Women in Laboring Families: England, 1860–1950," *Feminist Studies* 1 (1973): 107–23; Peter N. Stearns, "Working-Class Women in Britain, 1890–1914," in *Suffer and Be Still*, ed. Martha Vicinus (Bloomington: Indiana University Press, 1972), pp. 100–20; Elizabeth Roberts, *A Woman's Place* (New York: Basil Blackwell, 1984); Patricia Branca, *Silent Sisterhood* (London: Croom Helm, 1975); Wilson, *Money in the Family*; Pahl, *Money & Marriage*; Whitehead, "'I'm Hungry, Mum'"; Ayers and Lambertz, "Marriage Relations." For France, see Evelyne Sullerot, "Les femmes et l'argent," *Janus* 10 (1966): 33–39; Marie-

Françoise Hans, *Les femmes et l'argent* (Paris: Grasset, 1988); for French and English working-class households, see Louise Tilly and Joan Scott, *Women, Work, and Family* (New York: Holt, Rinehart and Winston, 1978). Marianne Gullestad, *Kitchen-Table Society* (New York: Columbia University Press, 1984), provides some wonderful data on working-class mothers in urban Norway, and Meg Luxton, *More Than a Labour of Love* (Toronto: Women's Press, 1980). For Canada, see David Cheal, "Family Finances: Money Management in Breadwinner/Homemaker Families, Dual Earner Families, and Dual Career Families," *Winnipeg Area Study Research Reports*, no. 38. For Israel, see Dafna N. Izraeli, "Money Matters: Spousal Incomes and Family/Work Relations Among Physician Couples in Israel," *Sociological Quarterly* (forthcoming). And for Argentina, see Clara Coria, *El Dinero en la Pareja Algunas Desnudeces Sobre El Poder* (Buenos Aires: Grupo Editor Latinoamericano, 1989).

68. Blumstein and Schwartz, *American Couples*, p. 56; Victoria Felton-Collins, with Suzanne Blair Brown, *Couples and Money* (New York: Bantam, 1990), p. 147. See Jean Lave, *Cognition In Practice* (Berkeley: University of California Press, 1988), pp. 131–41. On the relationship between gender, class, money and the distribution of family power, see also Robert O. Blood, Jr. and Donald M. Wolfe, *Husbands and Wives* (New York: Free Press, 1965); Mirra Komarovsky, "Class Differences in Family Decision-Making on Expenditures," in *Household Decision-Making*, vol. 4 of *Consumer Behavior*, ed. Nelson N. Foote (New York: New York University Press, 1961), pp. 255–65; Mirra Komarovsky, *Blue-Collar Marriage* (New York: Vintage, 1967); Constantina Safilios-Rothschild, "The Study of Family Power Structure," *Journal of Marriage and the Family* 32 (1970): 539–52; Lillian B. Rubin, *Worlds of Pain* (New York: Basic Books, 1976); Susan A. Ostrander, *Women of the Upper Class* (Philadelphia: Temple University Press, 1984); Rosanna Hertz, *More Equal Than Others* (Berkeley: University of California Press, 1986); John Mirowsky, "Depression and Marital Power: An Equity Model," *American Journal of Sociology* 91 (1985): 557–92. See also Phyllis Chesler and Emily Jane Goodman's *Women, Money and Power* (New York: Morrow, 1976) for an early statement on women's relationship to money; and for a recent study of women's socialization to money, see Jerome Rabow, Michelle Charness, Arlene E. Aguilar, and Jeanne Toomajian, "Women and Money: Cultural Contrasts," *Sociological Studies of Child Development* (JAI Press, 1992), vol. 5, pp. 191–291.

69. Arlie Hochschild, *The Second Shift* (New York: Avon, 1990), p. 221.

70. Blumstein and Schwartz, *American Couples*, p. 101. See also Jane Hood, *Becoming a Two-Job Family* (New York: Praeger, 1983), pp. 6–71. For England, see Jan Pahl, *Money & Marriage* (New York: St. Martin's Press, 1989), pp. 128–31; also Gail Wilson, *Money in the Family* (Brookfield, Vt.: Gower, 1987). For other cross-cultural comparisons, see Rae Lesser Blumberg, "Income under Female versus Male Control: Hypotheses from a Theory of Gender Stratification and

Data from the Third World," in *Gender, Family, and Economy: The Triple Overlap*, pp. 97–127.

71. See Blumstein and Schwartz, *American Couples*, p. 56; Hochschild, *The Second Shift*, p. 222. Blumstein and Schwartz also discuss how variations in the male-provider ideology as well as the social relations of gay male and lesbian couples and of cohabiting heterosexual couples modify the effect of money on couples' power structure; see *American Couples*, pp. 53–111. On some ethnic and racial variations in the relation between paid labor and household labor, see Beth Anne Shelton and Daphne John, "Ethnicity, Race, and Difference: A Comparison of White, Black, and Hispanic Men's Household Labor Time," and Scott Coltrane and Elsa O. Valdez, "Reluctant Compliance: Work-Family Role Allocation in Dual-Earner Chicano Families," in *Men, Work, and Family*, ed. Jane C. Hood (Newbury Park, Calif.: Sage, 1993), pp. 131–50, 151–75.

72. See Philip Blumstein and Pepper Schwartz, "Money and Ideology: Their Impact on Power and the Division of Household Labor," in *Gender, Family, and Economy*, ed. Rae L. Blumberg; pp. 261–88. On the significance of accounting systems, see Hertz, *More Equal than Others*, pp. 84–113. Using a national sample of respondents, Judith Treas concludes that the choice of domestic accounting systems depends primarily on considerations of efficiency (despite her data's indication that a wife's higher education promotes segregation of funds and that even in pooling couples, wives are more likely to withhold some of their income), "Money in the Bank: Transaction Costs and the Economic Organization of Marriage," *American Sociological Review* 58 (October 1993): 723–34.

73. Kathleen Gerson, *No Man's Land: Men's Changing Commitments to Family and Work* (New York: Basic Books, 1993), p. 192.

74. Lazear and Michael, *Allocation of Income Within the Household*, p. 147. See also Joanne Miller and Susan Yung, "The Role of Allowances in Adolescent Socialization," *Youth & Society* 22 (December 1990): 137–59, on how adolescents define their allowances either as an entitlement or earned household income. On the effect of kin networks on domestic money transfers, see Carol Stack, *All Our Kin* (New York: Harper and Row, 1975); Elizabeth Bott, *Family and Social Networks* (London: Tavistock, 1957).

CHAPTER 3 GIFTED MONEY

1. Lou Eleanor Colby, "When You Send Christmas Money," *Ladies' Home Journal* 27 (December 1909): 37.

2. "If You Run Out of Christmas Ideas," *Ladies' Home Journal* 23 (December 1905): 24. See also "New Ways to Give Christmas Money," *Ladies' Home Journal* 29 (December 1912): 70 and "The Ethics of Receiving," *Living Age* 279 (October 4, 1913): 57–60. On Christmas presents for slaves, see Eugene D. Genovese, *Roll, Jordan, Roll* (New

York: Vintage, 1976), p. 574. On love tokens, see footnote 35 in chapter 1 of this book.

3. I am indebted to American Express and Hallmark archive materials, especially archivist Stephen R. Krysko for his thorough and productive search of materials, and to Sally A. Hopkins, who provided much help with the Hallmark archives. Custodians of Western Union's archives were unable to establish the date when the company first promoted telegrams for gifts; the first available ad is from 1930. I am grateful to Mr. Krysko for this information.

See Ernest Dudley Chase, *The Romance of Greeting Cards* (Cambridge, Mass.: Harvard University Press, 1926), pp. 152–55; William Burnell Waits, Jr., "The Many-Faced Custom: Christmas Gift-Giving in America, 1900–1940," (Ph.D. diss., Rutgers University, 1978). By 1929, according to one estimate, Christmas dead letters handled by the Post Office contained an average of about ten thousand dollars in cash, one million in drafts and checks, and another million in greeting cards; see Ronald Millar, "Our Billion Dollar Christmas," *American Magazine* 108 (December 1929): 88.

4. See Ellen K. Rothman, *Hands and Hearts* (New York: Basic Books, 1984), pp. 76, 167–68; Waits, "The Many-Faced Custom," chap. 5; Chase, *The Romance of Greeting Cards.* On Mother's Day, see Leigh Eric Schmidt, "The Commercialization of the Calendar: American Holidays and the Culture of Consumption, 1870–1930," *Journal of American History* 78 (December 1991): 887–916; on birthday celebrations, Howard P. Chudacoff, *How Old Are You? Age Consciousness in American Culture* (Princeton, N.J.: Princeton University Press, 1989), pp. 126–37.

5. Jenna Weissman Joselit, "'Merry Chanuka': The Changing Holiday Practices of American Jews, 1880–1950," in *The Uses of Tradition,* ed. Jack Wertheimer (New York: Jewish Theological Seminary of America, 1992), p. 313. On the Americanization of Hanukkah, see also Andrew R. Heinze, *Adapting to Abundance* (New York: Columbia University Press, 1990), pp. 71–79. On the Bar Mitzvah, see Jenna Weissman Joselit, "'A Set Table': Jewish Domestic Culture in the New World, 1880–1950," in *Getting Comfortable in New York: The American Jewish Home, 1880–1950,* ed. Susan L. Braunstein and Jenna Weissman Joselit (New York: The Jewish Museum, 1990), p. 66. On Jewish holiday cards, see Luna Frances Lambert, "The Seasonal Trade: Gift Cards and Chromolithography in America, 1874–1910" (Ph.D. diss., George Washington University, 1980), p. 21.

6. Margaret Deland, "Concerning Christmas Giving," *Harper's Bazar* 38 (December 1904): 1157. For an excellent analysis that documents the commercialization of American holidays, see Schmidt, "The Commercialization of the Calendar." See also James H. Barnett, *The American Christmas: A Study in National Culture* (New York: Arno Press [1954] 1976), and Daniel J. Boorstin, *The Americans: The Democratic Experience* (New York: Vintage, 1974), pp. 157–64.

7. Benjamin R. Andrews, *Economics of the Household* (New York:

Macmillan Co., 1924), p. 512; Ernestine P. Swallow, "Children's Christmas Giving," *Journal of Home Economics* 8 (December 1916): 659–60. For examples of the inclusion of gifts in household bugets, see "Family Finance," *Good Housekeeping* 49 (December 1909): 635; Christime Frederick, *Household Engineering* (Chicago: American School of Home Economics, 1919), p. 273; Alice Bradley, *Fifty Family Budgets* (New York: Woman's Home Companion, 1923), p. 12.

8. *Correct Social Usage* (New York: New York Society of Self-Culture, 1905), pp. 518, 521. In his *Behavior in Public Places* (New York: Free Press, 1963), pp. 5–6, Erving Goffman offers a persuasive argument for the use of etiquette manuals as sociological evidence. Although etiquette manuals may not provide empirical evidence about actual behavior, Goffman argues, they still describe "some of the norms that *influence* the conduct of our middle classes." What's more, these guides give us "one of the few sources of suggestions about the structure of public conduct in America." For an historical account of American etiquette books, see Arthur M. Schlesinger, *Learning How to Behave* (New York: Macmillan, 1947).

9. *Harkavy's American Letter Writer and Speller, English and Yiddish* (New York: Hebrew Publishing Co., 1902), p. 701.

10. "New Ways to Give Christmas Money," p. 70; Mrs. Burton Kingsland, *The Book of Good Manners* (New York: Doubleday, Page & Company, 1910), p. 227; Lillian Eichler (Mrs. T. M. Watson), *The New Book of Etiquette* (Garden City, N.Y.: Doubleday, 1924), p. 77; Ethel Frey Cushing, *Culture and Good Manners* (Memphis, Tennessee: Students Educational Publishing Co., 1926), p. 291; Andrews, *Economics of the Household*, p. 50. On money gifts for weddings, see also Virginia Belle Van de Water, *Present Day Etiquette* (New York: A. I. Burt Co., 1924), p. 134. On the popularity of useful gifts in the 1910s and 1920s, see Waits, "The Many-Faced Custom," pp. 94–103; on cars as Christmas gifts, see the *New York Times*, December 24, 1911, sec. 8, p. 8.

11. For some important recent contributions that document and explain the persistence and significance of contemporary gift-giving, see David Cheal, *The Gift Economy* (New York: Routledge, 1988); James Carrier, "Gifts, Commodities, and Social Relations: A Maussian View of Exchange," *Sociological Forum* 6 (March 1991): 119–36; Michael Schudson, *Advertising, The Uneasy Persuasion* (New York: Basic Books, 1984); Theodore Caplow, "Christmas Gifts and Kin Networks," *American Sociological Review* 47 (June 1982): 383–92. For an earlier statement, see Barry Schwartz, "The Social Psychology of the Gift," *American Journal of Sociology* 73 (July 1967): 1–11. Studies of consumer behavior have also explored gift-giving; see Russell W. Belk, "Gift-Giving Behavior," *Research in Marketing* 2 (1979): 95–126; John F. Sherry, Jr., "Gift Giving in Anthropological Perspective," *Journal Of Consumer Research* 10 (September 1983): 157–68. For an economist's analysis of the significance of gift transfers in contemporary labor markets, see George A. Akerlof, "Labor Contracts as Partial Gift Exchange," *The Quarterly Journal of Economics* 97 (November 1982):

543–69. On the feminization of the gift economy, see Cheal, *The Gift Economy*, pp. 173–83; Caplow, "Christmas Gifts"; Eileen Fischer and Stephen J. Arnold, "More Than a Labor of Love: Gender Roles and Christmas Gift Shopping," *Journal of Consumer Research* 17 (December 1990): 333–45. Gift-giving—along with other activities such as visits, letters, and telephone calls—is part of what Micaela di Leonardo calls women's unpaid, largely invisible, but socially critical "kin work"; see "The Female World of Cards and Holidays: Women, Families, and the Work of Kinship," *Signs* 12 (Spring 1987): 440–53.

12. John Davis, *Exchange* (Minneapolis: University of Minnesota Press, 1992), p. 11. For the classic developmentalist view, see Marcel Mauss, *The Gift* (New York: Norton, [1950] 1990). Richard M. Titmuss's *The Gift Relationship* (New York: Vintage, 1971) provides a powerful update of Mauss with his comparison of paid versus voluntary blood transfusion services. Karl Polanyi's useful typology of reciprocal, redistributive, and market exchange assumes the dominance of the latter in capitalist societies; see *The Great Transformation* (New York: Beacon Press, 1957); Karl Polanyi, Conrad M. Arensberg, and Harry W. Pearson, eds. *Trade & Market in the Early Empires* (Glencoe, Ill.: Free Press, 1957).

13. For a critique of the notion that gift exchange and commodity exchange are fundamentally opposed, see Pierre Bourdieu, *Outline of a Theory of Practice* (Cambridge, Eng.: Cambridge University Press, 1977); Arjun Appadurai, "Introduction: Commodities and the Politics of Value," in *The Social Life of Things*, ed. Arjun Appadurai (New York: Cambridge University Press, 1986), pp. 1–63; Maurice Bloch and Jonathan Parry, "Introduction: Money and the Morality of Exchange," in *Money & the Morality of Exchange*, ed. J. Parry and M. Bloch (Cambridge, Eng.: Cambridge University Press, 1989), pp. 8–12. On the view that gifts and commodities are indeed opposed, see Lewis Hyde, *The Gift* (New York: Vintage, 1983), and C. A. Gregory, *Gifts and Commodities* (London: Academic Press, 1982). Jonathan Parry has suggested that the opposition of gifts to commodities is itself a cultural invention; the ideology of what Parry calls the "pure gift"—"altruistic, moral, and loaded with emotion"—develops, he contends, in opposition to a growing market sector where self-interested utilitarian exchange prevails; see "The Gift, The Indian Gift And The 'Indian Gift'," *Man* (1986) 21: 466. See Allan Silver, "Friendship in Commercial Society: Eighteenth-Century Social Theory and Modern Sociology," *American Journal of Sociology* 95 (May 1990): 1474–1504, for a similar argument.

14. Cushing, *Culture and Good Manners*, p. 288; W. C. Green, *A Dictionary of Etiquette* (New York: Brentano's, 1904), p. 272. On the growing popularity of Christmas cards, see Waits, "The Many-Faced Custom," chap. 5; Waits suggests that the unmanageable explosion of gift exchanges at the turn of the century, which included sending small, inexpensive gifts—gimcracks—to an increasingly wider circle of relations, was resolved by limiting gift-giving to kin and closer friends

and sending the more affordable and easier-to-select Christmas cards to less intimate relations.

15. Mrs. H. O. Ward, *Sensible Etiquette of the Best Society* (Philadelphia: Porter & Coates, 1878), p. 393; Deland, "Concerning Christmas Giving," p. 1159; Cushing, *Culture and Good Manners*, p. 287.

16. Mrs. Burton Kingsland, *The Book of Good Manners* (New York: Doubleday, Page & Company, 1910), p. 227; Eichler, *The New Book of Etiquette*, p. 78; Emily Post, *Etiquette* (New York: Funk and Wagnalls, 1922), p. 323.

17. C. B. Wheeler, "Gifts," *The Living Age* 242 (September 24, 1904): 797. On the problematics of turning food into a gift for friends rather than charity for the poor, see Waits, "The Many-Faced Custom," p. 328. After the 1920s, the grocery industry worked hard to promote the gifting of food. See also Ralph F. Lindner, "Groceries for Christmas Gifts," *Printer's Ink* (December 7, 1933): 698–99.

18. Edward Marshall, "Working Girls Bear Brunt of Holiday Giving," *New York Times*, December 15, sec. 5, p. 2, 1912. SPUG was an outgrowth of the National Civic Federation's New York Working Girls' Vacation Savings Funds organized a year earlier. The organization received much attention and praise from the press, and support from prominent political and religious leaders. One month after its organization in November, there were reportedly two thousand SPUG members; by December 14, the all-female organization had started accepting men. See the *New York Times*, December 18, 1912, p. 5.

19. *New York Times*, December 4, 1912, p. 2; "Worse than Careless Giving," *Outlook* (December 21, 1912): 833. See the *Outlook* editorial for the similarity of the working-girl's obligatory presents and those made to schoolteachers.

20. Eichler, *New Book of Etiquette*, pp. 61, 60; Catherine D. Groth, "The Giving of Christmas Presents," *Harper's Weekly* (December 25, 1909): 29.

21. Lambert, "The Seasonal Trade," p. 29.

22. Kingsland, *Book of Good Manners*, p. 228; Eichler, *New Book of Etiquette*, p. 78; Cushing, *Culture and Good Manners*, p. 292; Eliza Leslie, *Miss Leslie's Behaviour Book* (New York: Arno Press, [1859] 1972), p. 174.

23. Eichler, *New Book of Etiquette*, p. 75; *Correct Social Usage*, Pt. 2, p. 518; Eichler, p. 80.

24. Deland, "Concerning Christmas Giving," p. 1159.

25. With a book, we have many dimensions to draw on: subject, author, quality of production or illustrations. Or, as Natalie Zemon Davis points out, a dedication can personalize a book dramatically; "Beyond the Market: Books as Gifts in Sixteenth-Century France," *Transactions of the Royal Historical Society*, 5th ser., 33, (1983): 69–88. On the success of the American gift-book industry in the early nineteenth century, see Richard L. Bushman, *The Refinement of America* (New York: Alfred A. Knopf, 1992), pp. 283–85.

26. Georg Simmel, *The Philosophy of Money*, trans. Tom Bottomore and

David Frisby (London: Routledge & Kegan Paul, 1978), pp. 373, 376, 333, 227, 407, 269.

27. Mary Douglas and Baron Isherwood, *The World of Goods* (New York; Norton, 1979), p. 58; Colin Camerer, "Gifts as Economic Signals and Social Symbols," *American Journal of Sociology* 94 Suppl. (1988): 198; Cheal, *The Gift Economy* (New York: Routledge, 1988), pp. 131, 138, 122; and Cheal, "'Showing Them You Love Them': Gift Giving and the Dialectic of Intimacy," *The Sociological Review* 35 (1987): 165. See also P. Webley, S. E. G. Lea, and R. Portalska, "The Unacceptability of Money as a Gift," *Journal of Economic Psychology* 4 (1983): 223–38; Rik G. M. Pieters and Henry S. J. Robben, "Receiving a Gift," in *New Directions in Economic Psychology: Theory, Experiment and Application*, ed. S. E. G. Lea, P. Webley and B. M. Young (Cheltenham Eng.: Edgar Elgar, forthcoming).

28. Jonathan Parry and Maurice Bloch, "Introduction: Money and the Morality of Exchange," in J. Parry and M. Bloch, *Money & the Morality of Exchange*, p. 9. See also Rena Lederman, *What Gifts Engender* (New York: Cambridge University Press, 1986), pp. 231–33, and "Pearlshells *in* and *as* Mendi History," paper delivered at the Annual Meeting of the American Anthropological Association, Phoenix, Arizona, November, 1988; Maurice Bloch, "The Symbolism of Money in Imerina," in Parry and Bloch, *Money & the Morality of Exchange,* pp. 165–90; C. A. Gregory, "Gifts to Men and Gifts to God: Gift Exchange and Capital Accumulation in Contemporary Papua," *Man,* n.s. 15 (December 1980): 648–49.

29. "New Ways To Give Christmas Money," p. 70.

30. W. M. McNally, "Season's Greetings," *McNally's Bulletin,* no. 11 (New York: William McNally, 1925), pp. 79–80.

31. "Gifts of Money," *The Spectator* 81 (August 13, 1898): 206–7; *Correct Social Usage,* Pt. 2, p. 518.

32. See Mrs. John Sherwood, *Manners and Social Usages* (New York: Harper & Brothers, 1884), p. 257; Maud Cooke, *Social Etiquette* (Boston, 1896), p. 317; Green, *Dictionary of Etiquette,* p. 88. By the 1920s, according to Eichler's *New Book of Etiquette,* pp. 2–3, the custom of friends bringing silver presents for the baby "had vanished," and instead "to-day one sends flowers to the mother, if one is at all intimate, and perhaps a dainty bit of wearing apparel for the child."

33. Susan B. Anthony, "Men and Women: Their Province in the Household," *Independent* 54 (May 8, 1902): 1126.

34. Margaret Hamilton Welch, "The Wife's Share of the Income," *Harper's Bazar* 34 (April 6, 1901): 92–93; Alice Ives, "The Domestic Purse Strings," *Forum* 10 (September 1890): 108; "Husband Who Makes His Wife a Thief," *Ladies' Home Journal* 32 (1915): 16; Alvin F. Harlow, "When Lovely Woman Stoops to Stealing," *Collier's* 76 (August 22, 1925): 10.

35. Swallow, "Children's Christmas Giving," p. 659; Lillian M. Osgood, "Gift Shops," *The House Beautiful* 33 (December 1912): 21. See also Estelle Lambert Matteson, "The 'Many Happy Returns' Shop,"

Woman's Home Companion 39 (October 1912): 28. On women earning their own Christmas money, see Waits, "The Many-Faced Custom," pp. 146–50.

36. Louise Bolard More, *Wage-Earners' Budgets* (New York: Henry Holt and Company, 1907), p. 104. See Kathy Peiss, *Cheap Amusements* (Philadelphia: Temple University Press, 1986), p. 30. On working-class budgets that include gifts, see William C. Beyer et al. *Workingmen's Standard of Living in Philadelphia*, A Report by the Philadelphia Bureau of Municipal Research (New York: Macmillan Co., 1919), p. 85; Louise Marion Bosworth, *The Living Wage of Women Workers* (New York: Longmans, Green, and Co., 1911); Daniel Horowitz, *The Morality of Spending* (Baltimore: Johns Hopkins University Press, 1985), p. 121. The precise boundary between loans and "gifts of friendship" among working-class kin, friends, and neighbors needs further analysis.

37. See W. I. Thomas and Florian Znaniecki, *The Polish Peasant in Europe and America* (New York: Dover, [1918–20] 1958), pp. 358, 404, 433, 438. See also Walter D. Kamphoefner, Wolfgang Helbich, and Ulrike Sommer, *News from the Land of Freedom: German Immigrants Write Home* (Ithaca, N.Y.: Cornell University Press, 1991), pp. 471, 559; Sophonisba P. Breckinridge, *New Homes for Old* (New York: Harper and Brothers, 1921), p. 86; Elsa G. Herzfeld, *Family Monographs* (New York: James Kempster Printing Co., 1905), p. 58.

38. Itzhok Rivkind, *Yiddishe Gelt: A Lexicological Study* (New York: American Academy for Jewish Research, 1959), pp. 113, 190, 155, 102–7, 189–90, 237, 40, 188, xxii, xxiii, 54, 277, 93, 287, 120, 131, 177, 190, 149. Warm thanks to Mildred Teicher for translating portions of this text from Yiddish into English. On prostitutes' profits, see Deuteronomy 23:19, with commentary by Dr. J. H. Hertz, ed., *The Pentateuch and Haftorahs*, 2d ed. (London: Soncino Press, 1977), p. 848 n. 19. On *knipl* money, see *Weinrich Yiddish Dictionary* (New York: McGraw-Hill, 1968), p. 418; and on *shnuddering*, see Ewa Morawska, *Insecure Prosperity: Small-Town Jews in Industrial America, 1880–1940* (Princeton, N.J.: Princeton University Press, forthcoming) and Charles W. Smith, *Auctions: The Social Construction of Value* (New York: Free Press, 1989), p. 13. On how it was abolished by modernizing orthodox synagogues, see Jenna Weissman Joselit, "Of Manners, Morals, And Orthodox Judaism: Decorum within the Orthodox Synagogue," in Jeffrey S. Gurock, *Ramaz: School, Community, Scholarship, and Orthodoxy* (Hoboken, N.J.: Ktave Publishing House, 1989), pp. 30–31.

39. Isaac Metzker, ed., *A Bintel Brief* (New York: Schocken Books, 1971), p. 37.

40. Breckinridge, *New Homes for Old*, pp. 102–3. See also Elizabeth Ewen, *Immigrant Women in the Land of Dollars* (New York: Monthly Review Press, 1985), p. 237; Eugene E. Obidinski and Helen Stankiewicz Zand, *Polish Folkways in America* (Lanham, Md.: University Press of America, 1987), pp. 91–92; Marian Mark Stolarik, *Immi-*

gration and Urbanization: The Slovak Experience, 1870–1918 (New York: AMS Press, 1989), p. 98; Margaret F. Byington, *Homestead* (Pittsburgh: University of Pittsburgh Press, [1910] 1974), pp. 149–50; Caroline F. Ware, *Greenwich Village, 1920–1930* (New York: Harper and Row, [1935] 1965), p. 366.

41. On "treating," see Roy Rosenzweig, *Eight Hours for What We Will: Workers & Leisure in an Industrial City, 1870–1920* (New York: Cambridge University Press, 1983), pp. 57–64. On how Jewish immigrants adopted the custom of treating, see Heinze, *Adapting to Abundance*, p. 122.

42. Ralph D. Paine, "Christmas in Business Life," *The World's Work* 7 (December 1903): 4244. I have found no systematic historical treatment of changing systems of compensation in the United States. This topic offers a great opportunity for research and synthesis.

43. Anna S. Richardson, "For the Girl Who Earns Her Own Living," *Woman's Home Companion* 32 (December 1905): 27; Paine, "Christmas In Business Life," p. 4243.

44. *New York Times*, December 23, 1913, p. 1; December 13, 1911, p. 20; December 22, 1909, p. 1.

45. *New York Times*, December 23, 1914, p. 7; Sue Ainslie Clark and Edith Wyatt, *Making Both Ends Meet* (New York: Macmillan, 1911), pp. 5–6; T. D. MacGregor, *The Book of Thrift* (New York: Funk & Wagnalls, 1915), pp. 140–41. On Woolworth's bonus policies, see John K. Winkler, *Five and Ten* (New York: Robert M. McBride & Company, 1940), pp. 123–24.

46. Paine, "Christmas in Business Life," p. 4243; Richardson, "For the Girl Who Earns Her Own Living," p. 27.

47. Niles-Bement-Pond Company and Amalgamated Local No. 405, International Union, United Automobile, Aircraft & Agricultural Implement Workers of America, CIO (November 29, 1951), in *Decisions and Orders of the National Labor Relations Board*, 97 (Washington, D.C.: Government Printing Office, 1952), p. 172. See also Barnett, *The American Christmas*, pp. 93–95; Waits, "The Many-Faced Custom," pp. 387–92.

48. "Tips," *The Atlantic Monthly* 108 (December 1911): 857; "Tipping," *Living Age* 257 (May 23, 1908): 509; William R. Scott, *The Itching Palm* (Philadelphia: Penn Publishing Co., 1916), p. 119. As the terms "pourboire" and "trinkgeld" suggest, the tip was an earmarked currency from the start, designated to buy drinks for the server.

49. "The Reclamation of the Tip," *Outlook* 87 (October 26, 1907): 373; "Tip and Tipping," *Outlook* 87 (November 16, 1907): 593. In 1912 the Treasury Department allowed its officers and employees to include tips to hotel servants, railway porters, and steamship stewards in their traveling expenses; see *New York Times*, October 30, 1912, p. 12. On anti-tipping statutes, see Mississippi Laws 1912, chap. 136, sec. 4. For a discussion of other state laws against tipping, see Scott, *The Itching Palm*, pp. 122–43.

50. "Regulating Tips," *Scribner's Magazine* 45 (February 1909): 252;

Green, *Dictionary of Etiquette*, p. 170; Scott, *The Itching Palm*, p. 126.

51. "Foolish Christmas Giving," *New York Times*, December 28, 1910, p. 8.

52. Scott, *The Itching Palm*, p. 28. See also Courtney Kenny, "Jhering On Trinkgeld And Tips," 127 *The Law Quarterly Review* (July 1916): 318. Kenny's article is an insightful discussion of the reknowned nineteenth-century German jurist Rudolf von Jhering's pamphlet on tipping, which had gone through five editions. On the expansion of the criminal law of bribery in late-nineteenth-century America, see John T. Noonan, Jr., *Bribes* (Berkeley: University of California Press, 1984), p. 578.

53. Howells, "Matter of Tipping," *Harper's Monthly Magazine* 127 (July 1913): 312.

54. Scott, *The Itching Palm*, pp. 10, 37–38.

55. Richard Barry, "Tips," *Everybody's Magazine* 28 (January 1913): 67.

56. Scott, *The Itching Palm*, p. 24; "Regulating Tips," *Scribner's Magazine* 45 (February 1909): 252.

57. Rose Cohen, *Out of the Shadow* (New York: George H. Doran Company, 1918), p. 312.

58. Hamilton Holt, ed., *The Life Stories of [Undistinguished] Americans as Told by Themselves* (New York: Routledge, [1906] 1990), pp. 166–67.

59. "Tips," *Atlantic Monthly*, pp. 856–57.

60. Sloat v. Rochester Taxicab Co., 177 App. Div. Supreme Court of the State of New York at 60. See also "'Tips,' A Legal Source of Income," *American Law Review* 51 (June 1917): 463–64.

61. "Tips as a Part of Wages," *Virginia Law Register* 3 (July 1917): 206–7. On the persistent personalized aspects of tipping, see Greta Foff Paules, *Dishing It Out: Power and Resistance Among Waitresses in a New Jersey Restaurant* (Philadelphia: Temple University Press, 1991), pp. 23–47.

62. Eliza Leslie, *Miss Leslie's Behaviour Book*, p. 181; Cooke, *Social Etiquette*, p. 123.

63. Greene, *Dictionary of Etiquette*, p. 154; Leslie, *Miss Leslie's Behaviour Book*, p. 182.

64. Eichler, *New Book of Etiquette*, p. 81.

65. Cooke, *Social Etiquette*, pp. 124, 143–44; Cushing, *Culture and Good Manners*, p. 110; Emily Post, *Etiquette* (New York: Funk and Wagnalls Co., 1922), p. 311.

66. Post, *Etiquette*, p. 311.

67. Cooke, *Social Etiquette*, p. 143; Post, *Etiquette*, p. 310; Cushing, *Culture and Good Manners*, p. 110.

68. Beth Bailey, *From Front Porch to Back Seat: Courtship in Twentieth-Century America* (Baltimore: Johns Hopkins University Press, 1988), pp. 13, 23. On dating, see also Paula Fass, *The Damned and the Beautiful* (New York: Oxford University Press, 1977); and, for a general history of American courtship, Rothman, *Hands and Hearts*. In his fine account of the emergence of dating, John Modell observes that the system developed at the same time among college and high school students and points to some significant class and race differ-

ences in dating patterns; see *Into One's Own: From Youth to Adulthood in the United States, 1920–1975* (Berkeley: University of California Press, 1989), pp. 87, 89–92.

69. On brothel tokens, see Ted Schwarz, "Yellow Tokens and Red Lights," *Coins* 26 (August 1979): 70–72; "Wage-Earning Pittsburgh," *The Pittsburgh Survey*, ed. Paul Underwood Kellogg (New York: Survey, 1914), p. 360.

70. "Behind the Scenes in a Restaurant" (New York: Consumers' League of New York City, 1916), vol. 24, reprinted in *The Consumers' League of New York: Behind the Scenes of Women's Work*, ed. David J. Rothman and Sheila M. Rothman (New York: Garland, 1987). See also Dorothy Sue Cobble, *Dishing It Out: Waitresses and Their Unions in the Twentieth Century* (Urbana: University of Illinois Press, 1991), p. 42.

71. Eichler, *New Book of Etiquette*, vol. 1, p. 103.

72. Peiss, *Cheap Amusements*, pp. 54, 108–14. On "treating," see Kathy Peiss, "'Charity Girls' and City Pleasures: Historical Notes on Working-Class Sexuality, 1880–1920," in Ann Snitow, Christine Stansell, and Sharon Thompson, *Powers of Desire: The Politics of Sexuality* (New York: Monthly Review Press, 1983), pp. 74–87. Timothy J. Gilfoyle, *City of Eros: New York City, Prostitution, and the Commercialization of Sex, 1790–1920* (New York: Norton, 1992), p. 311, suggests that "as 'treating' grew more common, it undermined commercial sex." On Jewish courtship and treating, see Heinze, *Adapting to Abundance*, pp. 122–24.

73. Paul G. Cressey, *The Taxi-Dance Hall* (Chicago: University of Chicago Press, 1932), pp. 36, 84, 50, 48–49. Cressey suggests that taxi-dancing may have been another way for married women to obtain some "additional funds," p. 84. See also Leo Rosten, "Dime-a-Dance," in *People I Have Loved, Known, or Admired* (New York: McGraw-Hill, 1970), pp. 289–91, 297.

74. Lorraine Baric, "Some Aspects of Credit, Saving and Investment in a 'Non-Monetary' Economy (Rossel Island)," in *Capital, Saving and Credit in Peasant Societies*, ed. Raymond Firth and B. S. Yamey (Chicago: Aldine, 1964), p.41.

75. "New Ways To Give Christmas Money," p. 70; "Ways of Giving Money," p. 24; Colby, "When You Send Christmas Money," p. 37; Emily Rose Burt, *The Shower Book* (New York: Harper and Brothers, 1928), pp. 124–25.

76. "Buy, Buy Christmas," *Ladies' Home Journal* 47 (December 1930): 17; Frances A. Kellor, "The Housewife at Christmas," *Ladies' Home Journal* 24 (December 1906): 48.

77. Dudley Chase, *The Romance of Greeting Cards*, p. 152. William Leach, in *Consuming Visions*, ed. Simon J. Bronner (New York: Norton, 1989), p. 131, examines the general concern with display and decoration of commodities after the turn of the century.

78. "When You Send Christmas Money," p. 37. On English Christmas cards, see George Buday, *The History of the Christmas Card* (London: Salisbury Square, 1954), p. 165. On Valentine cards, see Gene

Hessler, "Valentine Money," *Coin Age* 19 (March 1983): 104–5; Frank Staff, *The Valentine and Its Origins* (New York: Frederick A. Praeger, 1969).

79. *New York Times*, November 6, 1910, p. 6. See also *New York Times*, December 23, 1914, p. 7; William O. Scroggs, "Christmas and the Payroll," *Outlook* (December 18, 1929): 621.

80. See Green, *Dictionary of Etiquette*, p. 91.

81. "Refused 'Godless' Coins," *New York Times*, December 26, 1907, p. 1.

82. Cooke, *Social Etiquette*, p. 319. See Paul Einzig, *Primitive Money* (New York: Pergamon Press, 1966), p. 136.

83. *American Express Service*, December 1917, pp. 22–23, in American Express archives.

84. See gift-certificate ads for Siegel Cooper Co., *The World*, December 9, 1906, p. 9; Simpson Crawford Co., *The World*, December 16, 1906, p. 8M. See also "Selling Christmas," *Business Week*, December 15, 1934, 5.

85. For Macy's "merchandise bonds" ad, see *The World*, December 9, 1906, p. 148; Simpson Crawford Co. ad, "Shoes for Christmas," *The World*, December 17, 1905, p. 6M; Mark Cross, "Cross Glove Certificates," *The World*, December 9, 1906, p. E5. Bridal registries, rumored to have originated after the Depression according to a *New York Times Magazine* article (June 6, 1993, p. 70) were another technique for gifting money that increased the discretion of the recipient.

86. "$400,000,000 in this Year's Christmas-Club Funds," *Literary Digest* 91 (December 26, 1926): 50. See also Lloyd M. Crosgrave, "Christmas Clubs," *Quarterly Journal Of Economics* 41 (August 1927): 732–39; Waits, "The Many-Faced Custom," pp. 60–67.

87. Winthrop P. Stevens, "Should Banks Pay Interest on Club Accounts?" *Bankers Magazine* (January 1940): 72; Crosgrave, "Christmas Clubs," pp. 736–7. I thank Jenna Weissman Joselit for the information on Hanukkah savings accounts.

88. Mildred Johm, "The Christmas Club Idea in Boston," *Bankers Magazine* 113 (December 1926): 841–42. Often the Christmas money was reserved for domestic necessities such as a washing machine or a daughter's new coat. Reportedly Christmas Club funds were also partly earmarked for the payment of insurance, taxes, or mortgages. See also Herbert F. Rawll, "A Three Hundred Million Dollar Idea," *Banker's Magazine* 111 (December 1925): 883–87.

89. "New Ways To Give Christmas Money," p. 70.

90. See Emily Post, *Etiquette* (New York: Funk and Wagnalls, 1937), p. 400; Joan Seidl, "Consumers' Choices: A Study of Household Furnishing, 1880–1920," *Minnesota History* 48 (Spring 1983): 194.

91. Andrews, *Economics of the Household*, pp. 50–51.

92. Mary Elizabeth Carter, *House and Home* (New York: A. S. Barnes, 1904), pp. 197–98. See also Edwin Kirkpatrick, *The Use Of Money* (Indianapolis: Bobbs Merrill, 1915), pp. 46–51. It seems that working-class families made a distinction between a child's wages and tips, with wages treated as collective domestic income, and tips as a

child's discretionary income. A mother expected her child to hand over his wages, but it was "a mark of high virtue" to surrender tips to the household; see *Boyhood and Lawlessness* (New York: Survey, 1914), p. 69. On children's strategies to obtain tips, see David Nasaw, *Children of the City* (New York: Anchor Press, 1985), pp. 80–87. For a more detailed analysis of the management and control of children's money, see Viviana A. Zelizer, *Pricing the Priceless Child: The Changing Social Value of Children* (New York: Basic Books, 1985), pp. 100–10. Barry Schwartz, in "The Social Psychology of the Gift," p. 5, notes that the difference between a child's Christmas present and the Hanukkah gift of cash, or *gelt*, is that "the giver of Hanukkah *gelt* inevitably surrenders to the recipient a measure of control because money, unlike a particular commodity. . . may be used in any way and thus becomes a more flexible instrument of the possessor's volition." We see, however, that as a gift, money can, in fact, be as restricted as a nonmonetary gift.

93. "How They Simplified Their Christmas: Some Suggestions Taken from Ideas Submitted by Journal Readers," *Ladies' Home Journal* 23 (November 1906): 42; Colby, "When You Send Christmas Money," p. 37.

94. "Two Thousand SPUGS in City Fight Useless Gifts," *New York Times*, December 18, 1912, p. 5; Thomas and Znaniecki, *The Polish Peasant*, p. 404. See also Witold Kula, Nina Assorodobraj-Kula, Marcin Kula, *Writing Home: Immigrants in Brazil and the United States, 1890–91*, ed. and trans. Josephine Wtulich (New York: Columbia University Press, 1986).

95. Thomas and Znaniecki, *The Polish Peasant*, p. 655.

96. On the popularity of premiums, see Susan Strasser, *Satisfaction Guaranteed: The Making of the American Mass Market* (New York: Pantheon, 1989).

97. Davis, *Exchange*, p. 53. American Express Research Study, conducted by CLT Research Associates, August, 1990. Only limited information was released from this proprietary study. Caplow's study of "Christmas Gifts and Kin Networks" in Middletown during the late 1970s found that, after clothing and toys, money was, along with food and beverages, the third most common gift item; most money gifts between kin were intergenerational, bestowed by the older generation to the young; see pp. 385–86. See also "The American Express Gift Cheque," *Special Report for Financial Institutions*, 1 (Spring 1989); Gift Cheque ads in American Express archives; Tiffany ad in the *New York Times*, December 23, 1990. On the resurgence of Christmas Clubs, see Martha Woodcock, "Savings Clubs Get Support," *Credit Union Times* 2 (December 9, 1991): 1. On the economic significance of the gift economy more generally, see John Davis, "Gifts and the U.K. Economy," *Man* 7 (September 1972): 409–29; Schudson, *Advertising*, pp. 137–43.

98. Elizabeth L. Post, *Emily Post's Etiquette* (New York: HarperCollins, 1992), p. 268.

99. Emily Post, *Etiquette* (New York: Funk and Wagnalls, 1952), p. 236.

Similar instructions appear in the 1992 edition. Post, *Etiquette*, p. 591.

100. There is an extensive literature on intergenerational transfers and assistance. For some recent data, see Alice S. Rossi and Peter H. Rossi, *Of Human Bonding: Parent-Child Relations Across the Life Course* (New York: Aldine de Gruyter, 1990); Joan Huber and Glenna Spitze, "Trends in Family Sociology," in *Handbook of Sociology,* ed. Neil Smelser (Newbury Park, Calif.: Sage Publications, 1988), p. 440; Barry Wellman and Scott Wortley, "Different Strokes from Different Folks: Community Ties and Social Support," *American Journal of Sociology* 96 (November 1990): 558–88; Dennis P. Hogan, David J. Eggebeen, and Clifford C. Clogg, "The Structure of Intergenerational Exchanges in American Families," *American Journal of Sociology* 98 (May 1993): 1428–58. For an important study of formal volunteering and other acts of "caring" for relatives, friends, and strangers by Americans, see Robert Wuthnow, *Acts of Compassion* (Princeton, N.J.: Princeton University Press, 1991). On friendship exchanges, see Graham Allan, *Friendship* (Boulder, Colorado: Westview, 1989); Allan Silver, "Friendship and Trust as Moral Ideals: An Historical Approach," *Arch. Europ. Sociol.* 30 (1989): 274–97. In *Asylums* (Garden City, N.Y.: Anchor Books, 1961), pp. 277, 280 n. 144, Erving Goffman refers to small "ritual" gifts of money exchanged by patients. On women as Christmas Club depositors, see "Christmas Club," *The Unidex Reports,* Summary of the Seventh Biennial Christmas Club Study (Easton, Penn.: Christmas Club A Corporation, September 1988). And on gift money spent for and by children, see James U. McNeal, *Kids As Customers* (New York: Lexington Books, 1992), pp. 26–31.

101. I thank Sha Re, Ochanomizu University, Tokyo, who shared valuable information from her master's thesis on "Gift Giving and Human Relations" in Japan, and Bai Gao for translating this information into English. See also Harumi Befu, "Bribery in Japan: When Law Tangles with Culture," in *The Self and the System,* ed. Elinor Lenz and Rita Riley (Los Angeles: Western Humanities Center, UCLA, 1975); "Gift-Giving in Japan," *Understanding Japan* 1 (November 1992): 1, 6.

CHAPTER 4 POOR PEOPLE'S MONEY

1. John Foster Carr, *Guida degli Stati Uniti per L'Immigrante Italiano* (New York: Doubleday, Page & Co., 1910), pp. 5, 64–66.

2. Letter to the General Director of the New York Association for Improving the Condition of the Poor, November 7, 1913, on file at the Community Service Society (CSS) Papers, Box 25, Rare Book and Manuscript Library, Columbia University.

3. Amy D. Dunn, "The Supervision of the Spending of Money in Social Case Work" (M.A. thesis, Ohio State University, 1922), pp. 72–74. Mrs. C also received a monthly $25 mothers' pension, and her rent and coal bills were paid by the Family Service Society.

4. Mary E. Richmond, *Friendly Visiting Among the Poor* (New York: The

Macmillan Company, [1899] 1907), p. 161; Frederic Almy, "Constructive Relief," *The Survey* 27 (November 25, 1911): 1265; Dunn, *The Supervision of the Spending of Money*, p. 9; Frank D. Watson, *The Charity Organization Movement in the United States* (New York: Macmillan Co., 1922), p. 159. For an account of why women's organizations began shifting to cash donations, see Elizabeth S. Clemens, "Organizational Repertoires and Institutional Change: Women's Groups and the Transformation of U.S. Politics, 1890–1920," *American Journal of Sociology* 98 (January 1993): 777–80.

5. H. P. S., "Do Your Christmas Planning Early," *The Family* 2 (February 1922): 239. Macy's ad, *The World*, December 9, 1906, p. 148; Siegel Cooper Co. ad, *The World*, December 16, 1906, p. M3. On pensions, see Mary E. Richmond, "Of Christmas Gifts," *The Survey*, December 24, 1910, reprinted in Richmond, *The Long View: Papers and Addresses* (New York: Russell Sage Foundation, 1930), pp. 302–3. Starting in 1909, newspapers used special Christmas appeals to raise one-year pension funds for selected dependent families; see J. Edwin Murphy, "Yearly Pensions as a Substitute for Christmas Baskets," *The Survey* 31 (December 13, 1913): 298–99. The New York Times Neediest Cases Fund was initiated in 1912.

6. Dunn, *The Supervision of the Spending of Money*, p. 8; Emma A. Winslow, "Food, Shelter, and Clothing," *The Survey* 37 (October 14, 1916): 45; Joanna C. Colcord, "Relief," *The Family* 4 (March, 1923): 14; Pearl Salsberry, "Christmas, 1924," *The Family* 6 (April, 1925): 38; H. P. S., "Do Your Christmas Planning Early," p. 239.

7. Thos. J. Riley, "Teaching Household Management," *The Family* 3 (March 1922): 17; Hazel Kyrk, *A Theory of Consumption* (New York: Houghton Mifflin, 1923), pp. 131, 291–92. Kyrk, a pioneer of consumer economics, was a professor of economics and home economics at the University of Chicago from 1925 to 1952. Her biographer points out that *A Theory of Consumption* "remains a classic exposition of the social basis of consumer behavior." See *Notable American Women: The Modern Period*, ed. Barbara Sicherman et al. (Cambridge, Mass.: Belknap Press of Harvard University Press, 1980), p. 405.

8. Dunn, *The Supervision of the Spending of Money*, p. 64; A. C. Pigou, *The Economics of Welfare* (London: Macmillan & Co., [1920] 1948), pp. 754, 756; Riley, "Teaching Household Management," pp. 16–17; Colcord, "Relief," p. 14; Edith Abbott and Sophonisba P. Breckinridge, *The Administration of the Aid-to-Mothers Law in Illinois*, U.S. Department of Labor, Children's Bureau, Publication no. 82 (Washington, D.C.: Government Printing Office, 1921), p. 27; John Graham Brooks, "Some Problems of the Family," *Proceedings of the Twenty-Eighth National Conference of Charities and Correction* (1901), p. 296.

9. Dunn, *The Supervision of the Spending of Money, p. 12*.

10. Michael B. Katz, *In the Shadow of the Poorhouse* (New York: Basic Books, 1986), p. 15.

11. Primary sources for the study of changing methods for dispensing relief include a wide variety of documents, ranging from annual reports and publications of private charitable organizations; national, state, and local reports on public relief; the annual proceedings of the National Conference of Charities and Correction to manuals for friendly visitors and instructions for American Red Cross workers, a settlement worker's diary, contemporary dissertations, histories and texts concerning charity work, home-economics and consumer-economics textbooks, budget studies, legal cases and materials, including magazines and journals specializing in social welfare and home economics, as well as insurance publications. A particularly valuable source, on file at the Rare Book and Manuscript Library of Columbia University, are the records of the Community Service Society, which was formed in 1939, merging the New York Association for Improving the Condition of the Poor and the New York Charity Organization Society.

The best single secondary source on the history of American welfare is Michael B. Katz, *In the Shadow of the Poorhouse* (New York: Basic Books, 1986). Other useful accounts include Michael B. Katz, *Poverty and Policy in American History* (New York: Academic Press, 1983); James T. Patterson, *America's Struggle Against Poverty, 1900–1985* (Cambridge, Mass.: Harvard University Press, 1986); Blanche Coll, *Perspectives in Public Welfare* (Washington, D.C.: Government Printing Office, 1969); James Leiby, *A History of Social Welfare and Social Work in the United States* (New York: Columbia University Press, 1978); Nathan I. Huggins, *Protestants Against Poverty: Boston's Charities, 1870–1900* (Westport, Conn.: Greenwood, 1971); Robert Bremner, *From the Depths: The Discovery of Poverty in the United States* (New York: New York University Press, 1956); Roy Lubove, *The Struggle for Social Security, 1900–1935* (Cambridge, Mass.: Harvard University Press, 1968); Walter I. Trattner, *From Poor Law to Welfare State* (New York: Free Press, 1979).

The relationship of gender to social-welfare policies is now being explored by a number of scholars, particularly with regard to the issue of mothers' pensions; see, for example, Theda Skocpol, *Protecting Soldiers and Mothers* (Cambridge, Mass.: Harvard University Press, 1992), and Mimi Abramowitz, *Regulating the Lives of Women* (Boston, Mass.: South End Press, 1988). However, the literature remains distressingly weak on the experience of African Americans with charity organizations, as well as on their earmarking practices more generally. For some hints in that direction, see Ivan Light, "Numbers Gambling among Blacks: A Financial Institution," *American Sociological Review* 42 (December 1977): 892–904; Ann Fabian, *Card Sharps, Dream Books, & Bucket Shops: Gambling in Nineteenth-Century America* (Ithaca, N.Y.: Cornell University Press, 1990).

12. Quoted in Huggins, *Protestants Against Poverty: Boston's Charities*, p. 24.

13. Dorothy G. Becker, "The Visitor to the New York City Poor,

1843–1920," *Social Service Review* 35 (December 1961): 383, 387.

14. Priscilla Ferguson Clement, *Welfare and the Poor in the Nineteenth-Century City: Philadelphia, 1800–1854* (Cranbury, N.J.: Associated University Presses, 1985), pp. 57, 69, 148. See also Benjamin Joseph Klebaner, *Public Poor Relief in America, 1790–1860*, (New York: Arno Press, 1976), p. 355.

15. See Clement, *Welfare and the Poor in the Nineteenth-Century City*, pp. 74, 160.

16. Association for Improving the Condition of the Poor (AICP), First Annual Report (1845). On the New York AICP, see Becker, "The Visitor to the New York City Poor" and *Frontiers in Human Welfare* (New York: Community Service Society of New York, 1948); and for the AICP more generally, see Watson, *The Charity Organization Movement in the United States*, pp. 76–93.

17. Becker, "The Visitor to the New York City Poor," p. 387 n. 20.

18. *Hand-book for Friendly Visitors Among the Poor*, Compiled and Arranged by the Charity Organization Society of the City of New York (New York: G. P. Putnam's Sons, 1883), p. 11; Robert Treat Paine, Jr., *The Work of Volunteer Visitors of the Associated Charities Among the Poor* (Boston: Geo. E. Crosby & Co., 1880), p. 5. On the scientific charity movement, see Katz, *In the Shadow of the Poorhouse*, pp. 58–84; Paul Boyer, *Urban Masses and Moral Order in America, 1820–1920* (Cambridge, Mass.: Harvard University Press, 1978), pp. 143–61; Watson, *The Charity Organization Movement in the United States*.

19. Katz, *In the Shadow of the Poorhouse*, p. 36.

20. Lillian Brandt, "The Passing of Public Outdoor Relief in New York City," February, 1933, p. 3, on file at the CSS Papers, Box 19, Columbia University. There was one exception to the ban on cash, since the "poor adult blind" still received small stipends. See also Barry J. Kaplan, "Reformers and Charity: The Abolition of Public Outdoor Relief in New York City, 1870–1898," *Social Service Review* 52 (June 1978): 202–14.

21. Charles Henderson, "Poor Laws of the United States," *The Charities Review* 6 (July/August, 1897): 481; Lewis B. Gunckel, "Outdoor Relief in Ohio," *The Charities Review* 7 (November, 1897): 761; General Laws of Minnesota, 1893, chap. 178, sec. 12, p. 316. There was one exception to the prohibition of cash relief: in cases where transportation was provided, it was permitted to give the pauper "a small sum of money... for the purchase of food" (on file at the Minnesota Historical Society). See also "Classified Statement Of Public Outdoor Relief in the Larger Cities of the United States in 1897," *Proceedings of the Twenty-Fifty National Conference of Charities and Correction* (1898), pp. 182–83. On Philadelphia's public cash relief policy, see Klebaner, *Public Poor Relief in America*, p. 352.

22. On the increase in urban poverty in the early nineteenth century and the concern with immigrants and intemperance, see Katz, *In the Shadow of the Poorhouse*, pp. 16–17. On poor people's gambling, see Fabian, *Card Sharps, Dream Books, & Bucket Shops*, chap. 1.

23. Michael Merrill, "Cash Is Good to Eat: Self-Sufficiency and Exchange in the Rural Economy of the United States," *Radical History Review* 4 (Winter 1977): 56–57.

24. Josephine Shaw Lowell, *Public Relief and Private Charity* (New York: G. P. Putnam's Sons, 1884), p. 66. On distinctions among contemporary pay systems, see Mark Granovetter and Charles Tilly, "Inequality and Labor Processes," in *Handbook of Sociology*, ed. Neil J. Smelser (Newbury Park, California: Sage Publications, 1988), pp. 206–7. Alex Keyssar suggests that the persistent preference for in-kind over cash relief for the unemployed between 1870 and the early 1920s reflected the charities' assumption that "relief was intended not to compensate for lost wages but to alleviate distress." *Out of Work* (New York: Cambridge University Press, 1986), p. 152.

25. Mrs. Charles Russell Lowell, "The Economic and Moral Effects of Public Outdoor Relief," *Proceedings of the Seventeenth National Conference of Charities and Correction* (1890), p. 89. Opposition to outdoor public relief was justified partly on the assumption that public monies were more likely than private donations to be regarded by the poor "as a right, as a permanent pension, implying no obligation on their part." Richmond, *Friendly Visiting Among the Poor*, p. 151. See also Amos G. Warner, *American Charities* (New York: Thomas Y. Crowell & Co., [1894] 1908), p. 242.

26. Levi L. Barbour, "Arguments Against Public Outdoor Relief," *Proceedings of the Eighteenth National Conference of Charities and Correction* (1891), p. 42; Leah Hannah Feder, *Unemployment Relief in Periods of Depression* (New York: Russell Sage Foundation, 1936), p. 142. On the various methods of relief for the unemployed during the winter of 1893–94, see Carlos C. Closson, "The Unemployed in American Cities," *Quarterly Journal of Economics* 8 (July 1894): 452–77.

27. Rev. S. Humphreys Gurteen, *A Handbook of Charity Organization* (Buffalo, N.Y.: published by the author, 1882), p. 176; *Hand-Book for Friendly Visitors*, p. 2.

28. Philadelphia City Archives, Minutes of the Guardians of the Poor, March 16, 1829, quoted in Clement, *Welfare and the Poor in the Nineteenth-Century City*, p. 72.

29. Cited by Klebaner, *Public Poor Relief in America*, p. 351, n. 2.

30. Gunckel, "Outdoor Relief in Ohio," p. 760.

31. New York Charity Organization Society (NYCOS), *Thirteenth Annual Report* (1894), p. 64. The term "charity work" is used in the twelfth annual report of NYCOS (1893), p. 11. On the popularity of almshouses in nineteenth-century America, see David J. Rothman, *The Discovery of the Asylum* (Boston: Little, Brown & Co., [1971] 1990), chap. 8; and on the persistence of outdoor relief, Katz, *In the Shadow of the Poorhouse*, pp. 3, 37. On the failure of most public and private work-relief projects, see Katz, p. 224; and on the controversy over work-relief wages during 1893–97, see Feder, *Unemployment Relief in Periods of Depression*, pp. 179–80.

32. General Laws of Minnesota (1893), p. 317.

33. *Hand-Book for Friendly Visitors*, p. 5; Lenora Hamlin, "Friendly Visiting," *The Charities Review* 6 (June 1897): 323. See also Zilpha D. Smith, "How to Get and Keep Visitors," *Proceedings of the Fourteenth Annual Conference of Charities and Correction* (1887), p. 159.

34. Hamlin, "Friendly Visiting," p. 323.

35. Paine, *The Work of Volunteer Visitors of the Associated Charities*, p. 15.

36. Katz, *In the Shadow of the Poorhouse*, p. 47.

37. *Report of the Special Committee on Outdoor Alms of the Town of Hartford* (Hartford, Conn.: Press of the Case, Lockwood & Brainard Co., 1891), pp. *xviii–xxi*; *lxvii*; *lx*; Warner, *American Charities*, pp. 241–42.

38. *Extracts from the Journals of Miss M. E. Remington, Missionary of the Welcome Hall Mission* (New Haven, Conn., 1892), pp. 49, 68.

39. See also Virginia Yans-McLaughlin, *Family and Community: Italian Immigrants in Buffalo, 1880–1930* (Ithaca, N.Y.: Cornell University Press, 1977), p. 153. Some settlement houses also established cooperative loan funds for poor immigrants; see Sheila M. Rothman, *Woman's Proper Place* (New York: Basic Books, 1978), p. 115–16.

40. Anna F. Hunter, "The Savings Society of Newport," *The Charities Review* 9 (September, 1899): 337; "Taking Care of the Cents," *The Charities Review* 5 (February 1896): 212.

41. *Hand-Book for Friendly Visitors*, p. 2; Gurteen, *A Handbook of Charity Organization*, pp. 183–84.

42. Anne Townsend Scribner, "The Savings Society," *Proceedings of the Fourteenth Annual Conference of Charities and Correction* (1887), pp. 148, 145; Mary Willcox Brown, *The Development of Thrift* (New York: Macmillan Co., 1899), pp. 62, 65.

43. Joseph Lee, *Constructive and Preventive Philanthropy* (New York: Macmillan Co., 1902), p. 22; Willcox Brown, *The Development of Thrift*, p. 17.

44. Scribner, "The Savings Society," p. 143.

45. Edward T. Devine, *The Practice of Charity* (New York: Dodd, Mead & Co., [1901] 1909), pp. 41–42. See also Emily W. Dinwiddie, "Thrift Promotion," *Social Work Yearbook* (New York: Russell Sage, 1933), p. 506.

46. Scribner, "The Savings Society," p. 148. On coal and shoe clubs in Philadelphia, see "A Co-operative Coal Club," *The Charities Review* 8 (July 1898): 214. For earlier unsuccessful attempts to organize a fuel fund for the poor in New York, see Raymond A. Mohl, *Poverty in New York, 1783–1825* (New York: Oxford University Press, 1971), pp. 251–52.

47. Willcox Brown, *The Development of Thrift*, p. 45; Hon. S. T. Merrill, "Relief Measures For Pauperism" (1889), *Papers on Pauperism, 1818–1889*, p. 9, on file at the Princeton University Library. On savings-banks history generally, and on savings banks for southern black freedmen, see David M. Tucker, *The Decline of Thrift in America* (New York: Praeger, 1991), chaps. 4 and 6; Fabian, *Card Sharps, Dream Books, & Bucket Shops*, pp. 128–36. On other philanthropic and commercial savings schemes for the poor, see Willcox Brown, *The Development of Thrift*, pp. 32–72.

48. Prospectus, Penny Provident Fund, quoted by Willcox Brown, *The Development of Thrift*, p. 45; Copy of Stamp Deposit Card, Penny Provident Fund of the City of New York, Rules and Conditions, on file at the Community Service Society Papers, Box 127, Rare Book and Manuscript Library, Columbia University.

49. Annual Report of the Committee on Provident Habits, *Tenth Annual Report of the New York Charity Organization Society* (1891), p. 25; *Annual Report of the Penny Provident Fund* (New York: Charity Organization Society of the City of New York, 1909), p. 2.

50. Elsa G. Herzfeld, *Family Monographs* (New York: James Kempster Printing Co., 1905), p. 6; Lee, *Constructive and Preventive Philanthropy*, p. 25. See also "Taking Care Of The Cents," pp. 212–13.

51. Willcox Brown, *The Development of Thrift* p. 47.

52. Scribner, "The Savings Society," p. 145.

53. Howard Brubaker, "The Penny Provident Fund," *University Settlement Studies* 2 (July 1906): 62. See also Annual Report of the Committee on Provident Habits, *Eleventh Annual Report of the Charity Organization Society of the City of New York* (1892), p. 37; Willcox Brown, *The Development of Thrift*, p. 46.

54. James H. Hamilton, "The Educational Aspects of Saving," *The Quarterly Journal of Economics* 13 (October, 1898): 67; J. H. Thiry, "The Early History of School Savings Banks in the United States," *Journal of the American Social Science Association* 25 (1888): 170; Annual Report of the Committee on Provident Habits, *Fourteenth Annual Report of the Charity Organization Society of the City of New York* (1895), p. 47; Elizabeth Tapley, "Small Savings and How to Collect Them," *The Charities Review* 5 (December 1895): 101. Annual Reports of the Penny Provident Fund mention factory workers and peddlers among their depositors. A 1906 study of the fund in New York rank-ordered the ethnicity of depositors: Jews led the list, followed by Germans, Italians, Americans, and Irish; there were few black depositors. See Brubaker, "The Penny Provident Fund," p. 62. Early savings banks had also attracted children as well as women depositors. For instance, 71 percent of the early depositors of the Boston Provident Institution for Savings, organized in 1816, were women and children; Tucker, *The Decline of Thrift in America*, p. 42.

55. E. W. Kemmerer, "The United States Postal Savings Bank," *Political Science Quarterly* 26 (1911): 475; statement by the director of the Postal Savings System in 1913 quoted by E. W. Kemmerer, "Six Years of Postal Savings in the United States," *American Economic Review* 17 (March 1917): 68; Peter Roberts, "The Foreigner and His Savings," *Charities and the Commons* 21 (January 30, 1909): 758; David S. Cohen, ed., *America the Dream of My Life: Selections from the Federal Writers' Project's New Jersey Ethnic Survey* (New Brunswick, N.J.: Rutgers University Press, 1990), p. 68. See also Lizabeth Cohen, *Making a New Deal: Industrial Workers in Chicago, 1919–1939* (New York: Cambridge University Press, 1990), pp. 75–76.

56. Kemmerer, "The United States Postal Savings Bank," p. 477; Jere-

miah W. Jenks and W. Jett Lauck, *The Immigration Problem* (New York: Funk and Wagnalls Co., 1913), p. 114; James H. Hamilton, "Savings Bank Legislation: What Is Needed?" *Charities and the Commons* 21 (February 6, 1909): 781. Postal savings accounts could be opened by anyone ten years of age or older, and deposits were received only in sums of a dollar or multiples of a dollar. In order to avoid competition with savings banks, no single account could exceed $500. For a comparative look at postal savings banks in England, France, Italy, and other countries, see James H. Hamilton, *Savings and Savings Institutions* (New York: Macmillan Co., 1902), chaps. 10–12.

57. Scribner, "The Savings Society," p. 149. Even advocates of postal savings banks recognized that letter carriers—the post office's equivalent of a visitor—were "not ideal savings banks missionaries"; although they might "distribute literature from house to house" describing the advantages of banking, they had "little time, and perhaps little inclination, to make many personal explanations." See Hamilton, *Savings and Savings Institutions*, pp. 302–3.

58. Kemmerer, "Six Years of Postal Savings in the United States," p. 51. See also S. P. Breckinridge, *New Homes for Old* (New York: Harper and Brothers Publishers, 1921), pp. 111–13. As European immigration declined, postal savings banks, which had grown yearly until 1917, began to lose depositors. Low interests rates of 2 percent on deposits had also discouraged potential clients. See Margaret H. Schoenfeld, "Trend of Wage Earners' Savings in Philadelphia," *Annals of the American Academy of Political and Social Science*, Suppl. to vol. 121 (September 1925): 47–52. According to Milton Friedman and Anna Jacobson Schwartz, *A Monetary History of the United States, 1867–1960* (Princeton, N.J.: Princeton University Press, 1971), p. 173 n. 64, postal savings deposits peaked to 4 percent of savings deposits in mutual savings banks in 1919, fell to 2 percent in 1929, but then climbed to 13 percent in 1933. On the creation of ethnic banks as a financial alternative for ethnic Chicagoans during the 1920s, see Cohen, *Making a New Deal*, pp. 75–83.

CHAPTER 5 WITH STRINGS ATTACHED: THE EARMARKING OF CHARITABLE CASH

1. Emma A. Winslow, "Food, Shelter, and Clothing," *The Survey* 37 (October 14, 1916): 45.

2. "How to Live on 24 Cents a Day," *The Survey* 36 (September 16, 1916): 598; Winslow, "Food, Shelter, and Clothing," p. 45; John B. Dawson, "The Significance of the Rise in Relief-Giving During the Past Five Years," *Proceedings of the Forty-Ninth Annual Session of the National Conference of Social Work* (1922), p. 234.

3. *Twenty-First Annual Report of the United Hebrew Charities* (New York: 1895), p. 15; *Thirty-Fifth Annual Report of the United Hebrew*

Charities (New York, 1909), pp. 33, 22; *Annual Report of the United Hebrew Charities* (New York, 1922), p. 13.

4. On the AICP, *Frontiers in Human Welfare* (New York: Community Service Society, 1948), p. 53; AICP, p. 3, October 17, 1914, Report on file at the Community Service Society (CSS) Box 82, Papers, Rare Book and Manuscript Library, Columbia University; Frederic Almy, Letter to Emma A. Winslow, March 16, 1917, on file at the CSS Papers, Box 130, Folder Home Economics, 1917–18; Emma A. Winslow, *Report of Study of Family Budgets in Relation to Family Case Work,* Pt. I: "The Use of the Budget by Other Social Agencies" (1916), p. 18, on file at the CSS Papers, Box 130, Columbia University; Amy D. Dunn, "The Supervision of the Spending of Money in Social Case Work" (M.A. thesis, Ohio State University, 1922), pp. 7–8.

5. *Report of the New York State Commission on Relief for Widowed Mothers* (Albany, N.Y.: J. B. Lyon Co., 1914), pp. 122–23.

6. *Thirty-Eighth Annual Report of the United Hebrew Charities* (1912), p. 9; Frank D. Watson, *The Charity Organization Movement in the United States* (New York: Macmillan Co., 1922), p. 325 and pp. 168, 324. See also Alex Keyssar, *Out of Work: The First Century of Unemployment in Massachusetts* (New York: Cambridge University Press, 1986), pp. 250–58; Robert H. Bremner, *From the Depths: The Discovery of Poverty in the United States* (New York: New York University Press, 1972), chap. 8.

7. See correspondence between donor and the New York Charity Organization Society, on file at the CSS Papers, Box 180, Columbia University. On November 22, 1910, New York newspapers reported, apparently erroneously, that the donor had distributed coupons for groceries and meats to the value of $1 to two thousand dependent families under the care of the Charity Organization Society and the Hebrew Charities. Yet subsequent correspondence from NYCOS suggests that at least the Charity Organization Society had used the coupons to buy meat wholesale at designated butchers as well as beds and clothing at Bloomingdales for the families.

8. Dunn, "The Supervision of the Spending of Money in Social Case Work," p. 9; Emil Frankel, *Poor Relief in Pennsylvania,* Commonwealth of Pennsylvania, Department of Welfare, Bulletin 21 (1925), p. 61; Ben B. Lindsey, "The Mother's Compensation Law of Colorado," *Survey* 29 (February 15, 1913), reprinted in Edna D. Bullock, *Selected Articles on Mothers' Pensions,* Debaters' Handbook Series (New York: H. W. Wilson Co., 1915), p. 18. See also *Public Outdoor Relief: An Inquiry into the Administration of Public Outdoor Relief in Dutchess County, New York, for the Three-Year Period, October 1, 1910 to September 30, 1913* (New York: State Charities Aid Association, 1913), pp. 14–15.

9. Letter from Emma Winslow to Frederic Almy, Secretary of the Buffalo Charity Organization Society, March 22, 1917. Winslow's letter responded to Almy's letter of March 16 praising Winslow's support of cash relief in her *Survey* article of October 14, 1916. In her letter,

Winslow notes that she had received other supporting letters; letters on file at the CSS Papers, Box 130, Rare Book and Manuscript Library, Columbia University; Emma H. Winslow, *Budget Planning in Social Case Work*, Committee on Home Economics, New York Charity Organization Society, Bulletin No. 3 (1919), p. 30; Dunn, *The Supervision of the Spending of Money*, p. 10.

10. Winslow, "Food, Shelter, Clothing," p. 46. A similar trend toward cash relief occurred in Germany at the turn of the century; by 1918, 85 percent of all home relief was in cash. Here, too, officials emphasized the "pedagogical" uses of cash relief; see George Steinmetz, *Regulating the Social: The Welfare State and Local Politics in Imperial Germany* (Princeton: Princeton University Press, 1993), pp. 157–63. Steinmetz suggests that German poor relief differentiated by gender; women were more likely than men to receive in-kind assistance (p. 165).

11. James H. Hamilton, "The Educational Aspects of Saving," *Quarterly Journal of Economics* 13 (1899): 49; Hazel Kyrk, *A Theory of Consumption* (Boston: Houghton Mifflin, 1923), pp. 28, 290, 40.

12. Kyrk, *A Theory of Consumption*, p. 131; Joseph Lee, *Constructive and Preventive Philanthropy* (New York: Macmillan Co., 1902), p. 21; Winslow, "Food, Shelter, and Clothing," p. 45.

13. Joanna C. Colcord, "Relief," *The Family* 4 (March 1923): 14; "How to Live on 24 Cents a Day," p. 598; Mary Willcox Brown, *The Development of Thrift* (New York: Macmillan Co., 1899), p. 67. See also Dunn, *The Supervision of the Spending of Money in Social Case Work*, p. 6.

14. Dunn, *The Supervision of the Spending of Money in Social Case Work*, p. 8; Winslow, "Food, Shelter, and Clothing," p. 45. To the argument that it was "cheaper for a society to make purchases than it is for the family," Winslow countered with evidence from a study of 500 food orders, showing that families purchased just as cheaply as social workers. But even when organizations, taking advantage of wholesale rates, did buy more economically, the educational benefits were lost. The "first interest" of social work, insisted Winslow, "should be to save families rather than money." See also Helen W. Hanchette, "Family Budget Planning," *Proceedings of the Forty-Sixth Annual Session of the National Conference of Social Work* (1919), pp. 410–11. The term "charity customer" is used by Frankel, *Poor Relief in Pennsylvania*, p. 69.

15. Winslow, "Food, Shelter, and Clothing," p. 45; "Do Your Christmas Planning Early," pp. 238–39.

16. Edward T. Devine, *The Principles of Relief* (New York: Macmillan Co., 1904), p. 117. See also Amos G. Warner, *American Charities* (New York: Thomas Y. Crowell, [1894] 1908), p. 282; Homer Folks, "Why Should Dependent Children Be Reared in Families Rather than in Institutions," *The Charities Review* 5 (January 1896): 142; R. R. Reeder, "The Dangers of Institutional Life," *Delineator* 75 (January 1910): 115.

17. See Dunn, *The Supervision of the Spending of Money in Social Case Work*, pp. 19–20; Thomas J. Riley, "Teaching Household Manage-

ment," *The Family* 3 (March 1922), p. 16. Significantly, an investigation of ten child-placing agencies conducted by the U.S. Children's Bureau in the early 1920s found that half of the agencies had established a policy that children in foster homes "should have a small but stated amount of spending money." See Viviana A. Zelizer, *Pricing the Priceless Child* (New York: Basic Books, 1987), p. 183.

18. Edward T. Devine, *The Practice of Charity* (New York: Dodd, Mead & Company, [1901] 1909), p. 77.

19. Dunn, *The Supervision of the Spending of Money in Social Case Work*, p. 14; Warner, *American Charities*, p. 90.

20. Robert Tucker, "Discussion of Needy Families," *Proceedings of the Twenty-Eighth Annual Session of the National Conference of Charities and Correction* (1901), pp. 374–75; John Lewis Gillin, *Poverty and Dependency* (New York: Century Co., 1921), pp. 83–84. Gillin was the sixteenth president of the American Sociological Society in 1926; Howard W. Odum, *American Sociology* (New York: Longmans, Green and Co., 1951), p. 135.

21. C. C. Carstens, "Public Pensions to Widows with Children," *Survey* 29 (January 4, 1913), reprinted in Bullock, *Selected Articles on Mothers' Pensions*, p. 164; Robert Biggs in *Proceedings of the Thirty-Eighth Annual Meeting of the National Conference of Charities and Correction* (1911), p. 297; Florence Nesbitt, *Household Management* (New York: Russell Sage Foundation, 1918), p. 20.

22. Kyrk, *A Theory of Consumption*, p. 20; James H. Hamilton, *Savings and Savings Institutions* (New York: Macmillan Co., 1902), p. 177; Nesbitt, *Household Management*, pp. 13, 15.

23. Ibid., pp. 18–19; Dunn, *The Supervision of the Spending of Money in Social Case Work*, p. 11.

24. Biggs, *National Conference of Charities and Correction* (1911), p. 297; Devine, *The Practice of Charity*, p. 77; Winslow, "Food, Shelter, and Clothing," p. 45. On the professionalization of social work, see Roy Lubove, *The Professional Altruist* (New York: Atheneum, 1973); and on social workers' abandonment of social reform, see Michael Katz, *In the Shadow of the Poorhouse* (New York: Basic Books, 1986), pp. 165–67.

25. Riley, "Teaching Household Management," p. 14. On working-class household budget studies, see Daniel Horowitz, *The Morality of Spending* (Baltimore, Maryland: Johns Hopkins University Press, 1985). On the collaboration of home economists with charity-organization societies, see Winifred S. Gibbs, "The Development of Home Economics in Social Work," *The Journal of Home Economics* (February 1916): 68–74; Dunn, *The Supervision of the Spending of Money in Social Case Work*, pp. 69–70; Benjamin R. Andrews, *Economics of the Household* (New York: Macmillan Co., 1924), pp. 119–20; Watson, *The Charity Organization Movement*, p. 412. In 1917, at the National Conference of Charities and Correction, a group of home economists and social workers met to discuss the relationship between both fields; see report on "Relationship Between Home Economics and Social Work" (1919), and

Emma Winslow, "Report of Home Economics Discussions at the National Conferences of Charities and Correction," both on file at the CSS Papers, Box 130, Rare Book and Manuscript Library, Columbia University. Winslow was the Chairman of the Social Work Committee of the American Home Economics Association.

26. Mark H. Leff, "Consensus for Reform: The Mothers' Pension Movement in the Progressive Era," *Social Service Review* 47 (September, 1973): 402; Theda Skocpol, *Protecting Soldiers and Mothers* (Cambridge, Mass.: Harvard University Press, 1992), p. 468.

27. Riley, "Teaching Household Management," p. 14.

28. Edward T. Devine, *The Principles of Relief* (New York: Macmillan Co., 1904), p. 24.

29. Jane Addams, "Social Settlements," *Proceedings of the Twenty-Fourth National Conference of Charities and Correction* (1897), pp. 345–46.

30. Mary Richmond, *Friendly Visiting Among the Poor* (New York: Macmillan Co. [1899] 1907), p. 154; Frederic Almy, "Constructive Relief," *The Survey* 27 (November 25, 1911): 1265; Devine, *The Practice of Charity*, p. 166.

31. Edward T. Devine, "Pensions for Mothers," *The Survey* 30 (July 5, 1913): 458; *Report of the New York State Commission*, p. 113.

32. "The Needy Mother and the Neglected Child," *Outlook* 104 (June 7, 1913), in Bullock, *Selected Articles on Mothers' Pensions*, p. 27. On "school scholarships," see Fred S. Hall, "Scholarships for Working Children," *Charities and the Commons* 21 (November 14, 1908): 279–82. Critics of mothers' pensions argued, however, that pensions in fact created an illegitimate financial interest in children's lives by turning a child into "a source of possible profit" to his or her mother; see "A Serious Step Backward" memorandum, New York Charity Organization Society, (c. 1912), on file at the CSS Papers, Box 188, Rare Book and Manuscript Library, Columbia University; Mary Richmond, "Motherhood and Pensions," *Survey* 29 (March 1, 1913): 775.

33. William Hard, "General Discussion," *American Labor Legislation Review* 3 (June 1913), in Bullock, *Selected Articles on Mothers' Pensions*, p. 186.

34. William Hard, "The Moral Necessity of 'State Funds to Mothers'," *Survey* 29 (March 1, 1913), in Bullock, *Selected Articles on Mothers' Pensions*, p. 105.

35. On veterans' pensions and on the political influence of women's organizations in shaping the mothers' pension movement, see Skocpol, *Protecting Soldiers and Mothers*. For early examples of cash pensions for women, see the *Sixth Annual Report of the American National Red Cross* (Washington, D.C.: Government Printing Office, 1911), pp. 20–22; Mary E. Richmond and Fred S. Hall, *A Study of Nine Hundred and Eighty-Five Widows* (New York: Russell Sage Foundation, 1913); Priscilla F. Clement, *Welfare and the Poor in the Nineteenth-Century City* (Cranbury, N.J.: Associated University Presses, 1985), p. 170; Michael B. Katz, *The Undeserving Poor* (New York: Pantheon, 1989), p. 67. For more general discussions of the gender-

ing of American social-welfare policies, see Skocpol, *Protecting Mothers and Soldiers;* Mimi Abramowitz, *Regulating the Lives of Women* (Boston: South End Press, 1988); Barbara J. Nelson, "The Gender, Race, and Class Origins of Early Welfare Policy and the Welfare State: A Comparison of Workmen's Compensation and Mothers' Aid," in *Women, Politics, and Change,* eds. Louise A. Tilly and Patricia Gurin, (New York: Russell Sage Foundation, 1990), pp. 413–35; Sonya Michel and Seth Koven, "Womanly Duties: Maternalist Politics and the Origins of Welfare States in France, Germany, Great Britain, and the United States, 1880–1920," *American Historical Review* 95 (October 1990): 1076–1108; Linda Gordon, "Social Insurance and Public Assistance: The Influence of Gender in Welfare Thought in the United States, 1890–1935," *American Historical Review* 97 (February 1992): 19–54; Wendy Sarvasy, "Beyond the Difference versus Equality Policy Debate: Postsuffrage Feminism, Citizenship, and the Quest for a Feminist Welfare State," *Signs* 17 (Winter 1992): 329–62.

36. *Sixteenth Annual Report of the Chicago Relief and Aid Society* (December 31, 1873), p. 7. The Chicago society's new policy was often cited and praised by later advocates of cash relief as the earliest favorable reference to cash grants for the needy. See, for example, Joanna C. Colcord, *Cash Relief* (New York: Russell Sage Foundation, 1936), pp. 9–10.

37. Devine, *The Principles of Relief,* p. 466.

38. Frederick Howard Wines, "The Flood at Shawneetown," *The Charities Review* 8 (June 1898): 180; Devine, *The Principles of Relief,* p. 465.

39. *The American Red Cross: Manual of Home Service,* 2d. ed. (Washington, D.C.: Department of Civilian Relief, December 1917), pp. 30, 6, 12. See also, Foster R. Dulles, *The American Red Cross: A History* (New York: Harper & Brothers, 1950), pp. 165–68.

40. Dunn, *The Supervision of the Spending of Money in Social Case Work,* p. 8.

41. Colcord, "Relief," p. 14.

42. Emma A. Winslow, *Report of Study of Family Budgets in Relation to Family Case Work,* Pt. 1, p. 15; Dunn, *The Supervision of the Spending of Money in Social Case Work,* p. 9.

43. Leff, "Consensus for Reform," pp. 401, 414; Michael B. Katz, *In the Shadow of the Poorhouse* (New York: Basic Books, 1986), pp. 128–29.

44. Edith Abbott and Sophonisba P. Breckinridge, *The Administration of the Aid-to-Mothers Law in Illinois,* U.S. Department of Labor, Children's Bureau Publication no. 82 (Washington, D.C.: Government Printing Office, 1921), pp. 28, 20–21.

45. U.S. Department of Labor, *Laws Relating to "Mothers' Pensions" in the United States, Denmark, and New Zealand,* Children's Bureau Publication no. 7 (Washington, D.C.: Government Printing Office, 1914), p. 22.

46. William H. Matthews, "Widows' Families, Pensioned and Otherwise," *Survey* 32 (June 6, 1914), in Bullock, *Selected Articles On Mothers' Pensions,* p. 49; *Laws Relating to "Mothers' Pensions",* p.

43; Abbott and Breckinridge, *The Administration of the Aid-to-Moth-ers Law*, pp. 39–40.

47. Dunn, *The Supervision of the Spending of Money in Social Case Work*, p. 9; "How to Live on 24 Cents a Day," p. 598.

48. Dunn, *The Supervision of the Spending of Money in Social Case Work*, p. 64; Colcord, "Relief," p. 14.

49. "Accounting Made Easy," *Charity Organization Bulletin* no. 153 (December 6, 1916), p. 1; "Efficiency Book for Housekeeping; How Best to Use Income," on file at the CSS Papers, Box 130, Rare Book and Manuscript Library, Columbia University.

50. *Report of the Massachusetts Commission on the Support of Dependent Minor Children of Widowed Mothers* (Boston: Wright & Potter Print-ing Co., 1913), p. 150; Emma H. Winslow, *Budget Planning in Social Case Work*, Committee on Home Economics, The New York Charity Organization Society, Bulletin no. 3 (September 1919), p. 31; Riley, "Teaching Household Management," p. 17; Dunn, *The Supervision of the Spending of Money in Social Case Work*, p. 14. As authorities increasingly defined consumer competence as a teachable skill, even in-kind relief or grocery orders, although second-best to cash, were turned into instructional tools. The United Charities of Chicago, for instance, sent the dependent housewife along with the social worker to buy food for the family, using the shopping expedition to "discuss prices, and food values, and to point out real economies as distin-guished from false economies"; see Dunn, *The Supervision of Money in Social Case Work*, p. 3. See also Frankel, *Poor Relief in Pennsylva-nia*, pp. 67–8.

51. Winslow, *Budget Planning*, pp. 3–5.

52. Gibbs, "The Development of Home Economics," p. 68.

53. New York *AICP*, October 17, 1914, p. 3. On file at the CSS Papers, Rare Book and Manuscript Library, Columbia University. The Red Cross relief program also adopted the budget method, and recom-mended to its workers the same household account book prepared by the American Home Economics Association and used by charity organizations to encourage dependent families to keep track of their expenditures. Porter R. Lee and Karl de Schweinitz, *Home Service* (Washington, D.C.: The American Red Cross, Department of Civilian Relief, July 1917), pp. 52–59.

54. Abbott and Breckinridge, *The Administration of the Aid-to-Mothers Law*, p. 25; Mary Bogue, *Administration of Mothers' Aid in Ten Local-ities*, U.S. Department of Labor, Children's Bureau Publication no. 184 (Washington D.C.: Government Printing Office, 1928), pp. 73, 36.

55. Andrews, *Economics of the Household*, p. 120; Dunn, *The Supervision of the Spending of Money*, p. 11; Colcord, "Relief," p. 14; Nesbitt, *Household Management*, pp. 59–60.

56. Abbott and Breckinridge, *The Administration of the Aid-to-Mothers Law*, pp. 27, 29. See also Hard, "The Moral Necessity of 'State Funds to Mothers'," in Bullock, *Selected Articles*, p. 104.

57. Letter by a NYCOS officer, October 22, 1908, on file at the CSS Papers, Box 105, Rare Book and Manuscript Library, Columbia University. See also Pearl Salsberry, "Christmas, 1924," *The Family* 6 (April 1925): 37–40.

58. See H. P. S., "Do Your Christmas Planning Early," *The Family* 2 (February 1922): 238–41; Salsberry, "Christmas, 1924," pp. 37–40.

59. Bogue, *Administration of Mothers' Aid*, pp. 55, 24; H. P. S., "Do Your Christmas Planning Early," p. 239; Salsberry, "Christmas, 1924," p. 39.

60. Winslow, *Budget Planning*, p. 23.

61. Ibid., p. 24; Bogue, *Administration of Mothers' Aid*, pp. 37, 39, 55.

62. Winslow, *Budget Planning*, pp. 5, 12, 17. The search for budget information did not stop at the family's doorsteps, but, Winslow added, was also to be obtained from "relatives, friends, employers, neighbors, schools, churches, social agencies, health agencies." The same was true for mothers' pensions investigations; see Bogue, *Administration of Mothers' Aid*, p. 34. Abbott and Breckinridge noted that while "every effort is made to protect the family's self-respect" in Cook County, Illinois, there was "no rule against visits to present neighbors"; see *The Administration of the Aid-to-Mothers Law*, p. 22.

63. Winslow, *Budget Planning*, p. 14; Mary Bogue, "Problems in the Administration of Mothers' Aid," *Proceedings of the Forty-Fifth Annual Session of the National Conference of Social Work* (1918), p. 355; Bogue, *Administration of Mothers' Aid*, pp. 64, 140.

64. Winslow, *Budget Planning*, p. 22; Dunn, *The Supervision of the Spending of Money*, p. 70.

65. Minutes, Home Economics Committee of the New York Charity Organization Society, October 5, 1926, and February 26, 1929; Margaret J. Bacon, "Savings and Insurance and Their Relation to the Family Budget," *Proceedings of the Twenty-Ninth New York State Conference on Social Work* (Rochester, N.Y., 1928), p. 97. The extent to which budget envelopes or the other earmarking strategies were adopted is unclear.

66. Grace Marcus, *Some Aspects of Relief in Family Casework* (New York: Charity Organization Society, 1929), pp. 9, 39, 63.

67. Gordon Hamilton, *Theory and Practice of Social Case Work* (New York: Columbia University Press [1940] 1967), pp. 91–92. See also Eleanor Neustaedter, "The Integration of Economic and Psychological Factors in Family Case Work," *Proceedings of the Fifty-Seventh Annual Meeting of the National Conference of Social Work* (1930), pp. 198–216; Cora Kasius, "A Review of Relief Practices," in *Relief Practices in a Family Agency*, ed. Cora Kasius (New York: Family Welfare Association of America, 1942), pp. 4–24; Beatrice H. Wajdyk, "The Use of Money in Modern Case Work Treatment," in *Meaning and Use of Relief in Case Work Treatment* (New York: Family Welfare Association of America, 1941), pp. 26–50; Dorothy L. Book, ed., *Family Budget Counseling* (New York: Family Welfare Association of America, 1944), pp. 7–15; Lubove, *The Professional Altruist*, pp. 110–17.

CHAPTER 6 CONTESTED MONIES

1. Mary F. Bogue, *Administration of Mothers' Aid in Ten Localities*, U.S. Department of Labor, Children's Bureau Publication no. 184 (Washington, D.C.: Government Printing Office, 1928), p. 55.

2. S. P. Breckinridge, *New Homes for Old* (New York: Harper and Brothers, 1921), p. 139. On working-class and immigrant mutual assistance societies, see John Bodnar, *The Transplanted* (Bloomington: Indiana University Press, 1985), pp. 120–30; Virginia Yans-McLaughlin, *Family and Community* (Ithaca, N.Y.: Cornell University Press, 1977), pp. 155–56; Kathy Peiss, *Cheap Amusements* (Philadelphia: Temple University Press, 1986), pp. 18–19; Lizabeth Cohen, *Making a New Deal* (New York: Cambridge University Press, 1990) pp. 65–67. Aside from organizational contributions, working-class families also made personal loans or gifts of money to kin and neighbors in times of distress. See Alex Keyssar, *Out of Work* (New York: Cambridge University Press, 1986), pp. 164–66.

3. *Extracts from the Journals of Miss M. E. Remington, Missionary of the Welcome Home Mission* (New Haven: 1892), p. 38.

4. On the use of Penny Provident savings for holiday presents, see Howard Brubaker, "The Penny Provident Fund," *University Settlement Studies* 2 (July 1906): 63; Annual Report of the Committee on Provident Habits, *Fourteenth Annual Report of the Charity Organization Society of the City of New York* (New York: 1895), p. 24.

5. Mrs. William E. Gallagher, "Expenditures of the Poor," *Proceedings of the Thirty-Ninth Annual Meetings of the National Conference of Charities and Correction* (1912), p. 119.

6. Emma A. Winslow, "Food, Shelter and Clothing," *Survey* 37 (October 14, 1916): 46.

7. Amy D. Dunn, *The Supervision of the Spending of Money in Social Case Work* (M.A. thesis, Ohio State University, 1922), pp. 6–7; *Report of the Special Committee on Outdoor Alms of the Town of Hartford* (Hartford, Conn.: Press of the Case, Lockwood, & Brainard Co., 1891), p. *xxi*.

8. Florence Nesbitt, *Household Management* (New York: Russell Sage Foundation, 1918), p. 47; Minneapolis Case (November 18, 1924) cited by Beverly Stadum, *Poor Women and Their Families: Hard-Working Charity Cases, 1900–1930* (Albany: State University of New York Press, 1992), p. 139. Stadum's analysis of three hundred social case records of poor wives and mothers living in Minneapolis, Minnesota, in the thirty-year period found that "regardless of prices in the marketplace and the limited resources with which they worked, women often resisted the imposition of this dollars-and-cents accountability." On the Italian housewives, see Virginia Yans-McLaughlin, *Family and Community*, p. 153.

9. Nesbitt, *Household Management*, p. 63.

10. Dunn, *The Supervision of the Spending of Money*, p. 57. See also Emma A. Winslow, *Budget Planning in Social Case Work*, Committee on Home Economics, New York Charity Organization Society, Bulletin no. 3 (September 1919), pp. 21–22, 31.

11. Gallagher, "Expenditures of the Poor," p. 119.

12. "Taking Care of the Cents," *The Charities Review* 5 (February 1896): 212; Edward T. Devine, *The Practice of Charity* (New York: Dodd, Mead & Company, [1901] 1909), p. 75.

13. Mary Willcox Brown, *The Development of Thrift* (New York: The Macmillan Co., 1889), p. 24; Breckinridge, *New Homes for Old*, p. 90; Florence Nesbitt, "The Family Budget and Its Supervision," *Proceedings of the Forty-Fifth Annual Session of the National Conference of Social Work* (1918), p. 364. See also Stadum, *Poor Women and Their Families*, p. 140.

14. Daniel Horowitz, *The Morality of Spending* (Baltimore: Johns Hopkins University Press, 1985), pp. 60–61. "Saloon money" was a hotly disputed currency; middle-class observers condemned saloon attendance as a dangerous squandering of money, while immigrant and working-class patrons saw it as a legitimate recreational expense. See Roy Rosenzweig, *Eight Hours for What We Will: Workers & Leisure in an Industrial City, 1870–1920* (New York: Cambridge University Press, 1985), chap. 2.

15. Elizabeth Tapley, "Small Savings and How to Collect Them," *The Charities Review* 5 (December 1895): 103, 101.

16. Annual Report of the Committee on Provident Habits, *Eleventh Annual Report of the New York Charity Organization Society* (1892), p. 36; Gertrude E. Palmer, "Earnings, Spendings, and Savings of School Children," *The Commons* (June 1903): 14.

17. Mary F. Bogue, *Administration of Mothers' Aid in Ten Localities*, U.S. Department of Labor, Children's Bureau Publication no. 184 (Washington, D.C.: Government Printing Office, 1928), pp. 188, 110; see also pp. 24, 90. On the mass-marketing of pianos between 1890 and 1912, and their popularity among immigrant families, see Andrew R. Heinze, *Adapting to Abundance: Jewish Immigrants, Mass Consumption, and the Search for American Identity* (New York: Columbia University Press, 1990), pp. 137–44.

18. Mary E. Richmond, *Friendly Visiting Among the Poor* (New York: Macmillan Co. [1899] 1907), p. 156.

19. G. V. L. Meyer, "Postal Savings Banks," *Charities and the Commons* 21 (February 20, 1909): 991. Also, 71 percent of the earliest depositors of the Boston Provident Institution for Savings, organized in 1816, were women and children; see David M. Tucker, *The Decline of Thrift in America* (New York: Praeger, 1991), p. 42. On women depositors in nineteenth-century savings banks, see also Hon. S. T. Merrill, "Relief Measures for Pauperism" (1889), in *Papers on Pauperism, 1818–1889*, no. 24, on file at Princeton University.

20. Edith Abbott and Sophonisba P. Breckinridge, *The Administration of the Aid-to-Mothers Law in Illinois*, U.S. Department of Labor, Children's Bureau Publication no. 82 (Washington, D.C.: Government Printing Office, 1921), p. 69.

21. Edward T. Devine, *The Principles of Relief* (New York: Macmillan Co., 1904), pp. 29–30. Gareth Stedman Jones takes the popularity of death

insurance among the English poor as a key indicator of a newly emerging working-class culture in London between 1870 and 1900, which was "impervious to middle-class attempts to guide it." Working-class patterns of saving, Jones argues, particularly among the unskilled and poorer artisans, were fundamentally different from those of the middle-class, and were oriented toward the "purchase of articles of display or for the correct observance of ritual occasions," not for the accumulation of capital. Death insurance allowed the poor to escape the humiliation of a pauper's funeral and "to be buried according to due custom." Charity organizers failed to recognize, according to Stedman Jones, that working-class and poor people's efforts to "keep up appearances" required "as careful a management of the weekly family budget as any charity organizer could have envisaged." But, Stedman Jones adds, "its priorities were quite different"; see Gareth Stedman Jones, *Languages of Class* (Cambridge, Eng.: Cambridge University Press, 1983), pp. 183, 199, 201. Paul Johnson's study of the working-class economy in Britain between 1870 and 1939 further documents the fundamental place of burial insurance and a "respectable funeral" in working-class culture, noting as well how middle-class observers decried "the profligacy of burial insurance" but were unable to explain its "entrenched position in working-class life." See Paul Johnson, *Saving and Spending: The Working-Class Economy in Britain, 1870–1930* (Oxford: Clarendon Press, 1985), pp. 47, 43. For an excellent historical account of the changing meanings of pauper funerals, see Thomas Laqueur, "Bodies, Death, and Pauper Funerals," *Representations* 1 (February 1983): 109–31.

22. Robert C. Chapin, *The Standard of Living Among Workingmen's Families in New York City* (New York: Russell Sage Foundation, 1909), p. 194; Louise B. More, "The Cost of Living for a Wage-Earner's Family in New York City," *Annals of the American Academy* 48 (July 1913): 109; Breckinridge, *New Homes for Old*, p. 93.

23. *Fifteenth Annual Report of the New York Charity Organization Society* (July 1896–June 1897), p. 25. The NYCOS proposed a "careful study of the reasons for this success" [of insurance agents] in order to "devise such substitutes as shall accomplish similar results without the attendant evils."

24. James B. Reynolds, "Some Other Aspects," *The Charities Review* 8 (May 1898): 146; Willcox Brown, *The Development of Thrift*, p. 63. On the history of American life insurance, see Viviana A. Zelizer, *Morals and Markets: The Development of Life Insurance in the United States* (New Brunswick, N.J.: Transaction Books, 1983). The insurance of children's lives, which was an enormously successful part of the industrial insurance business, was especially condemned; see Viviana A. Zelizer, *Pricing the Priceless Child: The Changing Social Value of Children* (New York: Basic Books, 1987), chap. 4.

25. Lucy Atwood Fay, "The Experience of Massachusetts," *The Charities Review* 8 (April 1898): 69.

26. Haley Fiske, "Industrial Insurance," *The Charities Review* 8 (March 1898): 37; Tapley, "Small Savings," p. 103; Reynolds, "Some Other Aspects," p. 148.

27. Willcox Brown, *The Development of Thrift*, p. 23.

28. Reynolds, "Some Other Aspects," p. 145. A study of 985 widows under the care of charity organizations in 1910 found that the women's small insurance policies were indeed used chiefly for the expenses of a "respectable burial"; see Mary E. Richmond and Fred S. Hall, *A Study of Nine Hundred and Eighty-Five Widows* (New York: Charity Organization Department of the Russell Sage Foundation, 1913), pp. 14–16.

29. Reynolds, "Some Other Aspects," p. 145. A report on funeral costs in the 1920s also noted the relatively lower funeral expenditures made by Jews in contrast to Irish and Italians; often the expenses were paid by Jewish burial societies; see John C. Gebhart, *The Reasons for Present-Day Funeral Costs*, A Summary of Facts Developed by the Advisory Committee On Burial Survey in the Course of an Impartial Study of the Burial Industry (c. 1926), p. 20, on file at the CSS Papers, Box 127, Rare Book and Manuscript Library, Columbia University.

30. Irving Howe, *World of Our Fathers* (New York: Harcourt Brace Jovanovich, 1976), p. 221; *Thirty-Seventh Annual Report of the United Hebrew Charities* (New York, 1911), p. 9.

31. Jane Addams, "Social Settlements," *Proceedings of the Twenty-Fourth Annual Session of the National Conference of Charities and Correction* (1897), pp. 339–40; Mary E. Richmond, *Friendly Visiting Among the Poor* (New York: Macmillan Co., 1907), p. 119.

32. Elsa G. Herzfeld, *Family Monographs* (New York: James Kempster Printing Co., 1905), pp. 43, 27, 44. On the Irish and Italians' expenses for "fine funerals," see also Louise Bolard More, *Wage-Earners' Budgets* (New York: Henry Holt and Co., 1907), p. 105.

33. *Report of the Special Committee of the Town of Hartford* (Hartford, Conn.: Press of the Case, Lockwood, & Brainard Co., 1891), pp. XXXI–XXXII; James Brown, *The History of Public Assistance in Chicago, 1833 to 1893* (Chicago: University of Chicago Press, 1941), pp. 106–7; Herzfeld, *Family Monographs*, p. 27.

34. William I. Thomas and Florian Znaniecki, *The Polish Peasant in Europe and America* (New York: Alfred A. Knopf, 1927), p. 1697; Helen W. Hanchette, "Family Budget Planning," *Proceedings of the Forty-Sixth Annual Session of the National Conference of Social Work* (1919), p. 412. On children's insurance as an alternative to a pauper burial for working-class families, see Zelizer, *Pricing the Priceless Child*, pp. 129–32.

35. "Industrial Insurance," *The Charities Review* 8 (March 1898): 1; Fay, "The Experience of Massachusetts," p. 70; Lee Frankel, "Industrial Insurance," *Proceedings of the Thirty-Sixth Annual Session of the National Conference of Charities and Correction* (1909), p. 377; "Industrial Insurance," *Charities and the Commons* 17 (October 1906–April 1907): 879.

36. Willcox Brown, *The Development of Thrift*, p. 171; Addams, "Social Settlements," pp. 339–40; Willcox Brown, *The Development of Thrift*, p. 155; Mary Willcox Brown, "Child Insurance," *The Charities Review* 8 (April 1898): 72.

37. Willcox Brown, *The Development of Thrift*, p. 171; "Child Insurance," p. 72; "Discussion on Industrial Insurance," *Proceedings of the Thirty-Sixth Annual Session of the National Conference of Charities and Correction* (1909), p. 382.

38. William H. Matthews, "Widows' Families, Pensioned and Otherwise," *Survey* 32 (June 6, 1914), in Edna Bullock, *Selected Articles on Mothers' Pensions*, Debaters' Handbook Series (New York: H. W. Wilson Co., 1915), p. 49; Winifred S. Gibbs, "The Development of Home Economics in Social Work," *The Journal of Home Economics* (February 1916): 69; "Informal Discussion," *Proceedings of the Forty-Sixth Annual Session of the National Conference of Social Work* (1919), p. 417. Significantly, Florence Nesbitt's influential *The Chicago Standard Budget for Dependent Families*, Bulletin No. 5 (Chicago: Chicago Council of Social Agencies, 1919), p. 7, allowed funds for "some form of insurance . . . against illness, death, or other misfortune," as "necessary to give freedom from pressing anxiety." Mothers' pension allowances in Erie County, New York, did not include insurance, while insurance was part of the widow's budget in San Francisco, as long as it was "not excessive and did not partake of the nature of saving"; see Bogue, *Administration of Mothers' Aid in Ten Localities*, pp. 95, 160.

39. Professor H. A. Phelps, "Insurance in 250 Unadjusted Families," *The Family* 7 (November 1926): 228; Joanna C. Colcord, "Relief," *The Family* 4 (March 1923): 14.

40. Dunn, *The Supervision of the Spending of Money*, pp. 19, 73; "Industrial Insurance," *Social Work Year Book 1933* (New York: Russell Sage Foundation, 1933), pp. 251–52. The general business of industrial life insurance continued to expand; in Philadelphia, between 1913 and 1923, insurance in force increased 140 percent; see Margaret H. Schoenfeld, "Trend of Wage Earners' Savings in Philadelphia," *Annals of the American Academy of Political and Social Science*, suppl. to vol. 121 (September 1925), p. 38.

41. Colcord, "Relief," p. 14; Dunn, *The Supervision of the Spending of Money*, p. 70.

42. See Janet Poppendieck, *Breadline Knee-Deep in Wheat: Food Assistance in the Great Depression* (New Brunswick, N.J.: Rutgers University Press, 1986), p. 172.

43. Margaret Wead, "Drifts in Unemployment Relief," *The Family* 13 (November 1932): 225.

44. See Poppendieck, *Breadlines Knee-Deep in Wheat*, pp. 105, 172–74. Hopkins strongly supported cash relief for providing the recipient with some choice: "although the amount may be small, it is a man's own business how he spends it"; see Harry Hopkins, *Spending to Save: The Complete Story of Relief* (New York: Norton, 1930), p. 105.

45. Dorothy Kahn, "The Use of Cash, Orders for Goods, or Relief in Kind, in a Mass Program," *Proceedings of the Sixtieth Annual Session of the National Conference of Social Work* (1933), pp. 273–75. Centralized collective arrangements to distribute relief goods, such as the traditional breadlines, soup kitchens, and commissaries, were particularly discredited among modern social workers, for they offered no opportunity to develop consumer competence among the poor. See Joanna C. Colcord, *Cash Relief* (New York: Russell Sage Foundation, 1936), pp. 18–26.

46. E. Wight Bakke, *The Unemployed Worker: A Study of the Task of Making a Living Without a Job* (Hamden, Conn.: Archon Books, [1940] 1969), pp. 375, 357, 359.

47. Colcord, *Cash Relief,* pp. 127, 153, 117, 130, 230.

48. Ibid., p. 165.

49. Bureau of Public Assistance, *Money Payments to Recipients of Old-Age Assistance, Aid to Dependent Children, and Aid to the Blind,* Circular no. 16 (Washington, D.C.: Federal Security Agency, Social Security Board, March 1944), pp. 24, *ii.*

50. Jane M. Hoey, "The Significance of the Money Payment in Public Assistance," *Social Security Bulletin* 7 (September 1944): 5.

51. Colcord, *Cash Relief,* p. 119.

52. Bureau of Public Assistance, *Money Payments,* pp. 29, 30, 27, 33.

53. Ibid:, pp. *ii,* 5–6.

54. "General Relief" *Social Security Bulletin* 1 (November 1938): 35–50.

55. Bureau of Public Assistance, *Money Payments,* pp. 6, 32.

56. Ibid., p. 14.

57. Ibid., pp. 22, 32.

58. Ibid., p. 6. For a clear restatement of the importance of unrestricted money payments, see "Eligibility and Payments to Individuals, 9/26/47" in U.S. Department of Health, Education, and Welfare, *Handbook of Public Assistance Administration,* Pt. 4 (Washington, D.C.: Social and Rehabilitation Service, Assistance Payments Administration, April 14, 1971). See also Elma H. Ashton, "Money Giving in Social Work Agencies: In Retrospect and in Prospect," *The Implications of the Federal Social Security Act for Social Work Agency Practice,* Federal Security Agency, Social Security Administration, Bureau of Public Assistance, Report no. 11 (Washington, D.C.: Government Printing Office, 1947), pp. 1–8. Textbooks on public-welfare administration as well as social-work texts emphasized the significance of the money-payment principle. See Arthur P. Miles, *An Introduction to Public Welfare* (Boston: D. C. Heath and Company, 1949), pp. 394–95; Arthur E. Fink, *The Field of Social Work* (Albany, N.Y.: State University of New York, [1942] 1949), p. 64; Herbert Bisno, *The Philosophy of Social Work* (Washington, D.C.: Public Affairs Press, 1952), pp. 38, 46.

59. Jerry R. Cates, *Insuring Inequality: Administrative Leadership in Social Security, 1935–54* (Ann Arbor, Michigan: The University of Michigan Press, 1983), pp. 116–17. Cates uses the term "gratuity" to describe public-assistance payments, p. 29.

60. Bureau of Public Assistance, *Money Payments*, pp. 21, 17.
61. Ibid., p. 10; Unites States Code, 87th Cong., 2d sess., 1: 1945.
62. Public Law 87–543, sec. 108(a); 76 *United States Statutes At Large* (1962), p. 189. On "money management" policies for welfare recipients, see Reed K. Clegg, *The Administrator in Public Welfare* (Springfield, Ill.: Charles C. Thomas, 1966), pp. 194–96.
63. See Houston Welfare Rights Organization v. Vowell, 391 F. Supp. 223 at 233 (1975); Memorandum To Welfare Specialists (Center on Social Welfare Policy and Law, December 21, 1984), p. 2; Timothy J. Casey and Henry A. Freedman, "The Case Against Direct Vendor Payments," *Public Welfare* (Winter 1979): 37; Arthur B. LaFrance, *Welfare Law: Structure and Entitlement* (St. Paul, Minn.: West Publishing Company, 1979), p. 420.
64. Neil Shafer, "Early Food Stamps Were Money at a Discount," *Bank Note Reporter* (March 1987): 22. On the first food-stamps program, see Kenneth Finegold, "Agriculture and the Politics of U.S. Social Provision: Social Insurance and Food Stamps," in *The Politics of Social Policy in the United States,* ed. Margaret Weir, Ann Shola Orloff, Theda Skocpol (Princeton, N.J.: Princeton University Press, 1988), pp. 219–20; Maurice MacDonald, *Food, Stamps, and Income Maintenance* (New York: Academic Press, 1977), pp. 1–4.
65. See Gary Burtless, "Public Spending for the Poor: Trends, Prospects, and Economic Limits," in *Fighting Poverty: What Works and What Doesn't,* ed. Sheldon H. Danziger and Daniel H. Weinberg (Cambridge, Mass.: Harvard University Press, 1986), pp. 21–24; Joseph E. Stiglitz, *Economics of the Public Sector* 2d ed. (New York: W. W. Norton & Co., 1988), p. 349; Robert Moffitt, "Incentive Effects of the U.S. Welfare System: A Review," *Journal of Economic Literature* 30 (March 1992): 1; "Economy Grows, Food Stamps Rise," *New York Times,* March 3, 1993, p. 23.
66. See Berger v. United States, 407 F. Supp. 312; U.S. Department of Agriculture, *Food Program Facts,* (Washington, D.C.: Food and Nutrition Service, October 1991), p. 4.
67. Stiglitz, *Economics of the Public Sector,* p. 349. On economists' support of cash transfers, see, J. R. Kearl et al., "What Economists Think: A Confusion of Economists?," *American Economic Review* 69 (May 1979): 34.
68. Case and Freedman, "The Case Against Direct Vendor Payments," p. 40.
69. Lester C. Thurow, "Government Expenditures: Cash or In-Kind Aid?," in *Markets and Morals,* ed. Gerald Dworkin, Gordon Bermant, and Peter G. Brown (Washington, D.C.: Hemisphere Publishing Corp., 1977), pp. 97–98. For two other provocative discussions of the in-kind versus cash dilemma, see Thomas C. Schelling, "Economic Reasoning and the Ethics of Policy," *The Public Interest,* no. 63 (Spring 1981): 60–61, and Steven Kelman, "A Case For Transfers," *Economics and Philosophy* 2 (1986): 55–73.
70. See the *New York Times,* July 26, 1991, and September 19, 1991.
71. On trading food stamps, see Edwina D. Andrews and Scott Geron,

"Surviving the '80s: How Public Aid Recipients Cope with Benefit Cutbacks," Report by Taylor Institute, Chicago (June 1984), p. 87. On children's insurance, see Kathryn Edin, "Surviving the Welfare System: How AFDC Recipients Make Ends Meet in Chicago," *Social Problems* 38 (November 1991): 464–65; Alex Kotlowitz, *There Are No Children Here* (New York: Doubleday, 1991), p. 17.

72. *Annie Mae Roberts et al. v. John Harder,* Connecticut Welfare Commissioner, 320 F. Supp. 1313 (1970).

CHAPTER 7 WHAT DOES MONEY MEAN?

1. Jorge Luis Borges, "Funes el memorioso," *Ficciones* (Madrid: Alianza Editorial, 1988), p. 129; my translation.

2. Georg Simmel, *The Philosophy of Money,* trans. Tom Bottomore and David Frisby (London: Routledge & Kegan Paul [1900] 1978), pp. 444–45.

3. Robert H. Wiebe, *The Search for Order, 1877–1920* (New York: Hill and Wang, 1968), pp. 40, 43.

4. Simmel, *Philosophy of Money,* pp. 365–66.

5. On the Ford Motor Company, see Stephen Meyer III, *The Five Dollar Day: Labor Management and Social Control in the Ford Motor Company, 1908–1921* (Albany: State University of New York Press, 1981), pp. 108–47. On efforts to introduce regulated payments for prisoners in the early part of the century and on orphan asylums, see chap. 1, n. 37 of this book.

6. Arthur Nussbaum, *Money in the Law* (Chicago: Foundation Press, 1939), p. 193; Joel Kurtzman, *The Death of Money* (New York: Simon & Schuster, 1993), pp. 88, 83. See also Thomas Wilson, *The Power "To Coin" Money* (New York: M. E. Sharpe, 1992), p. 24; Wayne E. Baker, "What Is Money? A Social Structural Interpretation," in *Intercorporate Relations,* ed. Mark S. Mizruchi and Michael Schwartz (New York: Cambridge University Press, 1987), p. 115.

7. James Coleman, *Foundations of Social Theory* (Cambridge, Mass.: Harvard University Press, 1990), p. 121.

8. Harrison C. White, "Varieties of Markets," in *Social Structure: A Network Approach,* ed. Barry Wellman and S. D. Berkowitz (New York: Cambridge University Press, 1988), p. 232. For other sociological critiques of the neoclassical model of markets, see Bernard Barber, "Absolutization of the Market: Some Notes on How We Got from There to Here," in *Markets and Morals,* ed. G. Dworkin, G. Bermant, and P. Brown (Washington, D.C.: Hemisphere, 1977), pp. 15–31; Mark Granovetter, "Economic Action and Social Structure: The Problem of Embeddedness," *American Journal of Sociology* 91 (1985): 481–510; Amitai Etzioni, *The Moral Dimension: Toward a New Economics* (New York: Free Press, 1988); Charles W. Smith, *Auctions: The Social Construction of Value* (New York: Free Press, 1989); Fred Block, *Post-Industrial Possibilities: A Critique of Economic Discourse*

(Berkeley: University of California Press, 1990). On the particular relationship of culture to market institutions and relations, see Paul DiMaggio, "Culture and Economy," in *Handbook of Economic Sociology*, ed. Neil Smelser and Richard Swedberg (Princeton: Princeton University Press and New York: Russell Sage Foundation, forthcoming). See essays in the *Handbook*, ed. Smelser and Swedberg, as well as essays in *The Sociology of Economic Life*, ed. Mark Granovetter and Richard Swedberg (Boulder: Westview Press, 1992), and *Beyond the Marketplace*, ed. Roger Friedland and A. F. Robertson (New York: Aldine, 1990). For a survey of the literature, including the work of anthropologists and historians, see Viviana A. Zelizer, "Beyond the Polemics on the Market: A Theoretical and Empirical Agenda," *Sociological Forum* 3 (Fall 1988): 614–34.

9.   See Chris Tilly and Charles Tilly, "Capitalist Work and Labor Markets," in Smelser and Swedberg, eds., *Handbook of Economic Sociology*.

10. Caroline Humphrey, "'Icebergs', Barter, and the Mafia in Provincial Russia," *Anthropology Today* 7 (April 1991): 8–13.

11. For an intriguing literary attempt to break down the dualism between the "marketable and the priceless" see Barbara Herrnstein Smith, *Contingencies of Value* (Cambridge, Mass.: Harvard University Press, 1988), p. 130.

12. Pierre Bourdieu, *Distinction* (Cambridge, Mass.: Harvard University Press, 1984); Michael Schudson, *Advertising: The Uneasy Persuasion* (New York: Basic Books, 1984), p. 160. For an early and classic statement, see Thorstein Veblen, *The Theory of the Leisure Class* (New York: Mentor, [1899] 1953). For further references on the culture of consumption literature, see n. 5 in chap. 1 of this book.

13. Andrew R. Heinze, *Adapting to Abundance* (New York: Columbia University Press, 1990), p. 223.

14. Jenna Weissman Joselit, "'A Set Table': Jewish Domestic Culture in the New World, 1880–1950," in *Getting Comfortable in New York: The American Jewish Home, 1880–1950*, ed. Susan L. Braunstein and Jenna Weissman Joselit (New York: The Jewish Museum, 1990), p. 33.

15. Lizabeth Cohen, *Making a New Deal: Industrial Workers in Chicago, 1919–1939* (New York: Cambridge University Press, 1990), pp. 105, 110, 123, 129.

16. The term is used by Kurtzman in *The Death of Money*, p. 15.

17. Robert N. Bellah et al., *The Good Society* (New York: Vintage, 1992), p. 90; Alan Wolfe, *Whose Keeper?* (Berkeley: University of California Press, 1989), p. 76.

18. See anthropologist Keith Hart's contention that computers and the spread of plastic money erode state control of currency, making money "less anonymous, more personalized," in "Heads Or Tails? Two Sides of the Coin," *Man* 21 (December 1986): 641–42.

INDEX

Working class *(continued)*
for domestic monies and, 32, 38;
wife's handling of husband's
wages in, 56–57; wife's personal
recreation money in, 60
Workmen's Compensation Act, 98

Yap Island, 21
Yellowbacks, 13
Yezierska, Anzia, 60–61
Young, Michael, 43

Znaniecki, Florian, 22, 183